Shakespeare
in the Age of Mass Incarceration

Shakespeare in the Age of Mass Incarceration offers invaluable insight into how Shakespeare appears in prison. Bringing together theater artists, currently and formerly incarcerated actors, and college-in-prison educators and students, the collection describes powerful encounters in classrooms and rehearsal rooms as they explore the complexity of "prison Shakespeare."

In this innovative volume, instructors from college-in-prison programs across the United States recount students' profound awe with Shakespeare, and their sometimes trenchant critiques. They also consider how their teaching has grown and changed as they learn from their incarcerated students. Theater artists, including founders of and participants in influential Shakespeare prison programs, illustrate evolving practices in the field. The collection also features discussion from directors of programs for returning citizens, addressing the formidable obstacles people face as they come out of prison.

Accessible and highly teachable, this collection offers useful perspectives for students of Shakespeare, prison arts and education programs, and social justice initiatives. Those interested in starting or contributing to Shakespeare programs or courses in prisons will find a wealth of practical information, and those who read or watch Shakespeare with interest, skepticism, or delight will discover points of connection with incarcerated people who do the same.

Liz Fox is Arts and Academic Programs Coordinator at the Kinney Center for Interdisciplinary Renaissance Studies at the University of Massachusetts Amherst, USA. She teaches literature courses for a variety of prison education programs.

Gina Hausknecht is Professor of English and the director of the Prison Learning Initiative at Coe College, USA.

Spotlight on Shakespeare
Series Editors: John Garrison and Kyle Pivetti

Spotlight on Shakespeare offers a series of concise, lucid books that explore the vital purchase of the modern world on Shakespeare's work. Authors in the series embrace the notion that emergent theories, contemporary events, and movements can help us shed new light on Shakespeare's work and, in turn, his work can help us better make sense of the contemporary world. The aim of each volume is two-fold: to show how Shakespeare speaks to questions in our world and to illuminate his work by looking at it through new forms of human expression. *Spotlight on Shakespeare* will adopt fresh scholarly trends as contemporary issues emerge, and it will continually prompt its readers to ask, "What can Shakespeare help us see? What can he help us do?"

Spotlight on Shakespeare invites scholars to write non-exhaustive, pithy studies of very focused topics—with the goal of creating books that engage scholars, students, and general readers alike.

Available in this series:

Shakespeare on Consent
Amanda Bailey

Shakespeare Through Islamic Worlds
Ambereen Dadabhoy

Shakespeare on the Ecological Surface
Liz Oakley-Brown

Shakespeare in the Age of Mass Incarceration
Edited by Liz Fox and Gina Hausknecht

For more information about this series, please visit: www.routledge.com/Spotlight-on-Shakespeare/book-series/SOSHAX

EDITED BY LIZ FOX AND
GINA HAUSKNECHT

Shakespeare
in the Age of Mass
Incarceration

LONDON AND NEW YORK

Designed cover image: tomozina, Getty

First published 2025
by Routledge
4 Park Square, Milton Park, Abingdon, Oxon OX14 4RN

and by Routledge
605 Third Avenue, New York, NY 10158

Routledge is an imprint of the Taylor & Francis Group, an informa business

© 2025 selection and editorial matter, Liz Fox and Gina Hausknecht; individual chapters, the contributors

The right of Liz Fox and Gina Hausknecht to be identified as the authors of the editorial material, and of the authors for their individual chapters, has been asserted in accordance with sections 77 and 78 of the Copyright, Designs and Patents Act 1988.

All rights reserved. No part of this book may be reprinted or reproduced or utilised in any form or by any electronic, mechanical, or other means, now known or hereafter invented, including photocopying and recording, or in any information storage or retrieval system, without permission in writing from the publishers.

Trademark notice: Product or corporate names may be trademarks or registered trademarks, and are used only for identification and explanation without intent to infringe.

British Library Cataloguing-in-Publication Data
A catalog record for this book is available from the British Library

ISBN: 978-1-032-58832-2 (hbk)
ISBN: 978-1-032-58833-9 (pbk)
ISBN: 978-1-003-45166-2 (ebk)

DOI: 10.4324/9781003451662

Typeset in Joanna
by Deanta Global Publishing Services, Chennai, India

Contents

List of Contributors   x

Foreword by Ved Price   xvii

Acknowledgments   xxi

Introduction: Why Is Shakespeare in Prison Today?   1
Liz Fox and Gina Hausknecht

Past and Present

Shakespeare's "Working-House of Thought": The Prison in Early Modern London   **One**   27
Matthew Ritger

Hope Needs to Be Loud: A Founding Member on Nearly 30 Years of Shakespeare Behind Bars   **Two**   43
Hal Cobb

Three Thousand Hours: Shakespeare and Awe in Prison   **Three**   54
Sarah Higinbotham

Interventions

The Cultural Invasion of Shakespeare in Prison
Four 69
dave rich

The Cultural Invasion of Shakespeare in Prison: Contexts and Futures **Five** 80
Jayme M. Yeo

Shakespeare at Auburn: Reflections on Teaching and Learning in the Prison Classroom **Six** 91
Julio C. Iglesias, Stephen K. Kim, and Chester "Al" Wood

"Prisoners of Our Actions": Teaching *Hamlet* on Rikers Island **Seven** 105
Brian Chalk

Playing Many Parts: The Challenges of Representing Incarcerated Shakespeares **Eight** 117
Grace Duffy, John S. Garrison, and Anthony Rhodd

Michael Chekhov Technique: A Trauma-Responsive Practice in Shakespeare in Prison **Nine** 130
Frannie Shepherd-Bates

Practices

"Presume Not That I Am the Thing I Was": Collaborative Theater Companies in English Prisons **Ten** 145
Rowan Mackenzie, Pheelix Obun, and Ian West

"Like Bright Metal on a Sullen Ground":
The First Six Months of a Prison
Shakespeare Program **Eleven** 162
Kate Powers

Wasps and Falcons: Figurative Language and
Teaching Shakespeare's Women **Twelve** 175
Karrah Davidson and Amanda Kellogg

Counter-Readings: Reimagining Shakespeare
in Prison Libraries **Thirteen** 188
Kevin Windhauser

I Was Octavius Caesar **Fourteen** 203
Reginald Sinclair Lewis

Futures

Within and Beyond: Shakespeare
Behind/BEYOND Bars **Fifteen** 215
Sammie Byron and Curt L. Tofteland

Time Out of Joint: Taking Shakespeare
from Prisons to Schools **Sixteen** 228
*Elder "Tariq" Beaudouin, Amiti Bey, Charles Hardy III,
Deena Hurwitz, Steve Rowland, Shamah ShaRize,
Mohendra Singh, and Caroline Young*

Marin Shakespeare Company and the Returned
Citizens Theatre Troupe **Seventeen** 239
Lesley Schisgall Currier

Bibliography 249
Index 262

List of Contributors

Elder "Tariq" Beaudouin was born in Haiti and came to the United States as a child, his father fleeing the horrors of Papa Doc Duvalier's regime. Tariq was a Muslim community organizer and was innocent of the crime for which he was convicted. He served 27 years and was deported to Haiti.

Amiti Bey is a former Black Panther who was a political prisoner for 40 years. Bey holds an MA in social work and is a writer, community organizer, husband, father, grandfather, educator, and activist.

Sammie Byron served 31 consecutive years of incarceration until he was paroled in 2014. He currently works as a Youth Training Facilitator at Goodwill Industries, where he uses his gifts to teach conflict resolution to students aged 16–24. He also facilitates classes for women overcoming domestic violence.

Brian Chalk is Professor of English at Manhattan College. He is the author of *Monuments and Literary Posterity in Early Modern Drama* (2015) and has published numerous essays on early modern literature and culture. His current project examines the relationship among dreaming, sleeping, and theatrical experience in Shakespeare's plays and poems.

Hal Cobb, incarcerated since 1995, is a founding member of Shakespeare Behind Bars and featured in Philomath Films' 2005 documentary. Winner of multiple PEN America Prison Writing

Awards, including 2010 First Place Non-Fiction Essay "The Pursuit of Character," adapted to "Prospero Behind Bars" for *Shakespeare Survey* (2013).

Lesley Schisgall Currier is founding Managing Director of Marin Shakespeare Company in San Rafael, California. A graduate of Princeton University, Lesley is an award-winning theater director and producer. In 2003, she started Shakespeare at San Quentin, which grew into Shakespeare for Social Justice, serving 14 California State Prisons and system-impacted youth.

Karrah Davidson is a high school English teacher in Durham, NC. She serves as an adjunct professor of Appalachian Studies at Radford University, where she received her MA in English Literature. She participated in several inside-out style programs, experiences which provided the foundation for her MA thesis: "English Pedagogy for Incarcerated Populations."

Grace Duffy graduated from Grinnell College with degrees in Spanish, English, and Peace & Conflict Studies. She was student coordinator for Grinnell's Liberal Arts in Prison Program. After graduation, she taught English in Madrid, Spain, and now works as a paralegal at an immigrant advocacy nonprofit in New York City.

Liz Fox is Arts and Academic Programs Coordinator at the Kinney Center for Interdisciplinary Renaissance Studies, University of Massachusetts. She teaches courses in a range of academic settings, including Wesleyan University's Center for Prison Education, Bard College's Clemente Course in the Humanities, and Bay Path University's American Women's College.

John S. Garrison's recent books are *The Pleasures of Memory in Shakespeare's Sonnets* (2024) and *Red Hot + Blue* (2024). Among other honors, he is a two-time recipient of a National Endowment for the Humanities fellowship, and he was named a Guggenheim Fellow in 2021.

Charles Hardy III is a Professor Emeritus of History at West Chester University of Pennsylvania, former president of the Oral History Association, and producer of award-winning radio and video documentaries and websites.

Gina Hausknecht teaches in the English Department and Social & Criminal Justice program at Coe College and directs its Prison Learning Initiative, which offers college courses in prison and community education about incarceration and reentry. She has published on Shakespeare and Milton and teaches about incarceration and restorative justice.

Sarah Higinbotham teaches Shakespeare at Emory's Oxford College, focusing on the intersections of literature and law. She also co-founded Common Good Atlanta in 2008, a nonprofit that bridges Georgia's universities and Georgia's prisons, with more than seventy faculty teaching inside seven prisons five days a week.

Deena Hurwitz is an international human rights attorney who founded and taught the human rights clinic at the University of Virginia School of Law for a dozen years. She has advocated for the rights of the Palestinian people for several decades and has published several books and articles, including *Human Rights Advocacy Stories* (2008).

Julio C. Iglesias is a continuing student of the Cornell Prison Education Program at the Auburn prison. During his time there, Julio earned an AA in liberal arts and finds enjoyment in literature, theory, and philosophy. He's striving to be a poet and, most of all, a great writer.

Amanda Kellogg is Director of Professional Development for James Madison University. She received her PhD in English from the University of North Texas. Her MEd (Educational Psychology) and her BA (English) are from the University of Virginia. Amanda has taught classes in Shakespeare in both jails and prisons.

Stephen K. Kim is a volunteer instructor and advisory board member for the Cornell Prison Education Program. He started teaching on the inside in 2020 after completing his PhD, and it has been one of his most meaningful teaching experiences. He is a lecturer at Cornell University.

Reginald Sinclair Lewis was formerly housed on Pennsylvania's death row, where he self-published three books that received wide acclaim. In 1988, he prevailed over 800 prolific prison poets to win first prize for poetry in PEN America's Prison Writing Awards. His poems, essays, and articles have appeared in over 100 publications.

Rowan Mackenzie is both practitioner and academic, working in a number of English prisons using Shakespeare as a tool for social change, creating non-offending identities and self-reflection. She has published and spoken widely on theater with marginalized communities and is the recipient of several prestigious awards for her work in the criminal justice system.

Pheelix Obun is currently serving a custodial sentence. During his sentence, he has become a founding member of Emergency Shakespeare and has attributed this to helping to shape his identity and give him the ability to plan for a future where he contributes positively to society.

Kate Powers is a stage director, college professor, and a teaching artist with Rehabilitation Through the Arts (RTA). A Drama League Directing Fellow and Fulbright Scholar in Shakespeare, she earned an MA at the Shakespeare Institute and an MFA in Directing & Social Justice at the University of Idaho.

Anthony Rhodd has published works in the University of Iowa's Prison Writing Project, an article with Dr. Mary Cohen in the *Journal of Religions*, and an abolition song "Over / Under" with community song-leader and activist Lyndsey Scott. In 2023, Anthony received Honorable Mention for Memoir in PEN America's Prison Writing Awards.

dave rich is a currently incarcerated critical race scholar. Having earned his AA, he is nearing completion of his BA from Belmont University. He has won numerous awards and professional publications for his writings. He is co-founder and leader of the incarcerated-persons-led, peer-to-peer mentoring project, the Brothers' HEARTS Initiative, whose mission is to "eradicate recidivism from within."

Matthew Ritger is Assistant Professor in the Department of English and Creative Writing at Dartmouth College, where he specializes in early modern literature and culture. He is currently at work on a book about the literary history of England's houses of correction during the sixteenth and seventeenth centuries.

Steve Rowland is a Peabody Award-winning documentary director, oral historian, and educator. He conducted over 230 interviews with Shakespeare artists, educators, and authors, and was the chief interviewer at the 2012 "Globe to Globe" festival at Shakespeare's Globe.

Shamah ShaRize's transformation began after reading *The Autobiography of Malcolm X* over 10 times while in solitary confinement for 4 years, 8 months, and 17 days. He is the owner of his own business, happily married with 4 children, and a powerful spoken word artist/motivational speaker and human rights advocate.

Frannie Shepherd-Bates is the founder and former director of Shakespeare in Prison, a program at Detroit Public Theatre. Her work with justice-impacted folks has been featured in several publications. She is also an active member of the Shakespeare in Prisons Network and the Art + Justice National Collective.

Mohendra "Tony" Singh was born in Guyana and moved to NYC with his family as a child. He served 27 years in prison and was deported to Guyana, a country he never knew. Tony fulfilled his long-time dream of becoming a loving father, works full-time in Guyana, and is a writer and educator.

Curt L. Tofteland brings 40 plus years of professional theater experience to his current role as a freelance theater artist—director, actor, producer, playwright, author, poet, teacher, program developer, prison arts practitioner, and consultant. He is the founder of the internationally acclaimed Shakespeare Behind Bars program, founded in 1995.

Ian West is a recently retired Governing Governor within His Majesty's Prison and Probation Service and a keen advocate of the work of Emergency Shakespeare and the rehabilitative potential which it offers to those incarcerated.

Kevin Windhauser holds a doctorate in English and Comparative Literature from Columbia University. He has worked in higher education in prison for nearly a decade, as program administrator, curriculum designer, and instructor of early modern literature. His writing has appeared in *The Journal of Prison Education Research* and *Shakespeare Studies*.

Chester "Al" Wood is a Cornell Prison Education Program graduate. He is always aspiring to become a better father and grandfather. He enjoys reading history and likes to learn about enhancing the future. He hopes to one day earn a BA and become a contributing member of society again.

Jayme M. Yeo is Associate Professor of English at Belmont University. She has developed award-winning projects on Shakespeare and regional US history and received grants from the NEH and Folger Shakespeare Library. Her most recent work appears in *Shakespeare Bulletin*, *College English Association Forum*, and *Teaching Social Justice through Shakespeare*.

Caroline Young is a Lecturer of English at the University of Georgia. She is a poet and teaches a range of critical and creative writing courses. She has passionately taught inside prisons for seven years and fosters collaboration between her university and incarcerated student classrooms through community-facing writing projects.

Foreword

Prison, paradoxically, motivates creativity. As an individual in the carceral system, I was constantly confronted with two choices: escape, figuratively speaking, or atrophy. In the adaptive struggle for survival, incarcerated people seek means to escape their immediate surroundings, to do anything at all that fosters connection to the world outside. Why further limit oneself in an environment that is already limiting? The imagination can either reach beyond the place of confinement or succumb to the numbing lack of positive stimulation. Arts and education in a carceral context open a space of liberation that allows for an essential act of forgetting. You can forget for the moment that you are in prison and imagine yourself elsewhere.

However, the value of this creative forgetting is often overlooked in conversations about arts and education prison programs. Instead, these programs are framed as "rehabilitative" and steeped in the language of transformation. Such narratives are premised on the assumption, long embedded in the history of American corrections, that an incarcerated person must become someone entirely different to be allowed to reenter society. This narrative of transformation is central to parole, commutation, and clemency, all of which press for the assertion that one has become a new person, entirely separate from the former self. This language is also the key to public sympathy: a criminal must change into someone who is not a criminal, the inner beast must be tamed. Transformation complete, the person behind bars can step outside, one of us.

It's true that the arts and education do something to you, but it may not be that they change you so much as they expand you. You are still you, and more. Education is fundamentally an exercise in expansion: of schema, knowledge base, horizon, understanding of self and world. Theater, a space of play, allows resistance to the constraints of prison and the larger culture. Education and theater are both profoundly individual *and* profoundly social. Both involve shifting the locus from the individual to a larger network. Education and the arts offer and allow an expansion of one's sense of self. While the conversion narrative is centered on the self, expansion creates space for the larger set of connections and commitments that typify a productive, functional adult human.

The transformation narrative insists on what you weren't, what you aren't. It is linked to assumptions that some people are inherently insufficient, essentially less-than. However, an expansion narrative tells it differently: you always had an unaddressed, undeveloped capacity. Something in you—something essential to you—stayed small, too vulnerable to grow. In an environment where good choices are slim, you don't have the opportunity to develop. You are pressed and shaped by powerful codes of conduct and survival. The real rehabilitative work may not be a transformation but an unmaking, a reaching back to the open, unhardened self. These are the acts of imagination that are fostered by education, by the arts, and by the connections forged by vulnerability.

Educational and arts spaces permit a kind of vulnerability that is not tolerated or tolerable elsewhere in prison. In the rehearsal space, the studio, or the classroom, one is allowed to be fun or funny, to let one's guard down; this becomes a place where identity-building can happen, better than in other places in prison. Participants can explore parts of themselves in a safe way, aspects of their personality that have been suppressed in an environment that is all about survival. The classroom offers an escape from an environment that's constantly telling you a story about yourself. Without this alternative, you can only conform to what the institution says you are—you don't get to develop your own story, explore your own sense of self. That storytelling, that reaching beyond, involves a vulnerability that is maladaptive in the prison and on the streets.

The carceral encounter with Shakespeare, in particular, invites opportunities for play, whether it be with texts, lines, or ideas that allow you to lift the veil of seriousness and the gravity of incarceration for a time. Beyond the earned status markers of higher ed and other rehabilitative programming, working with Shakespeare allows for an expansion into the space of joy. Studying and performing Shakespeare's complex and multilayered characters opens onto a creative space that both expands the sense of self and rewrites an earlier narrative. Shakespeare's plays, then, offer a form of resistance, the resistance of finding joy and connection with others in a space of punishment, not allowing the prison to force you into certain ways of being or define you by reducing you to a narrow set of social parameters or limiting your experience to a single story.

A new direction for the Alliance for Higher Education in Prison is to model taking the risk of showing up in authentic, vulnerable ways. In the shared work described in this book, there is tremendously important and serious work to do, but we also need to be willing to lift the veil of seriousness that confers respectability in higher ed and its surrounding spaces, to allow students, incarcerated actors, and those who work with them to be themselves.

Ved Price
Executive Director, Alliance for Higher Education in Prison

Acknowledgments

This project has benefited from the generous insights of practitioners, educators, and scholars committed to the arts and higher education in carceral settings as components of more just and equitable responses to crime and harm. We admire the care and thoughtfulness with which the authors in this volume have examined the complicated endeavor of teaching and volunteering in prisons, and the critical conversation among them about what Shakespeare contributes to this endeavor and to its complications. We have had many illuminating discussions over the course of making this book: in particular, many thanks to Sheila Cavanagh, Rebecca Ginsburg, Niels Herold, Scott Jackson, and Curt L. Tofteland for sharing their experience, wisdom, and networks. We learned a great deal from members of the Shakespeare Beyond Bars virtual group; we hope this volume will help create a world that understands your language. Thank you to our incarcerated students for their talents and perspectives. Many of the ideas in this book were generated by the members of the Shakespeare Association of America's 2021 seminar on teaching Shakespeare in prison: Casey Caldwell, Brian Chalk, Jenna Dreier, Sarah Higinbotham, Jean Howard, Bill Kerwin, Simone Waller, Kevin Windhauser. Thanks as well to the panelists and audience members of the 2023 Shakespeare Association of America "Carceral Shakespeare" roundtable. We appreciate Em

Daniels helping those of us teaching in prisons develop an appropriate pedagogy for carceral spaces. Our thanks to the Routledge team: John S. Garrison, Kyle Pivetti, Karen Raith, and Chris Ratcliffe. Finally, we are grateful to Matthew Brown, Jesse Hausknecht-Brown, Dan McGloin, and Douglas Shuga for conversation and support.

Introduction: Why Is Shakespeare in Prison Today?

Liz Fox and Gina Hausknecht

Why is Shakespeare in prison?

We might start by noting that practically everything is represented in United States prison life in some way, given the sprawling phenomenon of our carceral system. Ours is an age of mass incarceration. In early 2024, U.S. jails and prisons housed 2,000,000 people, up from a little more than 200,000 50 years before, with another 5,000,000 plus on probation or parole.[1] Racial disparity characterizes this system: as of this writing, those identifying as Black represent 13% of the U.S. population, over 37% of the prison and jail population, and 48% of the population serving life or "virtual life" sentences.[2] The 13th Amendment of the U.S. Constitution abolished slavery in 1865, with the exception of people lawfully convicted of a criminal act. As the American public is increasingly aware, the result of this exception has been the hyper-policing and surveillance of black and brown communities, "locking people of color into a permanent second class citizenship."[3] James Davis III, detailing what he calls "double double consciousness," tells us that "For the black prisoner specifically, the psychological effect of incarceration is concomitant to the resentment implicit in the reality of being black in spaces that are anti-black…Mass incarceration, as a manifestation of the law, embodies that enmity."[4] And it is shot through with paradoxes: crime rates have fallen since the

DOI: 10.4324/9781003451662-1

1990s as prison building has expanded.[5] Although there is growing bipartisan public support for prison reform, the continued political effectiveness of "tough on crime" rhetoric prevails in both major parties.[6] Despite the heightened public awareness of the costs and consequences of mass incarceration, prisons remain entrenched in local economies and retributive justice remains central to the American social compact.[7]

Shakespeare in the Age of Mass Incarceration brings to this contradictory web of realities further contradictions: in the chapters that follow, Shakespeare represents a profoundly liberatory force for incarcerated people, a means of critiquing the nature of prison itself, and a sustaining mechanism of oppressive, racist structures. Shakespeare-focused theater programs have thrived in U.S. prisons over the past 40 years. Through them, incarcerated people have found themselves in Shakespeare's work, drawn in by language, performance choices, or thematic challenges, recognizing a character's motivation, flaws, pain, and epiphanies. Prison Performing Arts director Agnes Wilcox noted the men she worked with were "amazed to find that William Shakespeare and Sophocles can reflect their lives in a play."[8] In theater games and exercises, rehearsals and productions, incarcerated actors work through Shakespeare's urgent questions: what is it to resist authority or mishandle one's own, to inflict damage and endure it, to be a self, to take responsibility, to forgive, to love? They do so in creative and trusting community, even within a space of desperate loneliness and anomie; in the words of Marin Shakespeare, "We practice being human together."[9] In many of these programs, participants enter into creative exchange with the plays themselves, generating their own responsive poems, stories, scenes, and monologues. To do any of this in a prison defies the governing logic of carceral spaces, organized around stripping away autonomy and compassion for self and others. Yet there is a potential danger, as well, of perpetuating an elitist cultural value system which situates Shakespeare at its apex and as its summative representation; the enduring fervent praise of Shakespeare's work for its "universal" truths about the human experience can mask an exclusionary discourse of particularities which elevates white Western cultures at the expense of other ways of knowing and being in the world, what Margo Hendricks calls the "lethal dichotomy in the idea of Shakespearean universality."[10] While Shakespeare prison programs are celebrated as engines of rehabilitation, Shakespeare may be most potent for marginalized people as a force not of assimilation but resistance; as Sophie Ward and Roy Connolly contend, "the value of Shakespeare's work for those who are disenfranchised lies not necessarily in its power to socialize or rehabilitate but rather in its edgy, festive, subversive and transgressive potential."[11] Nor does Shakespeare in prison fundamentally alter or address the larger realities of the carceral framework and may even obscure them. As Ayanna Thompson warns in "'Unicorns and Fairy Dust': Talking Shakespeare, Performance, and Social (In)Justice," "We've got to get us out of the system and a little Shakespeare production here and there is fine but that's...not change."[12] If the meanings of prison Shakespeare pile up in seeming opposition to each other, we might echo the words of Gloucester in the final act of *King Lear*, "that's true too."

In the appreciative accounts of this work, the value of Shakespeare is assumed. The prestige of these plays is a passport, both into the prison and into the public consciousness: "any diehard Shakespearean might recognize how his works appeal uniquely to the criminally accused, one of society's most marginalized populations."[13] Noting that Shakespeare programs attract a disproportionate share of attention among prison theater initiatives, Rob Pensalfini's comprehensive survey of these programs identifies the "'wow' factor" of "bringing together these two differently notorious phenomena: prisons and Shakespeare."[14] Shakespeare in prison shocks the imagination, seeming to yoke opposites: the lowest and the highest of cultural sites. The cultural capital accruing to Shakespeare resonates powerfully and it may do real work, sanding away at the assumed lesser humanity of incarcerated people, an assumption which keeps the carceral state in motion. Barry Edelstein, artistic director at The Old Globe, marvels at Shakespeare giving men at California's Centinela State Prison "a new language to speak things that they feel but don't know how to say…an idiom that could not be more remote from the one spoken here becomes their native tongue."[15] At the same time, the choice of Shakespeare, as opposed to other authors or performance texts, may reinforce the elitism that trades on Shakespeare's cachet, fostering a narrative of exceptionalism, one that is powerfully, if often covertly, racially charged.

Further, popular accounts of Shakespeare programs in prison tend to offer salvation stories. In these tellings, Shakespeare's value lies in its redemptive potential: Shakespeare programs fundamentally transform the people inside who encounter his work.[16] In her account of teaching Shakespeare in an Indiana supermax prison, Laura Bates describes the "deeper questions that examined the very core character of a man, whether he is a king or a convict; questions that could indeed change a prisoner's life."[17] Yet much is often downplayed in this romanticized, hopeful vision, flattening the complexity of engaging with Shakespeare in prisons. Heroizing dramatic change risks erasing the structural obstacles to that change.

These narratives certainly acknowledge, often in colorful detail, the difficulty of bringing Shakespeare into prison, but even those difficulties can feed into a satisfyingly linear narrative of reformation. Even while celebrating the successes of Shakespeare programs, such approaches risk defining them through metrics—reform, rehabilitation, recidivism—that over-simplify both the lived realities and the intrinsic injustices of mass incarceration. Although recidivism rates for those enrolled in higher education and prison arts programs are deeply impressive, they do not tell the full story of the impact of this work, excluding the contributions of and benefits to people serving life and de facto life sentences and masking the structural factors that make reentry harrowingly difficult. Reuben Jonathan Miller observes that "redemption is the currency in the American criminal justice system. But it's the felony record that excludes you from a job or a place to live, not the extent to which you've committed to a life of personal transformation and change."[18] The popular story of the incarcerated person transformed, despite the odds, by a rehabilitative program in the arts or education locates both the problem of crime and its solution squarely within the individual. Linking prison life-writing to the long history of the conversion narrative, Simon Rolston observes that "The prison individualizes punishment and demands that formerly incarcerated people be as highly individualized as possible and see their faults and their successes as only their own. But…a formerly incarcerated person's successful reintegration into social life after prison rarely happens without support from some kind of community."[19] The rehabilitative imperative in these narratives elevates personal failings and weakness over the entrenched inequities that propel mass incarceration and celebrates individual triumphs to the neglect of the interdependence that makes sustainable reentry possible.

Prisons, and carceral systems more broadly, are undergirded by a set of organizing purposes—incapacitation, punishment, deterrence, and rehabilitation—which sit in unequal and uneasy tension with each other. Which of these predominate in any given society or nation speaks powerfully to how that nation understands and enacts justice; the movement in this country over the past four decades has been increasingly toward the first two and away from the last, with devastating effects on our communities. "Rehabilitative" programs meant to ready incarcerated people for productive reintegration into the social fabric from which they were torn by their sentences have a long history in United States prisons. Participation in these programs is typically voluntary, although it is also imbricated in the prison's system of social control through rewards and incentives—only those with clean behavioral records are allowed access to the classroom and participation typically counts as "good time" toward release. Formal college education was one such program until the 1994 Crime Bill revoked Pell grant eligibility for incarcerated students, thus eliminating most college-in-prison programs.[20] Many other privately funded activities continued and flourished, including prison arts programs of many kinds, theater among them, with a subset of those focusing on Shakespeare.

The different models of how Shakespeare appears in carceral settings fall for the most part into two categories: prison education and prison arts. Although Shakespeare in prison has a longer history, including the now-famous "Robben Island Bible," organized Shakespeare prison theater programs first began in England in 1982 with the Royal Shakespeare Company's Cicely Berry and in the United States in 1988 with Jean Trounstine.[21] Formal education in prison developed gradually over the 20th century,[22] particularly through growing community college networks which led to the "golden age" of college in prison from the mid-1960s through the early 1990s. Between 1972 and 1994, there were an estimated 772 college-in-prison programs, supported mostly by federal and state funds.[23] However, this wealth of opportunity, which was undergirded by the logic of rehabilitation, was decimated by the 1994 Crime Bill. With the significant contraction of educational opportunities, prison theater programs expanded both in number and mission, many with a specific focus on Shakespeare.[24] The longest-running, most influential of the North American Shakespeare theater programs, Shakespeare Behind Bars (SBB), was founded by Curt L. Tofteland in 1995 at the Luther Luckett Correctional Facility in Kentucky.[25] Shakespeare performance in prison coalesced as a field with the inaugural Shakespeare in Prison Conference in 2013 and the Shakespeare in Prisons Network at Notre Dame provides resources and connections for practitioners. As indicated by the theme of the most recent Shakespeare in Prison Conference's opening ceremony, "The Future is Now: A Social Justice Roadmap," this transnational network increasingly reaches outward to invoke larger systemic change.[26]

Simultaneously, new work in early modern studies has recast Shakespeare and his contemporaries as important ground for social justice pedagogies. As Sharon O'Dair and Timothy Francisco argue in *Shakespeare and the 99%*:

> Shakespeare—the author, the plays, and the field—operates as a collective site for teasing out and making visible the complex, and often complicit relations between literary studies as an intellectual discipline and the profession as a

social organization, relations that result in a host of inequities across higher education, having to do with race, class, and gender but also with place, prestige, and resources.[27]

The ways in which Shakespeare calls attention to these inequities in traditional college classrooms are only amplified in prison, bringing into sharper focus the impact of such disparities on student experience. Indeed, Shakespeare can be a powerful lever for re-working our understanding of how institutions of higher education, both in and out of prison, can reclaim their democratizing function. This is work Shakespeare has long done on stage:

> while other theatrical works might be just as or even more effective as *literature* or as *theater* in the social justice arena, Shakespeare held a special place because his work was already part of *the larger cultural discourse* and therefore allowed access to and, importantly, funding for, social justice work.[28]

In *Teaching Social Justice Through Shakespeare: Why Renaissance Literature Matters Now*, Wendy Beth Hyman and Hilary Eklund call on humanists in the academy to "counter the forces that denigrate knowledge-based discourses, threaten humane values, and whitewash historical events."[29] In this context, Shakespeare becomes a window onto failure, recovery, and transformation not just on individual but on larger institutional levels.

It is time, then, to look beyond the "wow factor" of prison Shakespeare, and instead consider what Shakespeare both makes possible and occludes in the age of mass incarceration. Certainly, Shakespeare creates genuine opportunities for growth and intellectual engagement for people whose humanity is routinely erased by incarceration. As theater scholar and practitioner Rowan Mackenzie argues, "Shakespeare can alter the spatial constraints for those who feel imprisoned, whether physically or metaphorically, enabling them to speak, and to be heard, in ways they may previously have struggled with."[30] Yet the liberatory potential of education and performance is always circumscribed by the context in which it occurs, subject to the pressures of institutions that exist primarily to control rather than create. A 2024 Ithaka S+R report on self-censorship describes how navigation of that space by prison educators frequently involves omitting or downplaying, or appearing to downplay, racial and social justice issues.[31] However, in "The White Shakespearean and Daily Practice," Jean Howard credits her incarcerated students with motivating her investment in making Shakespeare studies "less white." Given their history of racial injustice in the carceral system:

> Why should they assume that the prison classroom will be a respite from or challenge to that system rather than an extension of it? To earn trust I have to own my whiteness and the role that I play in racist systems; and I have to acknowledge and embrace the kinds of knowledge and expertise they bring to the classroom.[32]

This volume encourages clear-sightedness about the paradox of prison education and arts programming: that to do this work at all, we are involved with the carceral state, and all benefits, all growth, are contained and mitigated by the space of the prison.

In other words, "why is Shakespeare in prison?" is a complicated question with a perhaps at times uncomfortably complex array of answers. *Shakespeare in the Age of Mass Incarceration* speaks to a broad range of very different encounters with Shakespeare in carceral contexts, exploring disconnections as well as connections, mistakes as well as successes. Shakespeare continues to churn into new shapes across the globe and occupy new sites, from law school curricula to therapeutic practices and, at the same time, increased awareness of the devastating impacts of mass incarceration informs an array of public discourses. Theater artists and educators who use Shakespeare in carceral spaces build on each other's work, engaging with the ravaging effects of those spaces and the lifelong consequences of incarceration. This book seeks to contribute to these larger conversations and movements: Shakespeare, as a common cultural property, offers a space for thinking through values, needs, pleasures, and aspirations that bind us to those who seem remote from us. In a growing and developing field of practice, the current volume proposes a number of interventions in how we think and talk about why—and how—Shakespeare is in prison. Each chapter explores one or more dimensions of the artistic, rhetorical, and ideological web of meanings that orbit around prison Shakespeare today. Together, they offer an extended dialogue both about the work itself—studying, teaching, acting, inhabiting Shakespeare—and how that work sits in inevitable tension with its carceral setting. Reflecting how many different ways Shakespeare appears in prisons, this collection brings together a wide range of practices, perspectives, and priorities. While there is a body of scholarship on prison theater arts programs, including those focused on Shakespeare, and an emerging critical discourse around prison pedagogy, there is less written to date on Shakespeare literature courses in prisons—a gap this volume addresses. Too, the existing discussion of Shakespeare in prison, both scholarly and public-facing, is for the most part on one side or the other: by, for, and about either theater practitioners or college-in-prison instructors. Moreover, relatively few of these conversations include currently or formerly incarcerated people writing about their experiences and perspectives on Shakespeare in prison. This book puts educators and theater artists in conversation with each other and with people enrolled in these programs about the shared work of engaging with Shakespeare's plays (and sometimes poetry) within and around prisons.

Perhaps most significantly, the book also attempts to hold multiple truths at once: prison encounters with Shakespeare can be powerful and even liberatory, and they can reinforce structures and histories of control and oppression. In the decades since the first Shakespeare prison programs launched, the field has grown more nuanced in its understanding of what harm and trauma look like and how they are perpetuated, even, at times, by those with the best of intentions. As educators and practitioners, we must remain vigilant to the idea that "the identities celebrated as universal by the standards of humanism and liberalism are almost always actually dominant particulars masquerading as universals."[33] In the essays gathered here, students, educators, and practitioners tell stories of profoundly meaningful experiences with Shakespeare's plays, and, through that lens, with themselves and each other. They also reflect on what they've learned along the way and what, they suggest, we still need to learn. In particular, those coming into prisons from the free world describe missteps of their own and of their fields; they catalog false assumptions about what it might mean to "do Shakespeare" in prison; they demonstrate humility and testify to their own growth. The book as a whole encourages trenchant conversation about the ethical limits of "rehabilitation" in the context of a deeply harmful carceral structure.

The chapters in this volume are grouped into four parts, each of which considers a facet of the rich and varied enterprise of carceral Shakespeare, with essays that examine its histories and impacts alongside essays that offer critical inquiry and suggest future directions. The first section, "Past and Present," offers a broad conceptual lens on Shakespeare and the site of the prison at either end of the 400 years that Shakespeare has sat at the center of Anglo-American literary culture. Matthew Ritger contrasts the omnipresence of London prisons in that bustling capital city with the paradoxical disappearance of modern carceral institutions from everyday view. Inflected by the values of Renaissance humanism, prisons and punishment were central to an early modern nation developing and refining its mechanisms of social control, with considerable tension around the purposes and methods of the infamous Bridewell prison. Those tensions reverberate through cultural discourses, including Shakespeare's plays; looking at how prison shows up in the plays, we see how the constant threat of imprisonment filters into characters' moral understanding of their own and others' actions.

Hal Cobb and Sarah Higinbotham each provide a window onto how Shakespeare shows up in prisons today, in theater arts and educational settings respectively, as a powerful engine for self-knowledge and connection, building capacity for the kind of individual and collective inquiry that undergirds human flourishing. A founding member of the influential Shakespeare Behind Bars, Cobb reflects on how SBB promoted his developing sense of self. As in many testimonies from prison, the Shakespearean experience is revelatory for Cobb: in playing a number of Shakespeare's women, in playing roles with challengingly personal relevance and revisiting them over time, and in playing in front of a documentary camera, Cobb sees himself and his peers in a series of unexpected ways that render him both deeply vulnerable and, ultimately, strengthened. Higinbotham, documenting the awe with which her incarcerated students get absorbed in Shakespeare, describes similarly powerful engagements among the men she has taught as they recognize their participation in a "transhistorical social network" that contrasts starkly with the prison's deprivation and isolation. Moral reckoning factors into both of these chapters yet when Higinbotham's students experience awe, they are absorbed into something larger than their own choices. In both of these pieces the communal contact with Shakespeare is immediate and local. It fosters connection to the other people in the room, allows for resistance in the face of the alienation of prison life, and also forges bonds across time and place.

Yet, for all of the recognition, joy, and validation the Shakespeare encounter offers in a variety of carceral contexts, the second section of the book, "Interventions," asks us to think carefully and candidly about ways in which assumptions and expectations around Shakespeare can erase other opportunities, voices, and realities. One motivation for this collection emerges from the anticipated proliferation of college in prison programs following the 2023 reinstatement of Pell eligibility for incarcerated students. We hope these essays will help those launching Shakespeare courses in the coming years steer around some potential pitfalls and toward critically engaged pedagogies. In a pair of companion essays, incarcerated student dave rich and English professor Jayme M. Yeo explore how classrooms that unwittingly participate in what Arthur Little Jr. calls the "white-people-making" of Shakespeare's poems and plays may replicate and reinforce racist structures of values.[34] In rich's formulation, the Shakespeare celebrated for offering us enduring truths about human nature represents "cultural invasion," as conceived by Paulo Freire. The authors in this section urge humility, flexibility, and critical self-examination around the default assumptions that accompany Shakespeare, often invisibly, into the prison.

The next two chapters offer honest accounts of how professors' expectations were challenged by their students' responses to the course material. In "Shakespeare at Auburn: Reflections on Teaching & Learning in the Prison Classroom," Stephen K. Kim and two of his students, Julio C. Iglesias and Chester "Al" Wood, each trace their deepening understanding of *The Tempest*, *Hamlet*, and *Othello*, respectively. Iglesias and Wood explore the effect of emotionally searing but ultimately productive identifications with the Ghost and with Othello, while Kim recounts how his students' resistance to his reading of Miranda and Caliban prods him toward a more reparative, empathetic view of both of them and a heightened sensitivity to the play's "uneasy entanglement with incarceration" (102). Brian Chalk's "'Prisoners of our Actions': Teaching *Hamlet* on Rikers Island" engages with the student-centered pedagogy of the inside-out model (courses in prison which enroll both campus-based and incarcerated students). Chalk describes with generous frankness his experience teaching one of the best-known accounts of prison Shakespeare, the "Act V" episode of *This American Life* which follows a group of men in a prison performing arts program rehearsing the final act of *Hamlet* at the Missouri Eastern Correctional Center. The chapter explores important ethical considerations concerning both this particular radio documentary and the vulnerabilities attendant on the carceral classroom.

Prison Shakespeare is both well-established and, appropriately and necessarily, in continual development; two final essays in this section offer in microcosm the critical reflexivity in the classroom and theatrical space that characterizes the current moment, moving away from celebratory narratives that surprise us with the humanity and charm of incarcerated people to a more critical inquiry that recognizes the need for structural as well as personal change. In the dialogue "Playing Many Parts: The Challenges of Representing Incarcerated Shakespeares," a Grinnell College professor, a recent Grinnell graduate, and an incarcerated student enrolled in Grinnell's Liberal Arts Prison Program reflect together on what each of them learned from their shared Introduction to Shakespeare course. This essay shrugs off some of the early tropes of Shakespeare-in-prison narratives, typically located in the educator's perspective and frequently foregrounding transformation and redemption. Rather than making Anthony Rhodd, the incarcerated student, new or whole, studying Shakespeare reignited and reinforced his individuality; John S. Garrison, the professor, noted that the students responded more to characters' heroism and self-awareness than to their guilt or sense of wrong-doing. Moving from the classroom to the rehearsal space in the final chapter in this section, Frannie Shepherd-Bates, founder and former director of Detroit Public Theatre's Shakespeare in Prison program, attends to how emotional engagement with the themes and patterns of the plays—violence, retribution, guilt, forgiveness, repair—may open onto painful or difficult reckonings. "Michael Chekhov Technique: A Trauma-responsive Practice in Shakespeare in Prison" describes an approach to theater-making with incarcerated people that reduces the risks and amplifies the healing capacity of memory as the basis for creative practice.

Shakespeare is in prison in a range of shapes and forms: the chapters in the "Practices" section describe several distinctive sites of engagement and some of the ways in which those sites were crafted. Emergency Shakespeare is a collaborative, democratically-run theater company in the U.K.; in a chapter co-authored by two of its co-owners, a theater artist and an incarcerated troupe member, and the warden of the prison who invited its creation, Rowan Mackenzie, Pheelix Obun, and Ian West chart the process, challenges, and rewards of building a collaborative theater company in a prison. Emergency Shakespeare, laying the foundation for connection, identity, efficacy, and autonomy among its members, counters some of the most devastating, dehumanizing effects of incarceration. Similarly, in "'Like Bright Metal on a Sullen Ground': The First Six Months of a Prison Shakespeare Program," theater artist Kate Powers charts the development of the first prison performing arts program in Minnesota, focusing on self-reflection, critical thinking, and playfulness. Powers traces the first six months of The Redeeming Time Project, drawing a disparate group of men through theater games into a space of mutual trust, inquiry, and experimentation. "Wasps and Falcons: Figurative Language and Teaching Shakespeare's Women" sketches out a new course focused on *The Taming of the Shrew*, taught, unexpectedly, in a men's prison. Detailing how the course ventured into the territory of gender and figuration in unanticipated ways, Amanda Kellogg and Karrah Davidson offer guidance for teaching figurative language in the particularly resonant space of the carceral classroom. While education and theater programs are available in some prisons, to some people, all U.S. prisons are mandated by law to guarantee access to libraries. Kevin Windhauser points out that prison Shakespeare is not always encountered in community. In "Counter-Readings: Reimagining Shakespeare in Prison Libraries," he explores some of what we know about Shakespeare's incarcerated readers, including

Malcolm X, and advocates for more investigation of these independent reading experiences. Reginald Sinclair Lewis' vibrant account of rehearsing Shakespeare in Pennsylvania prisons concludes this section. Lewis, a poet and essayist, brings to vivid life three years of on and off again engagement with a Shakespeare theater program. He details its origins during the last months of operation of the sprawling old Graterford prison, the move to the modern SCI-Phoenix, and the onset of COVID-19 a week before the debut of a new production of *Julius Caesar*.

Even as the pandemic triggered a small wave of decarceration, the formidable challenges of reentering society after a term of imprisonment remain, including legal discrimination in housing, education, and employment, all of which are the fundamental means by which people build independence and self-sufficiency. Ultimately, the goal of Shakespeare programs for incarcerated people is not better prison but better lives. The book's final section, "Futures," shows some of the pathways forged post-release by participants in Shakespeare prison programs who have continued their engagements with Shakespeare after incarceration. Sammie Byron, an alumnus of Shakespeare Behind Bars, has co-created and currently tours a one-man play, *Othello's Tribunal*, with SBB founding director Curt L. Tofteland; at the same time, Tofteland has crafted a "beyond" element to the original program. In a joint interview, they explore what Shakespeare BEYOND Bars has looked like for each of them and the deepening power of SBB over time. The second essay in this section follows a team of Formerly Incarcerated Teachers (FITs), men who studied Shakespeare in prison, offering discussion-based workshops to high school and college students under the auspices of the collaborative Time Out Of Joint (TOOJ) project. In bringing these teachers and students together to explore both Shakespeare's texts and Shakespeare-inspired "Prison Monologues" authored by the FITs, TOOJ builds capacity, for the FITs as educators and the students as inquisitive, empathetic learners. Marin Shakespeare Company's Returned Citizens Theatre Troupe (RCTT), an outgrowth of Marin's Shakespeare for Social Justice program in California prisons, hires RCTT members to create and perform original stories about their experiences of incarceration and reentry. Like TOOJ, RCTT addresses two of the pressing needs of those emerging from periods of incarceration: the daunting prospect of finding paid work, and meaningful, sustaining community. As essential as the benefits of RCTT are to its members, of at least equal value is what this powerful creative work imparts to its audiences: the first-hand knowledge that those who have been incarcerated are people, not prisoners—a recognition that goes a long way to repairing the community twice harmed by the violence of crime and incarceration. Shakespeare BEYOND Bars, Time Out Of Joint, and the Returned Citizens Theatre Troupe suggest best possible endpoints for Shakespeare prison programs.

Given these successes, why, then, may we want *less* Shakespeare in carceral spaces? We hope the answer will be obvious: to be a healthy, just society, we need less prison. The carceral state in America in the first decades of the twenty-first century responds to the trauma of crime (and the underlying traumas that contribute to crime) with more trauma, extending and reinforcing the racial inheritance of slavery by further devastating Black and brown communities. Danielle Sered, in calling for us to respond to violence with healing rather than additional violence, names how "In incarceration, we have protected and exacerbated the core dimensions of slavery, woven and rewoven them into what could have been a changing story of our nation, entrenched them ever more deeply into our economy, and built our politics in service, rather than in opposition, to the core myths, values, and practices that define structural racism."[35] The rehabilitative and educational work done in prisons needs to stay grounded in this reality. As dave rich powerfully argues, education's democratizing function cannot be realized "until better reckoning is made with the reality that for many Black (male) students the classroom has often better prepared them for prison than college" (69). The contributors to this collection demonstrate that prison arts practitioners and teachers can and do go into these fundamentally oppressive, racially fraught spaces equally tuned into the reach and the limitations of Shakespeare. New ways of addressing harm and healing will require imagination and empathy. Knowing that Shakespeare is in prison can encourage us to come to these texts—whether as performers, teachers, readers, or audiences—with appreciation for living art with real impact and it can remind us that we are connected to one another in profound, often invisible, ways.

A NOTE ON LANGUAGE

We support the use of person-first terms to describe those who have experience with the carceral system (from jail and prison to the juvenile legal system and community corrections), in keeping with the insight of the Underground Scholars Language Guide that language "is not merely descriptive, it is creative."[36] Words like "convict" and "felon" define people solely by their carceral status and, in doing so, reduce their identity to that status. Terms like "incarcerated people" and "returning citizens" decline to do so. Such language is the default for this volume, although we respect the choices of some of our contributors to make different decisions and we always affirm the autonomy of justice-impacted people to name themselves. We note that decarceration and more just responses to harm will not follow from simply using different words; as Reginald Dwayne Betts reminds us, we need policy change, not a sanitized vocabulary.[37]

NOTES

1 The Sentencing Project, "Growth in Mass Incarceration," https://www.sentencingproject.org/research/; Prison Policy Initiative, "Mass Incarceration: The Whole Pie 2024," https://www.prisonpolicy.org/reports/pie2024.html.

2 Prison Policy Initiative, https://www.prisonpolicy.org/research/race_and_ethnicity/. The Federal Bureau of Prisons reported 38.7% of those incarcerated in 2024 were Black, https://www.bop.gov/about/statistics/statistics_inmate_race.jsp.

3 Michelle Alexander, *The New Jim Crow: Mass Incarceration in the Age of Colorblindness* (New York: New Books, 2010), 13.

4 James Davis III, "Law, Prison, and Double-Double Consciousness: A Phenomenological View of the Black Prisoner's Experience," *Yale Law Journal Forum* 128 (2018–2019): 1126–1144 (1128).

5 FBI Crime Data Explorer, https://cde.ucr.cjis.gov/LATEST/webapp/#/pages/explorer/crime/quarterly; John Gramlich, "What the Data Says About Crime in the U.S.," April 24, 2024, https://www.pewresearch.org/short-reads/2024/04/24/what-the-data-says-about-crime-in-the-us/.

6 Haley Filippine, "The Return to Tough-on-Crime: The Media's Role in Rolling Back Reform," *Criminal Law Practitioner*, March 20, 2024, https://www.crimlawpractitioner.org/post/the-return-to-tough-on-crime-the-media-s-role-in-rolling-back-reform.

7 For a comprehensive picture of the economics of incarceration in the United States, see Jackie Wang, *Carceral Capitalism* (Cambridge, MA: Massachusetts Institute of Technology Press, 2018), 39.

8 Agnes Wilcox, "Denmark Is a Prison, and You Are There," *The Journal of the Midwest Modern Language Association* 38, no. 1 (2005): 116–22 (120).

9 https://www.marinshakespeare.org/shakespeare-in-prison/. For more on the importance of creative community inside, see Zeke Caliguiri,

"Foreword," *American Precariat: Parables of Exclusion*, eds. Zeke Caliguiri et al. (Minneapolis: Coffee House Press, 2023), ix–xvi.

10 Margo Hendricks, "'I Saw Them in My Visage': Whiteness, Early Modern Race Studies, and Me," in *White People in Shakespeare: Essays on Race, Culture, and the Elite*, ed. Arthur L. Little, Jr. (London: Bloomsbury, 2023), 191–98. See Jenna Dreier, "Decolonising Pedagogies in Prison Performance Programmes: Making Shakespeare Secondary," *Research in Drama Education* 26, no. 3 (2021): 477–493 (478) and chapters in this volume by dave rich and Jayme Yeo.

11 Sophie Ward and Roy Connolly, "The Play Is a Prison: The Discourse of Prison Shakespeare," *Studies in Theatre and Performance* 40, no. 2 (2020): 128–144 (129).

12 David Sterling Brown, "Unicorns and Fairy Dust": Talking Shakespeare, Performance, and Social (In)Justice with Ayanna Thompson and Farah Karim-Cooper," *Shakespeare Bulletin* 39, no. 4 (2021): 537–558 (556).

13 Karen Swallow Prior, "Why Shakespeare Belongs in Prison," *The Atlantic*, April 23, 2014.

14 Rob Pensalfini, *Prison Shakespeare: For These Great Shames and Deep Indignities* (New York: Palgrave Macmillan, 2016), 228.

15 Barry Edelstein, "Becoming King," *Where There's A Will* (podcast), November 2022, https://www.pushkin.fm/podcasts/where-theres-a-will-finding-shakespeare/becoming-king.

16 Two examples are Laura Bates' memoir *Shakespeare Saved My Life: Ten Years in Solitary with the Bard* (Naperville: Sourcebooks, 2013) and Jean Trounstine's *Shakespeare Behind Bars: The Power of Drama in a Women's Prison* (New York: St. Martin's Press, 2001).

17 Bates, 252.

18 Reuben Jonathan Miller, *Halfway Home: Race, Punishment, and the Afterlife of Mass Incarceration* (New York: Little, Brown & Company, 2021), 226. See also Ellen Condliffe Lagemann, *Liberating Minds: The Case for College in Prison* (New York: The New Press, 2016), 37–44; Erin L. Castro, "Racism, the Language of Reduced Recidivism, and Higher Education in Prison: Toward an Anti-Racist Praxis," *Critical Education* 9, no. 17 (2018), 1–14.

19 Simon Rolston, *Prison Life Writing: Conversion and the Literary Roots of the U.S. Prison System* (Waterloo: Wilfrid Laurier University Press, 2021), 240.

20 Jon Marc Taylor, "Alternative Funding Options for Post-Secondary Correctional Education," *Journal of Correctional Education* 56, no. 1 (2005): 6.

21 Pensalfini, 8, 15, 19. For Shakespeare circulating on South Africa's Robben Island to political prisoners including Nelson Mandela, see David Schalkwyk, *Hamlet's Dreams: The Robben Island Shakespeare* (London: Bloomsbury, 2013).

22 From a handful of correspondence courses in California to the creation of a Standing Committee on Education of the American Prison Association in 1930 and the founding of the *Journal of Correctional Education* in 1937, prison education became increasingly institutionalized with the growing awareness of the need for post-secondary education and collaboration with colleges and universities. See Carl C. Gaither, "Education Behind Bars: An Overview," *Journal of Correctional Education* 33, no. 2 (1982): 19–23; Thom Gehring, "Post-Secondary Education for Inmates: An Historical Inquiry," *Journal of Correctional Education* 48, no. 2 (1997): 46–55; and Meagan Wilson, et al. "Unbarring Access: A Landscape Review of Postsecondary Education in Prison and Its Pedagogical Support," *Ithaka S+R*, May 30, 2019.

23 Bard Prison Initiative, 25th Anniversary of the 1994 Crime Bill, 9-11-19, https://bpi.bard.edu/pell/

24 Pensalfini explores the "prison Shakespeare" phenomenon from a global perspective. For some specific accounts of Shakespeare in prison programs in other countries, see Ramona Wray, "The Morals of Macbeth and Peace as Process: Adapting Shakespeare in Northern Ireland's Maximum Security Prison," *Shakespeare Quarterly* 62, no. 3, (2011): 340–363; Marta Fossati, "Transforming *Romeo and Juliet* in a Juvenile Detention Centre in Italy: A Decolonising Approach to Prison Shakespeare," *Shakespeare in Southern Africa* 36 (2023): 33–45; and Kevin A. Quarmby, "'Shakespeare in Prison': A South African Social Justice Alternative," *The Arden Research Handbook of Shakespeare and Social Justice*, ed. David Ruiter (London: Bloomsbury, 2021), 190–206. For Shakespeare programs in the broader context of prison performance arts, see Jonathan Shailor's collection of essays *Performing New Lives: Prison Theatre* (London: Jessica Kingsley Publishers, 2011).

25 Many of the Shakespeare-centric theater programs in prisons today credit Tofteland and SBB for inspiration and support. Important U.S. programs that followed include Prison Performing Arts in St. Louis, Prison Creative Arts in Michigan, Marin Shakespeare, Shakespeare

Prison Project in Wisconsin, Laura Bates' Shakespeare in the SHU in Indiana, and Detroit Public Theatre's Shakespeare In Prison program. For a survey that studies many of these programs, see Amy Scott-Douglass, *Shakespeare Inside: The Bard Behind Bars* (London: Continuum, 2007). Jonathan Shailor describes the influence of SBB and others as he started a Shakespeare prison program in "Humanizing Education Behind Bars: Shakespeare and the Theater of Empowerment," in *Challenging the Prison-industrial Complex: Activism, Arts, and Educational Alternatives*, ed. Stephen John Hartnett (Urbana: University of Illinois Press, 2011). See Niels Herold, *Prison Shakespeare and the Purpose of Performance: Repentance Rituals and the Early Modern* (New York: Palgrave Macmillan, 2014) for a close look at the rehabilitative process of SBB.
26 The Fourth International Shakespeare in Prison Conference, https://shakespeare.nd.edu/service/shakespeare-in-prisons/sipc4/.
27 Sharon O'Dair and Timothy Francisco, *Shakespeare and the 99%: Literary Studies, the Profession, and the Production of Inequity*, eds. Sharon O'Dair and Timothy Francisco (Cham: Palgrave Macmillan, 2019), 5.
28 David Ruiter, "This Is Real Life: Shakespeare and Social Justice as a Field of Play" *The Arden Research Handbook of Shakespeare and Social Justice*, ed. David Ruiter (London: Bloomsbury, 2022), 3.
29 Hilary Eklund and Wendy Beth Hyman, "Introduction," *Teaching Social Justice Through Shakespeare: Why Renaissance Literature Matters Now*, eds. Hilary Eklund and Wendy Beth Hyman (Edinburgh: Edinburgh University Press, 2020), 2.
30 Rowan Mackenzie, *Creating Space for Shakespeare: Working with Marginalized Communities* (London: Bloomsbury, 2023), 1.
31 Ess Pokornowski, Kurtis Tanaka, "Between Two Systems: Navigating Censorship and Self-Censorship in Higher Education in Prisons," *Ithaka S+R*, April 3, 2024, https://sr.ithaka.org/publications/between-two-systems/.
32 Jean Howard, "The White Shakespearean and Daily Practice," *White People in Shakespeare: Essays on Race, Culture, and the Elite*, ed. Arthur L. Little, Jr. (London: Bloomsbury, 2023), 266, 273.
33 Kimberlé Williams Crenshaw, Luke Charles Harris, Daniel Martinez HoSang, and George Lipsitz, eds., *Seeing Race Again: Countering Colorblindness across the Disciplines* (Oakland: University of California Press, 2019), 3.

34 Arthur L. Little, Jr., "Introduction: Assembling an Aristocracy of Skin," *White People in Shakespeare: Essays on Race, Culture, and the Elite*, ed. Arthur L. Little, Jr. (London: Bloomsbury, 2023), 1–26 (1).

35 Danielle Sered, *Until We Reckon: Violence, Mass Incarceration, and a Road to Repair* (The New Press, 2019), 235.

36 Underground Scholars Language Guide: A Guide For Communicating About People Involved in the Carceral System, March 26, 2019, https://undergroundscholars.berkeley.edu/blog/2019/3/6/language-guide-for-communicating-about-those-involved-in-the-carceral-system.

37 Reginald Dwayne Betts, "Incarcerated Language," *The Yale Review*, October 1, 2018, https://yalereview.org/article/incarcerated-language.

Past and Present

Shakespeare's "Working-House of Thought": The Prison in Early Modern London

Matthew Ritger

One

But now behold
In the quick forge and working-house of thought
How London doth pour out her citizens ...

Henry V, Act V, Prologue, 23–25

Although the scale, impact, and methods of twenty-first century mass incarceration have developed to a degree that would seem to defy all comparison, the prison was also an important fact of life in Shakespeare's own time.[1] Arguably, institutions and experiences of incarceration were just as common then as now, although in different ways: smaller in numbers and scale but more normalized for the population as a whole. Incarceration was an omnipresent fact of life for writers, poets, and dramatists, whether highborn or low; indeed, a list of canonical English writers incarcerated in the sixteenth or seventeenth century is nearly synonymous with the table of contents for *The Norton Anthology of English Literature*: Henry Howard, Thomas Wyatt, Thomas More, Thomas Kyd, Christopher Marlowe, Thomas Dekker, Ben Jonson, John Donne, and John Milton all experienced imprisonment at one point or another.[2] (Shakespeare himself would seem to be the exception that proves the rule.) Some of these were for debts;

DOI: 10.4324/9781003451662-3

some had to do with controversial plays or writings; some were political prisoners.

Prison writing, often drawing upon the influences of Boethius, the Pauline epistles, and the penitential psalms, developed into a foundational genre for English literature, enabled in part by the differing norms of an era when access to spaces of confinement and written communications were much less tightly controlled.[3] Visitors, letters, pamphlets, books, and even prisoners themselves circulated widely, often without the levels of censorship or extractive fines and fees that work to disrupt the communications of those "inside" today. Rivkah Zim has recently delineated many points of comparison within the long history of writing from confinement, from the Christian tradition to the English Renaissance and in every century since.[4] Then as now, "the early modern prison was a site of culture," Molly Murray has argued, one that "ought to be considered alongside the court and the university as a place of significant textual, and literary, production."[5] The work of contemporary writers, such as Jimmy Santiago Baca, George Jackson, or Assata Shakur, might therefore be set in a tradition that includes Martin Luther King Jr. or Oscar Wilde but also John Bunyan, Thomas More, and Boethius.

But while prisons remain a prominent center of cultural production today, the sense of a paradox has intensified. In part, this is likely because, as Foucault famously pointed out, "modern" penitentiaries have increasingly obscured the physical nature of punishment and moved its practices out of the public eye.[6] In the United States in the late twentieth and twenty-first centuries, the effect continues to divide public consciousness. A racialized and class-stratified polarization has been constructed between those whose lives and communities are disproportionately impacted by carceral systems and those who frequently read or hear about prisons in the news and other media but may never set foot inside, or might even find it difficult to say where their own local, state, or federal sites of incarceration are located. The physical space of neoliberal prisons and penitentiaries compound that bifurcation by removing themselves further "out of sight and out of mind" for some: behind fences or concealed from main roads, in rural locations and at the edges rather than the center of urban life, or even hidden in plain sight through the widening dispersal of surveillance methods James Kilgore calls "e-carceration."[7]

Or perhaps what Foucault might have called a "repressive hypothesis" has been underway.[8] In the United States today, the same society that appears determined to render modern prisons and those they impact invisible also makes that system a topic of constant discourse in other spheres: tracked by headlines and journalistic exposés, spurred on by community organizing and activism, followed by cycles of political debate and academic inquiry, constantly represented and misrepresented in films, television, or streaming series, podcasts, or most recently, on TikTok.[9] Perhaps what is peculiar to modern societies, to adapt Foucault's phrasing, is not that they have consigned the prison to a shadow existence, but that they dedicate themselves to speaking of the prison almost *ad infinitum*, positioning prisons and those impacted as a secret while simultaneously promulgating and trafficking in innumerable representations and misrepresentations.[10] What John J. Lennon has recently called a "renaissance" of writing, journalism, fiction, poetry, art- and media-making by incarcerated and formerly incarcerated persons exerts both aesthetic and political power through the potential to diversify, particularize, and humanize the representational stereotypes that surround or even displace prison practices today.[11]

In Shakespeare's London, the prison's physical presence and representational strategies were by contrast more direct, central, and obvious, and the threats these institutions posed were more widely shared. Murray has called the early modern prison the "anti-panopticon."[12] Rather than secretive and austere institutions transfixed by surveillance methods, prisons and other sites of punishment were some of the most central locations around which the whole of early modern London revolved. Public stocks and whipping posts were a common feature in nearly every square and marketplace. The gallows at Tyburn were notorious, but so were notorious institutions of confinement whose names might still be familiar today: the Tower of London, Newgate, the Clink, the Marshalsea, "Bedlam" asylum, as well as Bridewell, England's first "house of correction." All of these institutions were busy crossroads of daily life in early modern London. A more recent comparison might be made to the women's House of Detention in Greenwich Village in Manhattan from 1932 to 1974, a location whose centrality and accessibility—even to those on the sidewalk—seems unthinkable now.[13] Audre Lorde described the "House of D," as it was known, "right smack in the middle of the Village": "Information and endearments flew up and down, the conversants apparently oblivious to the ears of the passerby as they discussed the availability of lawyers, the length of stay, family, conditions, and the undying quality of true love."[14] The permeability and proximity of the House of D in its original location (in 1974, the prison's population was removed to Riker's Island) offers an imaginative steppingstone toward understanding the centrally located carceral institutions of Shakespeare's London. Reconsidering both might also help to question the distinctions between public spheres, inside or outside, today, when the "prison industrial complex" remains such an important, though more hidden, hub of economic, legal, educational, and cultural activity.

The physical proximity of London's prisons was perhaps especially important for early modern writers, actors, and playwrights, for multiple reasons. Due to jurisdictional idiosyncrasies, carceral institutions of Shakespeare's day tended to be located in London's ancient "liberties," which were part of the city but technically not under its jurisdiction, and where the new public theaters, too, were allowed to thrive.[15] London's liberties were akin to red light districts and black sites compounded into one: brothels and bear baiting rings existed alongside jails and prisons of equally questionable legality. Thanks to the extralegal possibilities afforded by these areas, Shakespeare's outdoor amphitheater at the Globe stood within the liberty of the Clink prison. Shakespeare's indoor playhouse, in the former monastery at the Blackfriars, was located not just next door but across a gallery bridge from Bridewell, the house of correction, which was at that time the city's most innovative and therefore most controversial carceral institution. There was even a bridge between Bridewell and Blackfriars: a wooden gallery spanning the ditch of the Fleet river (paved over entirely centuries ago), which stood throughout Shakespeare's lifetime.[16]

The prison on the other side of that passageway was both a regular fact of life and a constant danger to Shakespeare and his company. From 1572, statutes classed traveling playing companies as vagrants or vagabonds, and therefore, despite the legal cover of their noble patronage, Shakespeare and his collaborators were liable at any time to be policed, whipped, confined, and set to hard labor in the prison next door, especially if their productions offended or seemed too likely to incite a crowd.[17] (On occasion, actors and playwrights were punished in precisely this way.[18]) Bridewell's threatening presence serves as a reminder that Shakespeare's own relations to the power structures of his time and place were constantly shifting and genuinely ambiguous. On the one hand, he and his company were court performers, whose productions were carefully curated by the Crown and censored by civic magistrates; on the other hand, companies like his were just as likely to be seen, definitionally, as a threat to the social order, policed alongside the "idle" poor who made up a large part of their public audiences.

The present volume might therefore be understood differently than at first appears. By exploring the many ways Shakespeare's works are read, performed, studied, discussed, and experienced within and around prisons today, nearly 400 years after Shakespeare's death, the essays in this volume make a strong case for the idea that context matters to the interpretation and reinterpretation of any literary text. But while the meanings and insights of Shakespeare's plays might be startlingly fresh in prison education programs and prison libraries today, I would argue that one reason for this is not only because those contexts are vital, new, or unexpected places to be thinking about Shakespeare, but also because such readings *restore* a submerged yet common part of the political context within which Shakespeare's plays were first composed, performed, and printed. Recalling to mind the practices of a prison whose three-story towers loomed over Shakespeare's indoor theater might help us to reconsider any number of Shakespeare's plays and their most salient formal interventions in the general context of early modern England's own systems of punishment, just as today we find vital meanings in re-reading, re-staging, or re-thinking Shakespeare's plays within the context of our own carceral systems.

Bridewell, the first of England's early modern "houses of correction," is the institution I would single out for comparison, not only because of the bridge that connected its complex to Shakespeare's indoor theater, but because of its ideological relevance to the carceral institutions of today. Bridewell, for (or rather, *with*) all its corruption, struggles, and hypocrisies, is one of the most intriguing examples of the relevance of this period in the history of punishment for our own. Bridewell was established in the 1550s as London's first house of correction and has come to be seen by historians of punishment as the first institution anywhere in early modern Europe to combine short-term, variable sentences of confinement with hard labor, work training, and in some cases education, with the stated goal of individual reform.[19] Centuries before the rise of the penitentiary, England's original house of correction already experimented with many of the changes Foucault considered constitutive of the "modern" reformist penal paradigm.[20] Although whippings remained a common and essential part of penology at Bridewell—or the "house of occupations," "house of labors," or "house of reformation," as it was sometimes called—there were also efforts to incorporate more proleptically "modern" reforms.[21] Punishments were tailored to fit the minor wrongs of vagrancy or vice, such as "idleness" or "nightwalking," by varying the length of sentences and the kinds of work to which each subject might be set. Common tasks included pushing the mill, beating hemp, or spinning thread and yarn, while the young in particular were apprenticed to trades and crafts including making shoes, pins, nails, or even manufacturing "Tennise balls."[22] These labors constituted a meaningful sentencing reform, at least compared to the threat of mass hangings that were standard in ancient statutes.

The house of correction incorporated many of the ideas of Renaissance humanism, even as it struggled and failed to live up to those ideals. Like many correctional institutions today, especially juvenile justice facilities, Bridewell was a somewhat ambiguous place: part prison, part workhouse and workshop, but also containing school rooms for orphans and young apprentices. Humanist influence is everywhere in Bridewell's rhetoric and its logic of justification. The purpose of the house of correction was to return petty offenders as "proffitable members of the common wealth," according to some of its earliest records.[23] "By labour and punishment of their bodies, their forward natures may be bridled, their evil minds bettered," explained one justicer's manual in the early-seventeenth century, compressing those humanist ideals of the dignity and malleability of the human being into their coercive inverse.[24] One particularly vivid example of Bridewell's cruel-yet-humanist rhetoric can be found in its earliest surviving chronicle history, which is written as a catechistic dialogue taking place between the personified humanist virtues of "Dignitie" and "Dutie."[25] Dignity and Duty attempt to head off the public debate that surrounded these prison projects from the start, but they also allude to the persistent doubt that perhaps "nothing is to be learned" in these houses of reformation.[26] "The name of Bridewell is in the eares of the people so odious that it killeth the creadit forever," Dignity admitted.[27] Even in its earliest years, Bridewell's reputation was so bad that Londoners were hesitant to hire a servant or apprentice whose name had "tasted of that soile."[28]

But while the "reformist" house of correction faced existential questions and public resistance even from the beginning, nothing comparable to an early abolitionist critique had yet emerged. The house of correction's corruption scandals, financial difficulties, and reports of shocking cruelty were well known, but in the later sixteenth and seventeenth centuries the official response was to double down on these new organizations, not to abandon them. Bridewell's own records show that, given its rates of recidivism, or "old guests" as they were called in the court books, the institution was clearly failing to keep its promise that repentance, correction, or reform could be brought about through its institutional means—and yet its model only seemed to grow in appeal.[29] Questions of ethics and practical viability continued to haunt England's houses of correction throughout the early modern period, and yet legislation continued to mandate the establishment of dozens of new organizations, each built on London's model, and each promoting themselves in the hope that, through the moral education of hard labor, anyone might "overthrow" their "vicious life of idleness."[30]

These unresolved problems already haunted the characters, or perhaps the idea of character itself, in so many of Shakespeare's plays. *Measure for Measure*, *The Tempest*, and *Hamlet* come most immediately to mind, but one might also suggest *Henry IV, Part 1*, where Prince Hal must reform his "idle" habits, or even less expected plays, such as the reparative romance of *The Winter's Tale*, to which I will now turn. *The Winter's Tale*, first performed in 1611, is one of the "late plays" most likely to have been staged at the Blackfriars (where Shakespeare and his company began performing after 1608) and thus in the actual shadow of Bridewell.[31] Carceral imagery adds a kind of crosshatching to the play's imagery from the very beginning. In Act 1, Scene 2, Hermione's efforts to persuade Polixenes to stay longer at court raise her husband's suspicions, and glaringly foreshadow her own unjust punishment. She plays at threatening detention:

> HERMIONE: ...Will you go yet?
>   Force me to keep you as a prisoner,
>   Not like a guest, so you shall pay your fees
>   When you depart and save our thanks. How say you?
>   My prisoner or my guest? By your dread 'Verily,'
>   One of them you shall be.
> POLIXENES: Your guest, then, madam.
>   To be your prisoner should import offending,
>   Which is for me less easy to commit
>   Than you to punish.
> HERMIONE: Not your jailer, then,
>   But your kind hostess.
>
> (1.2.52–62)

Hermione's persuasions take confinement and coercion as metaphor. When she succeeds, her husband Leontes flies into a jealous rage, accusing her of adultery, of being a "bed-swerver" and suggesting the child in her womb may have been fathered by Polixenes (2.1.93). "Away with her to prison," Leontes declares, swiftly literalizing and reversing Hermione's playful threat (2.1.103). Hermione exits defiantly: "When you shall know your mistress / Has deserved prison, then abound in tears / As I come out," she tells her women servants (2.1.120). The prison then becomes the metaphor for Hermione's womb as well as the injustice she suffers under Leontes' autocratic rule. "'My poor prisoner,'" Emilia reports Hermione saying to her newborn daughter, "'I am as innocent as you'" (2.2. 29–30). Paulina takes up the trope: "This child was prisoner to the womb and is / By law and process of great nature thence / Freed and enfranchised," she tells the Jailer, taking the infant into her care, outside the prison (2.2.59–60).

When Hermione's name is cleared by the oracle, the play's carceral metaphor turns itself inside out. Hermione remains in the position of civil death, perhaps even deceased, or confined to Paulina's "removed house" (5.2.105), where a statue in her memory—which she famously poses as in the final scene—embodies her frozen state of detention. Leontes, on the other hand, becomes the active penitent required to change and reform himself, not unlike those laboring in the house of correction. For 16 years, he "shuts up himself" and spends his days in prayer over the memorials to his son and wife (4.1.19). A soliloquy from Time, as the Chorus, and the long, pastoral interlude of Act 4, attempt to achieve the effect of time itself passing: "impute it not a crime," Time begs the audience, "that I slide / O'er sixteen years" (4.1. 4–6). "Once a day I'll visit / The chapel where they lie," Leontes promises, "and tears shed there / Shall be my recreation" (3.2.238). Recreation in this case will mean both consistent activity ("this exercise") and a reformation, a re-creation (3.2.239).

The conceit neatly reverses penal rhetoric of the house of correction next door. Hermione, who is guiltless, remains in isolation, a "dead likeness" of herself, much like a solitary confinement; Leontes, meanwhile, is the one who must undertake "this exercise" of ironic "recreation" or reform to "amend thy life" (as the Clown says to Autolycus, 5.2.150), not for a minor infraction of disorder, but for something potentially intractable. One has been cast out for nothing; the other has to work himself back to social rehabilitation for something that actually may be irreparable in secular terms—causing the death of his wife and elder child.

These asymmetries and injustices compound the faith-test of the finale. By the end of the 16 years and the end of the play, Cleomenes claims Leontes has done his time: "you have done enough, and have performed / A saintlike sorrow. No fault could you make / Which you have not redeemed—indeed, paid down / More penitence than done trespass" (5.1.1–4). "Forgive yourself," Cleomenes encourages Leontes (5.1.5). "Dear life redeems you," Paulina says, seemingly to Leontes, although it is Hermione who begins to stir (5.3.103). Hermione is the one who has been unjustly confined but not the one who needed to change or reform; Leontes is the penitent who has been his own house of correction, laboring to change his ways, but it has been a metaphorical, individual, and not institutional process, if we believe it—time in Paulina's "poor house" but nothing like an actual, carceral, workhouse.

Both sides of the chiasmatic structure might contain a double-edged critique of Bridewell next door. There is the injustice that Hermione, wrongly accused of a "crime" in which the law really ought to have no business in the first place, is the one whose freedoms are impacted. There is also the irony that Leontes, outside confinement and above the law, is the one who must daily try to create a change of heart, behavior, or the appearance of a duty to society done right, without or outside the institutional structures one might expect. Both ask that we imagine or reimagine how character is made, how people change, whether they do, by what means, and how we might know. Both contribute to the famously divided readings, interpretations, experiences, and stagings of the play's undecidable ending. And both position art itself as a medium for thinking about these questions.

NOTES

1 Wacquant suggests "hyper" rather than "mass" better describes the phenomenon; see Loïc Wacquant, "Class, Race, and Hyperincarceration in Revanchist America," *Socialism and Democracy* 28, no. 3 (2014): 35–56.
2 *The Oxford Dictionary of National Biography* offers concise accounts for each: Susan Brigden, "Howard, Henry, earl of Surrey (1516/17–1547), poet and soldier;" Colin Burrow, "Wyatt, Sir Thomas (c. 1503–1542), poet and ambassador;" Seymour Baker, "More, Sir Thomas [St Thomas More] (1478–1535), lord chancellor, humanist, and martyr;" J.R. Mulryne, "Kyd, Thomas (bap. 1558, d. 1594), playwright and translator;" Charles Nicholl, "Marlowe [Marley], Christopher (bap. 1564, d. 1593), playwright and poet;" John Twyning, "Dekker, Thomas (c. 1572–1632), playwright and pamphleteer;" Ian Donaldson, "Jonson, Benjamin [Ben] (1572–1637), poet and playwright," David Colclough, "Donne, John (1572–1631), poet and Church of England clergyman," Gordon Campbell, "Milton, John (1608–1674), poet and polemicist." See also *The Norton Anthology of English Literature, tenth edition, volume B: The Sixteenth and Early Seventeenth Century*, ed. Stephen Greenblatt (New York: W.W. Norton and Company).
3 Ruth Ahnert's *The Rise of Prison Literature in the Sixteenth Century* (Cambridge, UK: Cambridge University Press, 2013), offers a comprehensive yet succinct account.
4 See Rivkah Zim, *The Consolations of Writing: Literary Strategies of Resistance from Boethius to Primo Levi* (Princeton: Princeton University Press, 2014).
5 Molly Murray, "Measured Sentences: Forming Literature in the Early Modern Prison," *Huntington Library Quarterly* 72, no. 2 (2009): 147–167 (150).
6 Michel Foucault, *Discipline and Punish: The Birth of the Prison*, trans. Alan Sheridan (New York: Vintage Books, 1995), 9, 236–239.
7 See James Kilgore, *Understanding E-Carceration: Electronic Monitoring, the Surveillance State, and the Future of Mass Incarceration* (New York: The New Press, 2022).
8 This suggestion transposes an insight from Foucault's work on the history of sexuality, which noted how the supposed repression of sexual culture in the nineteenth century was accompanied by an explosion of discourses centered on sexuality in other ways (psychiatric, biological, therapeutic, confessional). Michel Foucault, *The History of Sexuality, vol. 1*,

trans. Robert Hurley (New York: Vintage Books, 1990), part two "The Repressive Hypothesis," 15–50.

9 Stevie Borrello, Daniel Fetherston, and Katherine Tutrone, "Prisoners Are Going Viral on TikTok," *Vice News*, November 12, 2020, https://www.vice.com/en/article/7k9bzd/prison-inmates-are-going-viral-on-tiktok.

10 "What is peculiar to modern societies, in fact, is not that they consigned sex to a shadow existence, but that they dedicated themselves to speaking of it *ad infinitum*, while exploiting it as *the* secret." Foucault, *History of Sexuality*, 35.

11 John J. Lennon, "The Prisoner and the Pen," *Esquire*, September 29, 2023, https://www.esquire.com/news-politics/a45191144/prison-free-writing-laws/.

12 Murray, 152.

13 For more on the House of D consider Angela Y. Davis, Gina Dent, Erica Meiners, and Beth Richie, *Abolition. Feminism. Now.* (New York: Haymarket Books, 2022).

14 Quoted in Angela Y. Davis et al., *Abolition. Feminism. Now.*, 18.

15 A concise overview is provided by Steven Mullaney's "Shakespeare and the Liberties," *Encyclopedia Britannica Book of the Year* (Published online, 2005), and more generally in Stephen Mullaney, *The Place of the Stage: License, Play and Power in Renaissance England* (Ann Arbor: University of Michigan Press, 1988).

16 Tony Dyson and Derek Gadd, "Excavations at 9–11 Bridewell Place and 1–3 Tudor Street, City of London, 1978," *Post-Medieval Archaeology* 15 (1981), 17.

17 14.Eliz. c.5, 1572; see Peter Roberts, "Elizabethan Players and Minstrels and the Legislation of 1572 Against Retainers and Vagabonds," in *Religion, Culture, and Society in Early Modern Britain*, ed. Anthony Fletcher and Peter Roberts (Cambridge, UK: Cambridge University Press, 1994), 29–55.

18 Following a performance of John Day's *The Isle of Guls* in 1606, several of the players and theatrical agents were thrown into Bridewell after staging their play in the Blackfriars. See Julie Sanders, "In the Friars: The Spatial and Cultural Geography of an Indoor Playhouse," *Cahiers Élisabéthains* 88, no. 1 (2015), 27.

19 Michael Ignatieff, *A Just Measure of Pain: The Penitentiary in the Industrial Revolution, 1750–1850* (New York: Penguin, 1978), 11: London's Bridewell was "the earliest forerunner of the penitentiary" and "the first use of confinement as a coercive education." Dario Melossi and Massimo Pavarini, *The Prison and the Factory: Origins of the Penitentiary System*, 40th Anniversary Edition (London: Palgrave Macmillan, 2018), 32: Bridewell is called "the most important example" before the penitentiary; its "social function and internal organization [were] ... already to a large extent those of the classic nineteenth-century model." Simon Devereaux and Paul Griffiths, eds., *Penal Practice and Culture, 1500–1900* (New York: Palgrave Macmillan, 2004), 4, 5.

20 Foucault, *Discipline and Punish*, 7, 121, 141; J. A. Sharpe, *Crime in Early Modern England, 1550–1750* (New York: Longman, 1999, 2nd ed.), 258; Pieter Spierenberg, "Four Centuries of Prison History: Punishment, Suffering, the Body, and Power," in *Institutions of Confinement: Hospitals and Prisons in Western Europe and North America, 1500–1950*, eds. Norbert Finzsch and Robert Jütte (Cambridge, UK: Cambridge University Press, 1996), 17–35; Philip Gorski, *The Disciplinary Revolution: Calvinism and the Rise of the State in Early Modern Europe* (Chicago: University of Chicago Press, 2003), 25.

21 Paul Griffiths, *Lost Londons: Change, Crime and Control in the Capital City, 1550–1660* (Cambridge, UK: Cambridge University Press, 2008), 18; Devereaux and Griffiths, eds., *Penal Practice and Culture*, 1500–1900, 23.

22 Paul Slack, "Hospitals, Workhouses, and the Relief of the Poor in Early Modern London," in *Health Care and Poor Relief in Protestant Europe, 1500–1700*, eds. Andrew Cunningham and Ole Peter Grell (London: Routledge, 1997), 229–247 (234–238); Griffiths, *Lost Londons*, 18, 253–254, 279; *Orders Appointed to be Executed in the Citie of London, for Setting Roges and Idles Persons to Worke, and for the Releefe of the Poore* (London: Printed by J. Charlewood for Hugh Singleton, 1587), B2ᵛ.

23 John Howes, *John Howes' MS, 1582: Being a Brief Note of the Order and Manner of the Proceedings in the First Erection of the Three Royal Hospitals*, ed. William Lempriere (London: Septimus Morgan, 1904), 10.

24 Michael Dalton, *The Country Justice, Containing the Practice of the Justices of the Peace*... (London: Printed by the Company of Stationers, 1661), fol. 122 (Dalton's handbook dates from 1618). "Forward" or "froward" dates from the fourteenth century: "perverse, difficult to deal

with… ungovernable,… 'naughty,'" as defined by the Oxford English Dictionary: *Oxford English Dictionary*, s.v. "froward, adj., adv., & prep.," https://doi.org/10.1093/OED/5702557197.

25 Quoted in John Abernathy Kingdon, *Richard Grafton, Citizen and Grocer of London* (London: Printed by Rixon and Arnold, 1901), 53.

26 R. H. Tawney, ed., *Tudor Economic Documents: Being Select Documents Illustrating the Economic and Social History of Tudor England*, vol. 3 (London: Longmans, 1924), 439.

27 Tawney, 438.

28 Tawney, 439.

29 Griffiths, 198.

30 Quoted in Kingdon, 53.

31 William Shakespeare, *The Winter's Tale*, ed. Frances E. Dolan (New York: Penguin Books), xxix. All subsequent citations are from this edition.

Hope Needs to Be Loud: A Founding Member on
Nearly 30 Years of Shakespeare Behind Bars

Hal Cobb

Two

Looking at Shakespeare Behind Bars (SBB) from the outside in, some surmise that we're just a bunch of inmates learning to become better liars and mastering the art of deception to become more accomplished criminals. Nothing could be further from the truth. Truth is the basis of SBB. It's the foundation we're built upon. We are pushed to find truth in the roles we take on and uncover personal parallels within Shakespeare's complex, completely human characters. It's rarely an easy or pleasant journey. It can be ugly, intimidating, frightening, unfamiliar, and overwhelming. Sometimes it's joyous and liberating. Often, one leads to the other.

When I arrived at Luther Luckett Correctional Complex (LLCC) outside of Louisville, Kentucky in mid-winter 1995, I had never been to prison before and didn't know what was in store. I began performing as a child as a way to escape who I was. I could hide behind a lyric or a character and pretend to be anybody else but me. I was approached by a staff psychologist in 1995 to be a replacement Prince of Verona in the fight scene from *Romeo and Juliet*. It turned out to be the birth of SBB and the end of acting as an escape for me.

I

One of the most important aspects of SBB is the fact that, as in Shakespeare's day, men play the female roles. I played

DOI: 10.4324/9781003451662-4

Sylvia in our first play production, The Two Gentlemen of Verona, in 1996, largely because no one else wanted to play a female, except for the very daring and delightful Billy Wheeler playing Julia, SBB's first guy-playing-a-gal-dressed-up-as-a-dude role. Curt L. Tofteland coached us to approach female characters just as we would any other: Lean into the text—everything we need to know about any character is there. Aside from initial catcalls from inmate audiences, there were no real external repercussions to showing up in a dress on stage in prison. For many SBB members, playing a female character is an internal hurdle to overcome, but when they do, it provides a most profound insight and personal change. We learn from the very beginning female characters aren't about how much wiggle and shake, affected gesturing, or falsetto vocalization you layer on, but, as with all of Shakespeare's characters, you simply tell the truth.

Over the years, I had the opportunity to play magnificent women from Shakespeare's canon: Gertrude in 2002's *Hamlet*; Portia and Calpurnia in the same 2004 production of *Julius Caesar* (in my mind, Ann-Margret vs. Nancy Reagan); Lady Macbeth in 2009; Lady Capulet in 2012's *Romeo and Juliet*; Richard III's Lady Anne in 2013; and Lady Macbeth's distant cousin Dionyza in 2015's *Pericles, Prince of Tyre*. Though each lady taught me great things, I perhaps learned the most from playing Gertrude.

Gertrude helped me to understand the women in my life: my mother, my former wives, my sisters, my daughter, my female friends. I found nothing textually to suggest that Gertrude knew anything about Claudius' plot to kill her husband and claim her along with the crown. As a widow, she has few options. As Queen, she knows a king-less Denmark is at risk of invasion from Norway. It is her duty to protect her country by marrying the closest heir, her brother-in-law. What other option did she have? Who is she if not Queen? Duty first also protects her status.

Having grown up in a southern, fundamentalist family, I began to look at the limitations society and the church had placed on the women in my life. They had been raised with very clearly defined gender roles to play, limiting their options. You can't argue with God, the church, or societal expectations without consequences, the ultimate being to burn in hell. It is one's Christian and womanly duty to marry, produce children, and submit to the man of the house as the church submits to God. No concern for one's personal hopes or desires.

I found myself more snugly in my mother's shoes as Gertrude becomes the mother of a murderer. How do you continue to love a child when they are responsible for the death of an innocent? My heart broke and grew empathetically as I began to understand the helplessness and pain I forced on my mother and other women in my life.

In our 2024 production of *As You Like It*, two men who had never played female roles took on Rosalind and Celia. The roles called to them because the "ride or die" quality of the characters mirrored their own personal friendship. They unashamedly threw themselves into the characters and were taken to places they couldn't anticipate. Glenn Guntle, an Army veteran once deployed to Iraq, discovered that as Celia he was the voice of women in the play. It was his job to rein in Chad Meadow's thoughtful Rosalind as she tested her masculine wings disguised as Ganymede. He had never looked at the world through a woman's eyes before. He admitted in Q&A sessions after public performances that he had never considered women's perspectives before, and that he had often taken women in his life for granted. For a man in a hyper-machismo environment to make a discovery like that is nothing less than astounding. It is the gift SBB members receive in playing Shakespeare's women.

II

The documentary *Shakespeare Behind Bars*, chronicling the nine-month process of preparing the 2002–2003 production of *The Tempest*, premiered at the Sundance Film Festival in January 2005 to great critical acclaim and went on to play at over forty film festivals around the world, winning eleven awards. It was broadcast on PBS, Sundance Channel, BBC, Starz/Encore, and other global channels. The film has been screened at more than 100 colleges and universities and has become part of high school and college curricula across the country and in places as far away as Australia and Japan as an introduction to both Shakespeare and criminal justice. Teachers and professors, along with their students, have journeyed to LLCC to observe the process of our rehearsals with amazing, challenging, and insightful Q&A sessions giving our work a more immediate sense of purpose and accomplishment.

My personal hope for the documentary was that it might be a bridge to reconciliation with estranged family and the extended community, an invitation to dialogue. Unfortunately, as a "trained actor" (a definition assigned to me by a prosecuting attorney), my participation in a prison acting company has been perceived as a miscarriage of justice since I get to partake in something I love instead of being punished. No dialogue with family or community members ensued.

Although I haven't seen the documentary for years, there are two moments burned into my memory. First, the scene where Curt is coaching me to access deeper feelings, digging into my "cabined, cribbed, [and] confined" heart to crack open Prospero. I stand there willing, yet confounded, with no idea how to break down walls installed as a toddler, beat into me before adolescence, shamed into me as a teenager, cemented over as an adult who takes his lover's life. I watch myself on film as a cloud covers my countenance, a steel security door unconsciously scrolls down in self-protection. I only knew how to withdraw, shut down. The next scene: a musical montage—me walking in the rain by steamed chow hall windows to retrieve my dinner—like the composer reached into my soul and scored its embedded sorrow and isolation.

As with all documentaries, participants are captured and frozen in time. The unintended consequence for me is I felt perceived as wallowing in self-pity rather than taking responsibility for my actions. What the documentary doesn't show is the growth I made in progressive years taking on roles like Leontes in *The Winter's Tale*, where I confront responsibility for a wife's death and abandonment of my daughter; with Malvolio in *Twelfth Night*—trapped in his puritanical (my fundamentalist) beliefs and desperate to be in love; and ultimately the title role in *King Lear*—self-absorbed to the point of blindness, ignorant of the consequences actions have on others until perhaps it's too late. The process of healing deep wounds can take more than one season.

III

In *The Winter's Tale*, Leontes, the King of Sicilia, appears to be responsible for the death of his wife, the death of one child, and the abandonment of another. Originally, for our 2010 production, two of us were drawn to the role of Leontes, both of us for similar reasons, both with similar crimes. It meant we would have to reenact portions of, and take responsibility for, our crimes. I'd previously taken the opportunity to work on deeper connections to roles with Titus Andronicus, Gertrude, and Prospero in *The Tempest*. I decided to take on the supporting role of Cleomenes, Leontes' close confidante and advisor, as James Prichard stepped up to the monumental task of facing his crime and victim through a Shakespearean character. I could be close enough to Leontes to vicariously garner benefits, as well as support a brave soul doing the work of a lifetime.

But being willing and being emotionally available are often at odds with each other, as I experienced when trying to access my heart while working on *The Tempest*, as caught for posterity's sake in the documentary. Automatic emotional defense mechanisms often kick in. Even though your spirit is willing, your body (where emotional memory is often stored) can be weak. Months into the 2010 *Winter's Tale* season, Prichard became overwhelmed and asked if we could switch roles.

Nearly a decade later, while searching for scenes for the SBB 25 Year Retrospective, *The Winter's Tale* Act 5, Scene 1 came immediately to mind: the repentant Leontes with faithful Cleomenes and Paulina—the ever-diligent victims' advocate. It was an opportunity for Prichard and me to return to our original casting. Prichard was still hesitant to tackle what he could not previously, but he knew he needed to do it and courageously faced his apprehension. It was difficult and glorious to hear and experience, but not as difficult as it was to confess publicly:

> LEONTES: Whilst I remember
>   Her and her virtues, I cannot forget
>   My blemishes in them, and so still think of
>   The wrong I did; which was so much,

> That heirless it hath made my kingdom and
> Destroy'd the sweet'st companion that e'er man
> Bred his hopes out of.
> PAULINA: True, too true, my lord:
> If, one by one, you wedded all the world,
> Or from the all that are took something good,
> To make a perfect woman, she you kill'd
> Would be unparallel'd.
> LEONTES: I think so. Kill'd!
> She I kill'd! I did so: but thou strikest me
> Sorely, to say I did; it is as bitter
> Upon thy tongue as in my thought: now, good now,
> Say so but seldom.
>
> (5.1.7–23)[1]

It was powerful to hear Prichard's ownership and experience the profound healing that takes place in SBB in moments like that. But this time, I found it difficult to internalize Cleomenes' opening remarks to Leontes:

> Sir, you have done enough, and have perform'd
> A saint-like sorrow: no fault could you make,
> Which you have not redeem'd; indeed, paid down
> More penitence than done trespass: at the last,
> Do as the heavens have done, forget your evil;
> With them forgive yourself.
>
> (5.1.1–6)

Words like that are easy to say to someone else, especially when you know they deserve to hear them. But when you try to say them to yourself...I choked out the words privately and publicly while memorizing, and repeated them silently in meditation as I drifted off to sleep for months before I could do so without tearing up. I still haven't quite learned how to embody them.

IV

As an inmate longing for redemption and forgiveness, I prefer plays and characters that offer and model those possibilities. I was drawn to characters like Prospero, Leontes, and Lear. Despite their inherent human character flaws (paranoia, abuse of power, drive for revenge, hubris) they learn their lessons and love breaks through to set them free. Conversely, Gertrude in Hamlet, Lady Macbeth in the Scottish Play, and Titus Andronicus die unredeemed. Titus left me feeling disjointed and numb for months after. He got the revenge he wanted, but it was hollow. Had he survived, would he have found peace? If the chains of fear and pain were to be broken, it would be up to his surviving grandson and future generations.

Prison is the perfect place for actors to explore the dark side of human nature. Many of us don't have to imagine the atrocities of a Shakespearean character. In the way SBB works, striving to find the truth of the text within ourselves, making personal emotional connections with the characters we portray, there is a therapeutic effect. As uncomfortable as dredging up personal demons can be, I've learned that I don't have to keep secrets anymore. You're only as sick as your secrets. As I own my past and take responsibility for my choices and actions, I purge the power they've held over me.

I was so myopically focused on being forgiven in our 2002–2003 journey with The Tempest that I totally missed the glaring fact that for 95% of the play Prospero is focused on revenge. It made me revisit Prospero in 2023 for the Retrospective. In Act 5, Scene 1, he stumbles on forgiveness by accident as he's about to wreak havoc on those who have wronged him. Prospero relishes that his payback project has gathered to a head and summons Ariel to report how his magical torment is affecting his enemies. Ariel's description of his enemies' contrition and the unintended effects of his actions on his good old, innocent friend Gonzalo is the straw that breaks the camel's back:

> ARIEL: Your charm so strongly works 'em
>   That if you now beheld them, your affections
>   Would become tender.
> PROSPERO: Dost thou think so, spirit?
> ARIEL: Mine would, sir, were I human[e].
>
> (5.1.21–25)[2]

As the forgiveness scene unfolds Prospero has to enact the insights he's gained. He chooses to forgive. Forgiveness is not some magical or mystical feeling that sweeps over someone, even when faced with the unanticipated consequences of seeking revenge. It is a tough choice, and not a one and done thing. Forgiveness must be repeated as often as is necessary.

Prospero chooses to forgive twice. First, he forgives his enemies while they are still entranced and cannot hear him. Then he chooses to forgive them face to face when his magic fades and they are back to themselves. Alonzo, King of Naples and co-conspirator against him, shows contrition and asks for forgiveness, which Prospero most easily grants. But when faced with an unrepentant Antonio, his own flesh and blood, "whom to call brother / Would even infect my mouth," he struggles (5.1.150–151). Can he live up to his intention: "Yet with my nobler reason 'gainst my fury / Do I take part: the rarer action is / In virtue than in vengeance" (5.1.34–35)?

Jerry (Big G) Guenthner as Antonio almost smugly dared me as Prospero to forgive him. When I choked out the words "I do forgive / Thy rankest fault / all of them," his countenance changed as we embraced, to one who desperately desired forgiveness (5.1.151–152).

Shakespeare is a master at understanding and illuminating human nature and he doesn't hold back in *King Lear*. Illuminating may be the wrong term as he exposes the profound, ever-present dark side and ugliness of humanity through many of his characters. Like Lear, the damage I've done to my family, friends, and community was rooted in self-absorption, lack of self-awareness, and inconsideration. Lear is never purposely a jerk. As a king, raised and surrounded by sycophants, he was never told no. In contrast, as a cowering child striving to be the best little boy in the world, it seemed like I never heard yes. Both backgrounds can result in a sense of narcissistic entitlement. Underneath it all, Lear and I want to love and be loved—to atone, to be forgiven, reconciled with, and loved by the dear ones we wronged the most. Unfortunately, the effect of Cordelia's forgiveness, though profound, is short lived. Like King Lear, my personal growth, redemption, and ability to take responsibility may have come too late. Life, at present, has the same sense of unease that many are left with at the conclusion of Shakespeare's great tragedy.

V

Ultimately, we as SBB members have to open up, reveal ourselves, and become vulnerable in an environment that discourages and devalues such honesty at every turn. Vulnerability is a strength we learn, and it is the key to self-discovery, transformation, and change. Honesty and vulnerability are what sets SBB apart from any other program, class, or seminar found in prison. We don't allow each other to hide behind a false front, or skate across the surface of a deeper connection, memory, or emotion. We embrace each other during these difficult discoveries. We hold a safe, supportive, non-judgmental space for each other to find and assimilate our own truths, take responsibility for our own actions, and develop into the men we often didn't know we could be.

Being incarcerated for 29 years with no out date can drain hope out of a man. After numerous parole board hearings, Red in *The Shawshank Redemption* muses, "Hope is a dangerous thing." Now anticipating a fifth parole board hearing, I profoundly understand what he means. It can leave one as melancholy as Jaques. Paraphrasing a recent public service announcement on recovery: HOPE NEEDS TO BE LOUD TO BE HEARD. Isolation and depression can be deafening. Shakespeare Behind Bars is the loudest hope I've found in prison. It is the only program that provides continuity and a sense of community. It has helped me to know, express, and hold on to who I truly am, in spite of my past and current surroundings.

NOTES

1. William Shakespeare, *The Winter's Tale*, eds. Barbara A. Mowat and Paul Werstine (Washington, DC: Folger Shakespeare Library, 1998).
2. William Shakespeare, *The Tempest*, eds. Barbara A. Mowat and Paul Werstine (Washington, DC: Folger Shakespeare Library, 1994).

Three Thousand Hours: Shakespeare
and Awe in Prison

Sarah Higinbotham

Three

It may seem that prison would be a place devoid of awe. But in the Shakespeare classroom early one December morning in 2018, in a Georgia state prison where I had been teaching for ten years, I began class by defining "awe": "an emotional response to perceptually vast stimuli that defy one's accustomed frame of reference."[1] I asked, "when have you experienced awe? When have you felt an emotional response to something more vast, more boundless than you typically encounter?"

Some shared vibrant memories of musical concerts, of surviving a car accident, of the birth of their children, of an act of self-sacrifice by a cellmate, of a home-cooked dinner that we shared (their first homemade food in ten years), of shared laughter and insight with visiting Emory and Morehouse students, and of witnessing the moral courage of the people with whom they were incarcerated.

But many of their responses centered on encountering Shakespeare's characters. Glenn relayed the epiphany he experienced when Hamlet distances himself from his action, speaking of himself in the third person, even while apologizing to Laertes, "Give me your pardon, sir: I've done you wrong..." Then a sudden shift four lines later, within the same speech: "Was it Hamlet wronged Laertes? Never Hamlet..."[2] Glenn quoted the lines, then quietly said that

DOI: 10.4324/9781003451662-5

"Never Hamlet" paralleled how *he* had disassociated since he had been in prison. Realizing that he shared moments of disconnection with the "brilliant and fucked-up guy Hamlet" filled him with awe. Shep also turned to Hamlet, stating that he experienced awe when he realized that Hamlet is a "denizen of the ghetto" just like himself, simultaneously shattered by a family member's death but not allowed to grieve because of what Shep called "ghetto politics." Shep then shared how the death of his brother—"his king"—affected him just as the king's death left Hamlet: angry, lost, erratic, and desperate. Shep's realization invoked his awe.

For Jayme, awe came in the character of Shylock, whose assertion of his humanity against a powerful system transcended Jayme's lived experience. Jayme said he was "awed" by watching a man "pushed past the limits of his bond," and I realized that Jayme and others perceived Shylock's literal "bond" with Antonio in their implicitly broken social contracts with the state. Brand's awe moment was Angelo's soliloquy in *Measure for Measure*, when Angelo confronts his own limitations by acknowledging that "blood, thou art blood" and confessing that for most of his life, he had "wrench[ed] awe from fools."[3] When Angelo faced "his own bluster and cons," Brand said, and realized he is flawed, "yeah, I felt awe. Nothing but awe. Because that was me."

In these and other "awe moments," the incarcerated students connected moments in Shakespeare's plays with their own emotions, feelings, and thoughts—evoking an epiphany: they saw themselves as part of a transhistorical social network. It was a continuum they didn't know existed. Until they studied Shakespeare in prison, their only association with the Shakespeare brand was that of a remote and irrelevant cultural icon. Then they read Shakespeare, and debated about his plays and poetry, and criticized his plots, and articulated flaws in his art, and performed his work. They did not approach the historical person of Shakespeare as an icon nor did they idolize his work; rather, they rejected closed, hegemonic readings and they mirrored what Mikael Bakhtin saw in Shakespeare's plays: a "godlike freedom" that is "eternally mobile," open to and activating connections between their lives and the emotional lives of Shakespeare's characters.[4] That freedom allowed them to identify with Shakespeare's characters in ways that was not didactic or even redemptive. And those revelations invoked awe.

That *Shakespeare's* characters felt what *they* felt, and articulated their own emotions, and allowed them to transcend a highly-policed environment with criticism and even laughter, moved them to awe. And the science of awe demonstrates that when awe is triggered by a vast sense of shared community, human beings respond by bonding even more closely with those in proximity to them.

Dacher Keltner, one of the foremost psychologists studying awe, links just such a shift to how awe functions: "Our default mind," Keltner writes in 2023, "blinds us to this fundamental truth, that our social, natural, physical, and cultural worlds are made up of interlocking systems. Experiences of awe open our minds to this big idea. Awe shifts us to a systems view of life."[5] Incarcerated lives, so defined by physical and interpersonal isolation, shift to a systems-orientation: incarcerated readers of Shakespeare shared that they suddenly sensed how they were part of a unified whole. It is a powerful emotion, often relayed with a huge smile or a slow head shake of incredulity. It is a kind of beloved community that I myself have felt awed by in every prison class I've taught.

Thus, as I listened to the men quoting Shakespeare plays from memory—often from plays we had not discussed for over a year—and to the ways that Shakespeare had fostered a sense of emotional vastness, I shared their awe. That first awe discussion remains one of the most enlightening moments in more than 3,000 epiphany-filled hours inside prison classrooms.[6] I began to sense the profound ways that reading, discussing, and performing Shakespeare inside prison fosters awe, and how emerging cognitive research on awe helps us understand some of the power that we harness when awe is evoked, especially amid the sterility, shame, violence, sensory deprivation, and loneliness of prison. In this chapter, I aim to connect the science of awe to what I have observed in 16 years of teaching inside prisons, both in my students and in myself: how Shakespeare-in-prison fosters cognitive openness, strengthens communities, animates creativity, and transforms both our brains and our bodies.[7] The science of awe has revealed how awe is a powerful, radical force to transform us.

Of course, the correlation of positive emotions with learning is as ancient as Plato's *Republic*.[8] John Milton's *On Education* is a profound reflection on the role of emotions in learning.[9] More recently, and particularly in the United States since the 1980s, universities and schools have prioritized the connection of social and emotional learning to foster whole-student success.[10] Increasingly, trauma-informed pedagogy has revealed the correlation between trauma and learning.[11] Directly-impacted people like my now-released students Charles Tarwater and David Evans have published on their perspectives about the emotional and psychological benefits of college in prison.[12] And other chapters in this book evidence the myriad of social and emotional gains of studying Shakespeare in prison.[13]

But what about awe? We knew so little about awe until the early 2000s, when the first psychological studies on awe began. But the results were, well, jaw-dropping. While emotions like joy, gratitude, and safety are psychologically beneficial, it turns out that experiencing awe has distinctly "prosocial" effects, which means that awe motivates us to form strong social networks.[14] Awe makes us more generous. It reduces our interest in material things. It increases our likelihood of helping others. But it doesn't just shift our attention from our own interests to that of others, it fosters a deeper understanding of ourselves and our motives—orienting us more inclusively with the people around us. Remarkably, while awe is documented to embrace wonder, science demonstrates that awe does not subordinate reason: in fact, a controlled study proved that "awe leads to more rigorous thought," demonstrating that college students experiencing awe "were more discerning between what is a strong argument, grounded in robust scientific evidence, and a weak argument, based on a single individual's opinions."[15] Awe seems to be an emotion that activates our hearts, our social bonds, and our minds.

I taught my first Shakespeare play inside prison in 2008 and, as of this writing, facilitated a Shakespeare class inside prison as recently as Monday. I will teach *King Lear* inside a men's prison tomorrow. I have taught *Hamlet*, *Twelfth Night*, *Much Ado About Nothing*, *Henry V*, *Tempest*, *Merchant of Venice*, *Measure for Measure*, the sonnets, and dozens of individual scenes. I have taught full Shakespeare courses inside three different men's state prisons, one women's state prison, and two transition centers. We have acted the plays together, discussed them, and the incarcerated scholars have written thousands of pages of essays about the plays. Students from Emory University,

Georgia State University, Georgia Tech, Spelman College, and Morehouse College have visited for combined discussions and to perform the plays. In 2019, I proposed and received a grant to support teaching people after their release, and that weekly Atlanta class still thrives. Across all these experiences, and overwhelmingly, the prison-impacted people whom I teach use the language of "awe" to respond to Shakespeare: "*Hamlet* blows me away," "*King Lear* jolted me," "I am amazed at every scene," "I had goose bumps." They shake their heads and whistle. Sometimes it was just, "*damn*." They smile, they laugh, they gasp. Other awe indicators were the knowing smile at a powerful soliloquy, or the awe sound: "*whoa*."[16] Once it was Lyric stopping at the classroom door before walking in, holding up his book, and saying "this is serious art. I told my mom on the phone, I'm reading serious art, mom." When I asked what "serious art" means, he just slowly shook his head back and forth and whistled: two embodied awe responses.

All of these responses are documented as "awe."[17] The incarcerated students approach Shakespeare with deep critical and cerebral attention, but they repeatedly turn to the language of wonder, astonishment, bewilderment, veneration, and even reverence to frame their experiences.

That December morning five years ago, with my opening question, "when have you experienced awe?" had been a curious step toward understanding more about how the emotion of awe was functioning in our college-in-prison program. I had been reading cognitive psychological studies about awe as an emotion that activates community and fosters "non-defensive strength," in addition to enlarging perspective, growth-mindedness, and inclusive identification.[18] I was growing to understand how hundreds of emerging psychological studies were demonstrating that awe fosters "prosocial behavior," or behavior that benefits others: increased concern for others' welfare, gratitude, compassion, and helping behaviors, in addition to deprioritizing self-interest, signaling appreciation, and inhibited competition.[19] How awe decreases aggression.[20] I was seeing all of those attributes inside prison and after release. I admired (and often envied) the profound authenticity that I witnessed in the incarcerated scholars with whom I discuss literature every week—the ways they pursued academic and personal goals, against all odds. I read studies that connected the emotion of awe with just such "self-pursuit."[21]

I have copied and distributed Paul Piff et al.'s 2015 article about awe in *Journal of Personality*—cited over 1,000 times—and engaged in metacritical discussions of how awe is functioning inside our shared intellectual space.[22] Now the scholars regularly identify and connect awe to their college-in-prison experience. And they have been quick to identify and describe awe in a variety of texts aside from Shakespeare, too: for Jojo, it was when "[he] read lines in Milton's *Paradise Lost* and realized they were quoted in [his] favorite movie, *The Crow*." For R.C., it was Walt Whitman's "Song of Myself," which he said expressed something inarticulable that he had also felt. (He added, laughing, "hey! I thought I was crazy for thinking this way, but here Whitman says the same thing!") For Moe, it was his peers' "genius, right here in this room. When I hear them quoting and explaining Shakespeare, I feel awe." For both Lyric and Noe, it was a lecture on graffiti as a cultural export and a significant art form; Lyric added "wait—street art? College professors take that seriously? And my mind was blown."

And for Tim, it was when he learned how to integrate and cite sources in his essays: "For me," Tim said, "awe was this idea of entering into an academic *conversation* while writing, instead of just writing as a single person from a single perspective. In this program, I realize my ideas are always talking to others, both in books, and my peers and professors." As someone who regularly teaches first-year writing as part of my annual teaching load at Emory, I was hearing Tim express that *citing sources* was a form of collective effervescence: *whoa*.[23] I have often pondered how I can help my Emory students reach that level of awe when learning how to format their Works Cited pages.

These wide-ranging discussions of awe are now what come to mind when people visit the prison classroom and ask me, "why does college in prison *work*?" I think they are seeking to account for what they see in the space: the moral courage, the beloved community, the intellectual curiosity, the brilliant conversations, the original interpretations, the multidisciplinary connections between texts. The aliveness to the material and each other. The generosity, attentiveness, and care evidenced in classroom discussions. Perhaps they want to know what accounts for the dramatically lower recidivism rates in college in prison programs. Or they may be accommodating their own preconceived ideas about what people inside prison can achieve, or what the study of the humanities can offer. Increasingly, I want to answer the "why Shakespeare in prison works" question with a single word: awe.

As for my own lived experiences, as the daughter of a university professor and a public school teacher, mine was a childhood of awe: camping in our Volkswagen van in the national parks with my family for weeks at a time; sitting in the symphony hall as a second grader, listening to *Peter and the Wolf*; gazing above my head at the life-size body of a Blue Whale, suspended in the Smithsonian's Natural History Museum. Swimming in the ocean, reading *Lord of the Rings*, singing *a cappella* in a nineteenth-century wooden church while standing next to my grandparents. My adult life is similarly filled with awe, teaching the English Renaissance to undergraduate students, traveling to academic conferences where I encounter the ideas of my colleagues, attending the college theater productions, concerts, and guest lectures that my life as a professor opens to me. These are some of what a life of privilege affords. The goosebumps, the tears, the *whoa*.

As I conclude this exploration of awe and Shakespeare in prison, I recognize that most of what our incarcerated students experience is not wonder and astonishment but the "awful": intimidation, humiliation, dehumanization, institutionalization, the deprivation of social interaction, of color, of taste, of touch. They experience intense competition for scarce resources, rather than collective effervescence. They live in a tightly-regimented, sensory-deprived routine rather than encountering nature, theater, and symphonies. They are serving long sentences, surrounded by panoptic guard towers, stupefying boredom, and the omnipresent threat of sexual and physical violence. Prison narrows one's field of view in every imaginable sense. And demographically, most people in prison have already experienced childhoods high in early trauma.[24]

Perhaps those factors are why Brand responded to Angelo's soliloquy in *Measure for Measure* as he did, memorizing the speech and performing it to a two-minute standing ovation by his peers, an ovation that included hugging, laughter, and fist pumps. I was initially baffled that Brand chose Angelo's speech, because it was not one that we had discussed in class, nor (I admit) had I ever really appreciated it. Angelo delivers the soliloquy after he tells Isabella that only if she sleeps with him will he pardon Claudio. Otherwise, he will torture her brother to death. Once alone, Angelo confronts his own flaws, and by extension his own humanity:

> When I would pray and think, I think and pray
> To several subjects. Heaven hath my empty words,
> Whilst my invention, hearing not my tongue,
> Anchors on Isabel. God in my mouth,
> As if I did but only chew his name,
> And in my heart the strong and swelling evil
> Of my conception.
>   O place, O form,
> How often dost thou with thy case, thy habit,
> Wrench awe from fools, and tie the wiser souls
> To thy false seeming! Blood, thou art blood.
> Let's write "good angel" on the devil's horn.
> 'Tis not the devil's crest.[25]

I came to understand that Brand's existence before and during his incarceration involved a lesser sort of awe that is "wrenched" from us, intimidation, extortion, and terror. Shakespeare offered him a glimpse of what moving from terror to awe can look like. In Angelo's confession, Brand saw a different kind of awe, one that is "in the upper reaches of pleasure and on the boundary of fear," an "awe [that] is felt about diverse events and objects, from waterfalls to childbirth to scenes of devastation…Fleeting and rare, experiences of awe can change the course of a life in profound and permanent ways."[26]

Brand saw in Shakespeare's Angelo someone who was discovering his humanity—flawed as it was—in community with other people.

NOTES

1. Paul K. Piff, et al., "Awe, the Small Self, and Prosocial Behavior," *Journal of Personality and Social Psychology* 108, no. 6 (2015): 883.
2. William Shakespeare, *The Tragedy of Hamlet*, eds. Ann Thompson and Neil Taylor (London: Bloomsbury, 2016), 5.2.231. I share these examples with the scholars' permission and have changed their names. Our program refers to the incarcerated students as "scholars," holding that "scholar" is a state of mind. When I am distinguishing between

the incarcerated students and the Emory University and Morehouse College undergraduate students who often join class for discussion, I use "host students" for the incarcerated people and "travelling students" for the Emory and Morehouse people, language that was democratically decided upon by a combined discussion of both groups.

3 William Shakespeare, *Measure for Measure*, ed. J.W. Lever, 2nd series (London: Bloomsbury, 2016), 2.4.15.

4 Mikhael M. Bakhtin, *Problems of Dostoevsky's Poetics*, ed. and trans. Caryl Emerson (Minneapolis: University of Minnesota Press, 2013), 202.

5 Dacher Keltner, *Awe: The New Science of Everyday Wonder and How It Can Transform Your Life* (New York, Penguin Press, 2023), 248.

6 I first taught a three-hour, weekly class inside a Georgia state prison in 2008 and have taught continually for the last 16 years, sometimes teaching at two different prisons on the same day. As a requirement for some grants, I have been required to document contact hours; I have calculated time spent inside at somewhere above 3,680 hours.

7 Keltner, 56–57.

8 David L. Blank, "The Arousal of Emotion in Plato's Dialogues," *The Classical Quarterly* 43, no. 2 (2009): 428–439.

9 See Sarah Higinbotham, "Education as Repair," *To Repair the Ruins: Reading Milton*, eds. Mary C. Fenton and Louis Schwartz (Pittsburgh: Duquesne University Press, 2012).

10 Diane M. Hoffman, "Reflecting on Social Emotional Learning: A Critical Perspective on Trends in the United States," *Review of Educational Research* 79, no. 2 (2017): 533–556.

11 Cinzia Pica-Smith and Christian Scannell, "Teaching and Learning for this Moment: How a Trauma Informed Lens Can Guide Our Praxis," *International Journal of Multidisciplinary Perspectives in Higher Education* 5, no. 1 (2021): 76–83.

12 Charles Tarwater, "The Mind Oppressed: Recidivism as a Learned Behavior," *Wake Forest Journal of Law and Policy* 6 (2016): 357–369; David Evans, "The Elevating Connection of Higher Education in Prison: An Incarcerated Student's Perspective," *Critical Education* 9, no. 11 (2018): 1–13.

13 See also Emma Marie Heard, et al., "Shakespeare in Prison: Affecting Health and Wellbeing," *International Journal of Prisoner Health* 9, no. 3 (2013): 111–123; Rob Pensalfini, *Prison Shakespeare: For These Deep Shames and Great Indignities* (London: Palgrave Macmillan, 2016); as well as the work of

Sammie Byron and Curt L. Tofteland; Rowan Mackenzie, Pheelix Obun, and Ian West; and Frannie Shepherd-Bates in this volume.
14 Piff, et al.
15 Keltner, 39–40, citing Vlad Griskevicius, Michelle N. Shiota, and Samantha L. Neufield, "Influence of Different Positive Emotions on Persuasion Processing: A Functional Evolutionary Approach," *Emotion* 10 (2020): 190–206.
16 Keltner, 44, 55–59, 98, 131, 157, 158. Keltner traces the "body movements and sounds that were our earliest language of awe," 55.
17 Keltner, 29–43.
18 Joshua D. Perlin and Leon Li, "Why Does Awe Have Prosocial Effects? New Perspectives on Awe and the Small Self," *Perspectives on Psychological Science* 15, no. 2 (2020): 291–308.
19 Fang Guan, et al., "Awe and Prosocial Tendency," *Current Psychology* 38 (2019): 1033–1041; Jin Li, "The Effect of Preceding Self-Control on Prosocial Behaviors: The Moderating Role of Awe," *Frontiers in Psychology* 10 (2019): 1–9; Jennifer E. Stellar, et al., "Self-Transcendent Emotions and Their Social Functions: Compassion, Gratitude, and Awe Bind Us to Others Through Prosociality," *Emotion Review* 9, no. 3 (2017): 200–207.
20 Ying Yang, et al., "Elicited Awe Dereases Aggression," *Journal of Pacific Rim Psychology* 10 (2016).
21 Tonglin Jiand and Constantine Sedikides, "Awe Motivates Authentic-Self Pursuit via Self-Transcendence: Implications for Prosociality," *Journal of Personality and Social Psychology* 123, no. 3 (2022): 576–596.
22 Piff, et al.
23 Keltner braids the universal vocalization of "whoa" throughout his 2023 book on awe in brilliant and humanizing ways.
24 In a special issue on Trauma, Addiction, and Criminality, for example, a study found that 44.7% of incarcerated men experienced physical trauma in childhood; see Nancy Wolff and Jing Shi, "Adult Behavioral Health Problems and Treatment," *International Journal of Environmental Research and Public Health* 9, no. 2 (2012): 1908–1926.
25 Shakespeare, *Measure for Measure*, 2.4.1–17.
26 Dacher Keltner and Jonathan Haidt, "Approaching Awe, a Moral, Spiritual, and Aesthetic Emotion," *Cognition and Emotion* 17, no. 2 (2003): 297.

Interventions

The Cultural Invasion of Shakespeare in Prison

dave rich

Four

Shakespeare's *Hamlet* or Lorraine Hansberry's *A Raisin in the Sun*: these were the options presented to my classmates and me early in my college in prison experience. The settling smog from the especially tense 2016 election of President Donald J. Trump created a palpable race-fatigue that made *Hamlet* an easy escape for the majority-white class as we settled back into our patriarchal norms. And although I was outspoken enough to lend my voice to the conversation, I became tight-lipped when it came to advocating for Hansberry's racially charged play. Not wanting to be "that" guy, I cast my vote for *Hamlet* and the rest of the class soon followed. As I reflect back on this experience, I can now see how my education up to that point failed to equip me to explore topics of interest to me.

Education cannot be the "great equalizer of conditions" that Horace Mann posits it to be until better reckoning is made with the reality that for many Black (male) students the classroom has often better prepared them for prison than college.[1] Once in prison, education continues to divorce this demographic from its history by privileging Eurocentric values at the expense of cultivating any sense of cultural identity.[2] In this essay, I suggest that this trend of colonizing education—what Paulo Freire has called "cultural invasion"—is reproduced by Shakespeare in Prison

DOI: 10.4324/9781003451662-7

(SiP) programs when they fail to produce the praxis many carceral students crave.³

Historian Carter G. Woodson first surmised that American education has served the purpose of colonial oppression in the lives of Black persons, noting that the early education of Black Americans largely assimilated them to colonial thinking and acclimated them to the brutal treatment of slavery and post-Civil War racial oppression. Of antebellum educators he writes, "these earnest workers had more enthusiasm than knowledge," for their labor was more of "an effort toward social uplift than actual education."⁴ While Woodson focuses largely on Black education, Jarvis Givens and Ashley Ison have recently argued that this education was part of a larger project of racialization that extended to all American schooling.⁵ According to them, Black and Native American education historically existed as separate entities alongside white education in a multilateral, racialized approach that tiered citizenship and instituted racial hierarchy and domination.⁶ American education today has elements of colonialism embedded in it that are left over from this history. In fact, Sharon Stein has argued that modern institutions of education "are a primary means by which colonial structures of being are reproduced and naturalized. This affects both those deemed to be 'modern subjects' and those deemed to be their 'others,' albeit in very different ways."⁷

With the term "cultural invasion," Freire signals the ways that education departs from its goals of liberation, transformation, or self-efficacy. Freire lays the responsibility for this departure largely at the feet of educators themselves, who often omit to take into account the identities and desires of many of their students. Many educational efforts have failed, he says, "because their authors designed them according to their own personal views of reality, never once taking into account (except as mere objects of their actions) the men-in-a-situation to whom their program was ostensibly directed."[8] When SiP programs neglect to account for their own participants in collaboration with them, they are in danger of reproducing the colonial harms of American education.

This potential for harm is an urgent problem because the colonial elements of education are amplified in a prison setting, where dehumanization, racism, abuse of power, and other injustices are, through their ubiquity, normalized in the lives of incarcerated racial minorities. Prison efforts focused on rehabilitation that I have experienced as a Black man center whiteness and deny Black identity in ways that replicate the educational harms Woodson identifies. In this sense, prison inherits its racism from slavery.[9] Incarcerated scholar Andre Pierce describes this phenomenon, writing:

> When I appear before the parole board, I will be faced by individuals who are commissioned by the state to understand my Black body as having been legitimately dominated. As such, the parole board's central concern will be whether I have accepted my domination and have been morally corrected by its violence.[10]

And again:

> To say that I have been rehabilitated, as a Black man, is to say that my betterment has been facilitated by a racist system that denies that I have the human capacity for moral reflection. On the contrary, the system of imprisonment has threatened to undo my sanity. It is a system that is rooted in racist ideologies that equates my Black body with inferiority. It denies me the possibility of true moral uprightness, character development and intellectual competency.[11]

What Pierce names here is the cumulative effect of years of subordinating rehabilitative programming. What he, I, and thousands of other incarcerated Black men have experienced are classrooms that offer something of benefit but at too great a cost of racial harm.

Presumably prison program facilitators do not set out with the intention of upholding white supremacy, yet their placement within racist incarcerating institutions, combined with these programs' rendering of marginalized authors as "unnecessary voices," sends just this message.[12] This has been my experience in various academic and vocational classrooms where othering is normalizingly common. Take for instance my stint in cosmetology where the textbooks we studied from only made a passing reference to dreadlocks—one of the more prevalent hairstyles of the mostly Black prison population. The message sent was clear: this hairstyle was outside the margins.

This lauding of whiteness is not limited to classrooms only but extends to every area of the incarcerated experience. Religious services, for instance, represent another arena of institutionalized values. Working as the clerk of the Chapel department privies me to the harassment and over-scrutinization that non-Christian and Black Christian services are regularly subjected to. This, while standard Christian services enjoy a great ease. While religious volunteers from the former are met with skeptical mugs and their services interrupted by the blurring radio and chiming keys of the security presence, the latter often encounter no such resistance while holding services and even are afforded the luxury of visiting the housing areas. This ease contributes to the all-too-common view in Black carceral circles that Christianity is a "white man's religion." The library, too, is a place of reinforced harms. Here, books are categorized using the Dewey decimal system. Laminated markers identify where one section ends and where the other begins: law textbooks, science-fiction, classical literature. A section designated by a sticky note reading "African American literature" lies sectioned off—segregated, if you will—from the rest. The little island contains a mixture of all genres in no particular order other than by the author's last name. Not far, another section stretches the length of the library entitled "General Geography & History" (Dewey #900–990). A chart further detailing the section lists #960–969 as "General History of Africa." It currently contains four books, one of which happens to be in the wrong section. In an environment as inherently biased as this one, more is required than to not be racist; as Ibram X. Kendi illustrates, one must be "actively anti-racist."[13]

Against this backdrop, SiP organizations and individuals aim to produce human flourishing by immersing incarcerated students or participants in the world of Shakespeare. These include organizations which use theater as a means of personal transformation. Steeped in whiteness disguised as default, Shakespeare's work often speaks to a specific population even as it unwittingly alienates others. Rather than studying in-depth Shakespeare's handling of race, many SiP facilitators have chosen to focus on the topics they deem most relevant. When a "race neutral" or "default white" approach is used, everyone is disadvantaged.

A familiar formulation is that SiP programs offer "education through experiential knowledge,"[14] wherein "actors develop a deep relationship with the characters they play, which bring them to understand their own motivations and behaviors."[15] Through performance, incarcerated actors pick up skills such as learning "how to understand other people, to listen to others, to see how their story belongs also to others, and to find new solutions and ways of working through conflicts."[16] As a result, these skills cultivate "their ability to communicate ideas and feelings,"[17] resulting in the transformation of the participant and the prison.[18] That is to say, SiP facilitators are hopeful to heal the traumas that lead to prison with theater and literature. However, there is potential for cultural invasion when the needs of an incarcerated person, particularly of color, are assumed.

In Amy Scott-Douglass' account, the Shakespeare Behind Bars (SBB) approach to race in its early years seemed to largely ignore its existence. SBB "members hardly even mention race," records Amy Scott-Douglass in 2005, "they don't talk about race when it comes to their own group dynamics, and they don't talk about race in Shakespeare's plays."[19] This position led them to "edit racism out of Shakespeare,"[20] and, in at least one instance, replace a racist line with a sexist one—opting to refer to Julia of Shakespeare's *Two Gentlemen of Verona* not as a "swarthy Ethiope," but as a "witch," as if one form of disparagement is more tolerable than the other.[21] This avoidance of racial realities does little to aid carceral students in grappling with their racially charged environments. Elsewhere, Scott-Douglass details the cultural invasion tendencies of SBB illustrated by an exchange with one of its participants, Ron, where it becomes obvious that the issue of race is of greater significance to the incarcerated actor than to the facilitators: "I think about it [race/racism], you know what I'm saying? But at the same time, it's kind of counterproductive to have thoughts about certain things."[22] Here, Ron's need to explore racial issues was impeded by the well-meaning efforts of SBB facilitators, who in this instance had not created an atmosphere that allowed racial questions and contradictions to fully emerge.

Jean Trounstine's program, which in many ways sparked a movement, was also not immune to colonizing impulses. Describing one of her productions, Trounstine tells the story of incarcerated participants who are implicitly compelled to compromise their identities to make room for this othering variety of education. One such participant is Bertie, whom Trounstine describes as "a beautiful, feisty Jamaican of nineteen."[23] Trounstine goes on to describe the transformation Bertie undergoes as a result of her participation in the production. Bertie's Jamaican "accent grew less noticeable after five plays, and her confidence grew stronger."[24] Here, Trounstine draws a telling correlation between assimilation and confidence, as if the latter can only be found in the former. To be fair, Trounstine does make an effort at inclusivity. Unlike programs that focus exclusively or predominantly on Shakespeare, Trounstine's program employs a wide array of literature to assist her participants to find themselves in the material they cover. For instance, some of her groups, such as those discussing Toni Morrison and other authors of color, center a Black perspective.[25] Providing opportunities for Black incarcerated persons to see themselves in great pieces of literature creates space for them to begin the work of untangling internalized racist self-loathing.

In following Trounstine's model, opportunities do occur for incarcerated persons to engage with Shakespeare in ways that afford them the chance to make Shakespeare their own. Take, for instance, Scott-Douglass' reference to participants' performance of "Shakespeare rap" in the Prison Performing Arts Program,[26] where Black carceral actors critique American race relations. In doing so, these performers demonstrate the potential for SiP programs to move incarcerated minorities toward self-advocacy and social activism.[27] "Shakespeare rap" serves a very specific purpose within the carceral theater writes Scott-Douglass, as it "holds the government as least partly responsible for the disproportionate percentage of black people in prison."[28]

As SiP programs have expanded in number and sophistication, more SiP facilitators have incorporated the findings of Shakespeareans who have long contended with ways of making Shakespeare more inclusive. Researcher Ian Smith lays out the need for a study of Shakespeare through a racially literate lens, one that examines the racial framework that "inhibits and constrains the practices of reading and interpretation" of Shakespeare.[29] Building on this, proponents of premodern critical race studies highlight the need for their labor as a way of "outing whiteness."[30] When their logic is applied to Shakespeare they argue that they "make visible the racial marks and bruises it deploys on its way not just to white-people-making but to the seemingly benign institutionalization of Shakespeare as the innocent, humanistic emblem of white superiority and white supremacy."[31] Their assertion that it is the ethical responsibility of all Shakespeareans to seek out and address the "(in)visible" uses of whiteness[32] mirrors Dreier's imperative that SiP facilitators apply a decolonizing lens to interrogate their choice to study Shakespeare in carceral spaces.[33] Such an approach, she argues, allows for a shift in the power dynamics from white facilitators to participants, enabling them the freedom to do with Shakespeare what they will, even if that includes rejecting him.[34]

For incarcerated minorities seeking to better themselves, whiteness as a starting point is a normalized harm, one that we have learned to settle for because often there is no alternative.

For instance, in my years of incarceration I have encountered no Black or Indigenous studies. June Jordan's cry for curricular equity has not yet reached the penitentiary: "Black students, looking for truth, demand teachers least likely to lie, least likely to perpetuate the traditions of lying...For us, there is nothing optional about Black Experience and/or 'Black Studies': we must know ourselves."[35] In this vein, applying a critical race lens to Shakespeare, though it is a necessity, only addresses the tip of the iceberg. Incarcerated minorities are still left to bear what Jordan refers to as the "whiplash of white studies,"[36] in endeavoring to be the best versions of themselves. Informed by my 14 years of incarceration and 34 years inhabiting this Black body, I assert that what is needed, what is desired by many incarcerated minorities, is a Freirean educational experience, one where facilitators collaborate with participants to determine not only the subjects to be investigated, but the tools with which they are investigated; this demands a centering of participants' cultural backgrounds and experiences rather than a positing of distant "universal human truths."

Mwisho[37]

NOTES

1 Michelle Alexander, *The New Jim Crow: Mass Incarceration in the Age of Colorblindness* (New York: New Books, 2010), 12; Myles Moody, "From Under-Diagnoses to Over-Representation: Black Children, ADHD, and the School-to-Prison Pipeline," *Journal of African American Studies* 20, no. 2 (2016): 152–163 (161); Brenda L. Townsend Walker, "Teacher Education and African American Males: Deconstructing Pathways from the Schoolhouse to the 'Big House'," *Teacher Education and Special Education* 35, no. 4 (2012): 320–332.

2 Patrick Elliot Alexander, "Education as Liberation: African American Literature and Abolition Pedagogy in the Sunbelt Prison Classroom,"

South: A Scholarly Journal 50, no. 1 (2017): 9–21; Satra Taylor, et al., "Why Race Matters for Higher Education in Prison," Peabody Journal of Education 96, no. 5 (2021): 588–597.

3 Paulo Freire, Pedagogy of the Oppressed (New York: Bloomsbury Academic, 2014), 152.

4 Carter G. Woodson, The Miseducation of the Negro (Buffalo: E World Inc., 2012), 17.

5 Jarvis R. Givens and Ashley Ison, "Toward New Beginnings: A Review of Native, White, and Black American Education Through the 19th Century," Review of Education Research 93, no. 3 (2023): 319–352.

6 Givens and Ison, 324.

7 Sharon Stein, "Beyond Higher Education as We Know it: Gesturing Towards Decolonial Horizons of Possibility," Studies in Philosophy and Education 38, no. 3 (2019): 143–161 (151).

8 Freire, 94.

9 Alexander, 13; Caroline Cheung, "Abolition Pedagogy is Necessary," Journal of Higher Education in Prison 1, no. 1 (2021): 51–68 (52); Angela Y. Davis, Are Prisons Obsolete? (New York: Seven Stories Press, 2003); bell hooks, Teaching to Transgress: Education as the Practice of Freedom (London: Routledge, 1994); James Kilgore, "Bringing Freire Behind the Walls: The Perils and Pluses of Critical Pedagogy in Prison Education," The Radical Teacher, no. 90 (2011): 57–66 (59).

10 Andre Pierce, "The Violence of Carceral Logics," Resentencing: Poetry, Stories, Essays, and Visual Arts Reflecting on Incarceration with a Different Type of Sentence 1 (2022): 151–152 (151).

11 Pierce, 152.

12 Jenna Dreier, "Decolonising Pedagogies in Prison Performance Programmes: Making Shakespeare Secondary," Research in Drama Education: The Journal of Applied Theatre and Performance 26, no. 3 (2021): 477–493 (479).

13 Ibram X. Kendi, How to Be an Antiracist (New York: Random House Publishing Group, 2019), 12.

14 Rowan Mackenzie, "'Study Is Like Heaven's Glorious Sun'—Learning Through Shakespeare for Men Convicted of Sexual Offenses," Humanities 10, no. 1 (2021): 1–16 (11).

15 Mariacristinia Cavecchi, "Brave New Worlds. Shakespearean Tempests in Italian Prisons," Special Issue, Other Modernities: Journal of Literary and Cultural Studies (2017): 1–21 (7).

16 Pamela J. Monaco, "Removing the Bars of Collaborative Shakespeare," *Actes des congress de la Societe Francaise Shakespeare*, no. 37 (2019).
17 Jean Trounstine, "Beyond Prison Education," PMLA 123, no. 3 (May 2008): 674–677 (676).
18 Jenna Dreier, "From Apprentice to Master: Casting Men to Play Shakespeare's Women in Prison," *Humanities* 8, no. 3 (2019): 1–24 (2).
19 Amy Scott-Douglass, *Shakespeare Inside: The Bard Behind Bars* (London: Continuum, 2007), 46.
20 Scott-Douglass, 57.
21 Scott-Douglass, 57–58.
22 Scott-Douglass, 58.
23 Trounstine, 675.
24 Trounstine, 675.
25 Jean Trounstine, "Changing Women's Lives Through Literature," *The Women's Review of Books* 32, no. 3 (2015): 27–29 (27).
26 Scott-Douglass, 63.
27 Dreier, "Decolonising Pedagogies," 481.
28 Scott-Douglass, 65.
29 Ian Smith, *Black Shakespeare: Reading and Misreading Race* (Cambridge, UK: Cambridge University Press, 2022).
30 David Sterling Brown, Patricia Akhimie, and Arthur L. Little, Jr., "Seeking the (In)Visible: Whiteness and Shakespeare Studies," *Shakespeare Studies* 50, no. 3 (2022): 17–23 (20).
31 Brown et al., 20.
32 Brown et al., 20.
33 Dreier, "Decolonising Pedagogies," 479.
34 Dreier, "Decolonising Pedagogies," 482.
35 June Jordan, *CivilWars* (Boston: Beacon Press, 1969), 52.
36 Jordan, 53.
37 "Mwisho" is Swahili for "the end." It is my small ode to and acknowledgement of those before me.

The Cultural Invasion of Shakespeare
in Prison: Contexts and Futures

Jayme M. Yeo

Five

The relative scarcity of racially engaged scholarship on Shakespeare in Prison (SiP) would be startling if it did not mimic a similar omission in Shakespeare scholarship generally. As Ian Smith argues, this scarcity is less a direct denial of the prevalence of racial formation in Shakespeare's work so much as it is a kind of "scholarly act of deferral and displacement" that diminishes its importance. Smith argues this oversight stems from "systemic whiteness," which renders "whiteness itself as a source of racial blindness."[1] As premodern critical race scholars including David Sterling Brown, Patricia Akhimie, and Arthur L. Little, Jr. have pointed out, this "critical invisibility of whiteness" is in danger of "reproduc[ing] white superiority and supremacy in [Shakespeare's] name."[2] It is only from a position of privilege that race seems less significant than it is.

In many ways, SiP practitioners and scholars have enacted a similar kind of "deferral and displacement" regarding their own programs and participants. As dave rich's work in this volume witnesses, this deferral has the potential to magnify racial harms experienced by participants who already inhabit a space of intense systemic and interpersonal racism. As a result, our programs may not reach their full potential for work that might amplify voices, increase representation, and invite all participants to develop more critical understandings

DOI: 10.4324/9781003451662-8

of race in Shakespeare's plays and in our world today. Taking rich's argument seriously calls us to an urgent reassessment of our work that might allow us to build on our successes and identify and redress our oversights. This work of reassessment, of careful self-reflective practices, is iterative; if we can identify and critique our colonialist practices now, it is because the infrastructures created by previous practitioners provide space for renewed commitments to justice in an evolving world. In their turn, future practitioners will revise their own programs beyond any suggestions I might make here as they encounter new challenges and perspectives. Each generation builds on the work of the previous one. My attempt here, then, is to describe the context that has led us to a watershed moment in our practices and scholarship, where we are beginning to look at Shakespeare's colonial heritage more carefully and shape our programs in more meaningful response to that history. I will also briefly highlight some pathways toward decolonial practices that might inform program changes as we move forward.

Early SiP programs often focused on psychological transformation and drama therapy; many had (and continue to have) an explicit goal of supporting participants' flourishing in an otherwise dehumanizing space. The scholarship documenting this work reports that participants frequently experience intellectual and emotional benefits, including increased self-confidence, emotional resilience, and critical thinking.[3] Taken together, this work represents what Rob Pensalfini has referred to as a "universalizing message of Shakespeare being used to teach and liberate."[4] As programs have proliferated and evolved, more recent work highlights other goals, including transforming institutional systems and building bridges between "insiders" and "outsiders."[5] As this more recent work has begun embracing prison abolition or redressing institutional harm, it has also simultaneously (as rich argues) unearthed troubling oppressions embedded in some of our practices and vocabularies, derived from the histories of education, incarceration, and bardolatry. While psychological transformation contributes to the healing of marginalized participants, it also can subtly mimic institutional expectations of "rehabilitation" by regulating behaviors or opinions: for instance, by privileging stories of positive change and diminishing non-transformative or even negative accounts of SiP. In this way, SiP programs "may actually collude with punitive practices [of carceral education...] in the name of personal growth and self-actualization."[6] As Jenna Dreier has compellingly argued, SiP programs raise "unavaoidable parallels [...] between the work of the British colonizer in centuries past who used Shakespeare's texts to inscribe Western religious and moral values under the guise of literary education."[7] In other words, even as our work empowers participants, it may also paradoxically constrain them by interpellating them into a subjectivity that centers European language, culture, or values.

Here is one illustration of this paradox: Sheila Cavanaugh and Steve Rowland tell the story of Casper, an SiP participant who was in a parole hearing that was going poorly until one woman on the committee recognized him from an online video about the facility's SiP program:

> they had a long chat about Shakespeare and how prisoners can be enlightened by reading and talking about the plays. His ability to talk about feminism, manhood and power convinced her that he had, in fact, reformed. Casper was given parole [...] He works as a counsellor to young men in NYC. Recently married, he now has a new daughter and continues to be remorseful for his choices as a teenager.[8]

On the one hand, Casper's participation in SiP programs demonstrably contributed to his flourishing. His knowledge of Shakespeare helped lead to his parole and he has since built a rewarding career and started a family—all meaningful accomplishments. On the other hand, the parole board member's assessment of his "enlightenment" affirms settler-colonial educational imperatives. Even the supportive account of Casper's story subtly reinforces the parole board's assumptions with its uncritical commentary on Casper's institutional rehabilitation and moral reform. And the role of Shakespeare's work itself also bears scrutiny: would Casper's parole hearing have been a success if the video had been about an August Wilson or Luis Valdez program?

Casper's story ultimately illustrates the complexity of the problem: the issue here is not that working with Shakespeare did not lead to human flourishing, but that it did so in part through complicity with the very systemic oppressions (bardolatry, institutionalized ideals of rehabilitation, focus on criminality) that SiP programs often seek to overcome. Celebrating transformative encounters with Shakespeare while at the same time bearing witness to how those encounters may also perpetuate injustice is challenging work; often, the promising potentials of this work are intertwined with their oppressive possibilities and nearly every program has a blend of practices that are both (and sometimes simultaneously) helpful and harmful. In this context, rich's work raises a haunting question: how might we teach and perform Shakespeare in prison without reproducing these colonial harms? While the answer to this question partly involves utilizing decolonial practices, the more profound response identified by rich and echoed here is simply to keep this question in front of us as a call to courageous and continual examination and revision of our programs in collaboration with our participants.

To begin this work of self-examination, we might identify the contexts from which harmful practices most often emerge. The illustration above, for instance, demonstrates that the very carceral system we work within prompts us toward complicity with colonialism by lowering recidivism and other markers of institutional success.[9] Stories like Casper's can determine administrative approval, access to students and facilities, and public and private funding. And for those programs that are offered for college credit, there are additional curricular and accreditation imperatives that further determine program content. It is also worth acknowledging that these institutional values sometimes do align with our own learning goals and genuine desire for positive life outcomes for our participants: we want our participants to experience Shakespeare's work in ways that lead them toward emotional, intellectual, and social wellbeing. However, as rich cautions via Paolo Freire, there is a danger that these imperatives predetermine specific goals for our participants, precluding them from exploring goals that might differ from our own.

Another reason why we have overlooked the issue of colonialism in our work is that we are reading too much Michel Foucault and not enough Michelle Alexander. Neils Herold writes that "any book on prison theater [...] would be remiss in not beginning with at least a nod to Michel Foucault,"[10] and yet, Foucault's work offers only limited understanding of the dynamics of race in the American carceral system. Similarly, our programs might also benefit from looking more systematically to our own field for guidance on racial equity, including the robust conversation on premodern critical race studies, which urges us away from "outmoded readings of race as Black" in order to shift our gazes toward racial formation as a category of cultural identity-making.[11] Taken together, the scholarship on race in prison and in history might helpfully inform our understandings of the harmful potentials contained within a program focused solely on a settler-colonial author and guide us toward more informed considerations for our programs.

At the heart of this work is decentering power: the colonizing power of white supremacist heteropatriarchy, the pedagogical power of the facilitator, and the cultural power of Shakespeare's work. To some extent, as rich notes, we have a road map for what this decentering might look like via critical pedagogues such as Freire and bell hooks. At the same time (and as the saying goes), the map is not the territory; there is no single model for a decolonial SiP program. A for-credit college class in a more restrictive administrative environment, for instance, might borrow from Universal Design for Learning or culturally-sensitive teaching practices to offer instructor-led programming that maximizes student visibility and choices.[12] A voluntary performance workshop in a more progressive setting, on the other hand, might be able to grant authority to its participants to make programmatic decisions. I take rich's call to be less a petition for specific organizational structures than a request for continual self-reflection and reorientation toward the cultural context of Shakespeare and the cultural needs of all of our participants.

While this self-reflection may result in different programmatic changes, a central guiding principle that rich calls for is that we develop our goals in collaboration with our participants. This suggestion aligns well with recent scholarship on inclusive pedagogy, which holds that one of the first principles of course design is to prioritize relevance to students' lives: "motivation scholars suggest focusing on issues that are personally meaningful to students, such as those that relate to their cultural experiences, goals, and interests."[13] Our ability to offer relevant programming must begin, then, with a metacognitive assessment of what we know about the motivations of the people in our programs, and how we know what we know.[14] Many of us use entrance surveys or introductory discussions to take a baseline of participant motivations, but we ought to examine or reexamine those tools frequently. What assumptions or elisions are embedded in our questions? What steps do we take to reassess participant motivation throughout the program? There are gaps to be minded here. If we begin, for instance, with the question "Why did you join a Shakespeare program?" we may be assuming both choice and preference for Shakespeare over other opportunities.

If we take our questions about goals to be a starting point for a longer conversation, then how we continue the conversation matters. We should first be as intentional and transparent about our own motivations as we ask our participants to be with us. And second, we should be willing to honor our participants' responses even when those responses don't align with our own goals—for instance, when participants indicate that they want to learn more about political resistance or to center marginalized voices, history, and art. Honoring these goals might entail deeper discussions with participants and outside stakeholders about infrastructural limitations; it could mean revising programming; it might entail stepping into positions of pedagogical discomfort as we open ourselves to possibilities that can transform us as much as our participants.

While there is no single model for a decolonial SiP program, there are practices (some of which are by no means new to SiP programs) that we can implement or build on as we move toward more inclusive programs in the future. One practice identified by rich includes presenting Shakespeare as one artist in a diverse list of playwrights, which increases representation and contextualizes Shakespeare's racial formations by providing alternatives to them.[15] This approach has always been the case with programs such as Rehabilitation through the Arts or Jean Trounstine's program, but in the wake of the #BlackLivesMatter and "We See You White American Theater" movements, more programs are adopting culturally diverse reading lists. In 2020, for instance, Marin Shakespeare Company, which offers drama therapy-inspired programs to currently incarcerated actors, committed to adding "culturally conscious contemporary monologues to the curriculum."[16] Alongside cultural diversity, our reading lists might expand to make visible multiple forms of identity, including sexuality, gender, religion, age, physical ability, body shape, neurodiversity, and intersectional identities.

Another decolonizing strategy, identified by Dreier, includes "prioritizing participants' knowledge and artistic agency" and favoring care for participants over production standards.[17] This prioritizing of care happens, for instance, when participants "speak back" to Shakespeare by interpreting, responding to, or changing Shakespeare's text. These practices take place regularly within SiP programs and frequently result in productions or adaptations that, Ramona Wray argues, deserve much more of our critical attention than we have previously given.[18] As rich points out, they occur when participants write a song inspired by *Julius Caesar* that critiques contemporary politics,[19] or when they "interpret or adapt the text" for a performance.[20] We have the ability to amplify these productions not only by publicizing them on social media and other platforms (as, for instance, Detroit Public Theater's Shakespeare in Prison Program frequently does), but also by highlighting these productions as worthy of serious academic inquiry.

A final strategy, less represented in the literature of SiP, involves engaging students in a conversation about racial formation in text and performance more explicitly. This conversation might occur over formal readings on premodern race, for instance, or in pedagogical opportunities identified by Ayanna Thompson and Laura Turchi when participants explore personal connections and dissonances with the text. In this context, facilitators might invite conversations surrounding, for instance, casting choices: "If *who* they are matters, when Mercutio and Tybalt are a petite Latina and heavy-set white male, students need to talk about dimensions of the performance that meld the actor and the character in exciting and complicated ways."[21] In order to nurture the kind of program that rich calls for—one that works to heal racial oppression— we need to be willing to read Shakespeare "bravely" (in the words of Farah Karim-Cooper), not only interrogating explicit racism in Shakespeare's most well-known "race plays," but also by exploring the anxieties, fears, and desires that cohere in the process of race-making in *all* of Shakespeare's work.[22]

While these efforts might give us some starting places for pursuing racial justice in the context of an SiP classroom, ultimately best practices are only best within a given time and place. Emerging needs and shifting political, cultural, and institutional contexts dictate that our work will and should continuously evolve. As this essay calls for ever more nuanced cultural power dynamics, it also acknowledges that the work of justice is recursive, requiring continual self-revision in response to social change. The important thing is not, therefore, that we build perfectly just programs (as though such a thing were possible), but that we work with humility, transparency, and a collaborative spirit to create self-reflective programs capable of identifying and responding to injustices embedded within our work. The injunction here is not to conform to a specific set of practices but rather to embrace transformation that is supported by careful programmatic evaluation and meaningful collaboration with participants, even (and especially) when those evaluations and collaborations challenge our very notion of what it means to teach Shakespeare in prison. It means that we ought always to seek out more ethical practices even when those practices are unfamiliar, difficult, or uncomfortable. As we cultivate deeper attitudes of listening and openness towards the needs of our participants, perhaps the "courageous lens" of reading might turn not only onto Shakespeare, but on ourselves as well, helping us to develop programs that change our work both inside and out.

NOTES

1 Ian Smith, *Black Shakespeare: Reading and Misreading Race* (Cambridge, UK: Cambridge University Press, 2022), 3–4.

2 David Sterling Brown, Patricia Akhimie, and Arthur L. Little, Jr., "Seeking the (In)Visible: Whiteness and Shakespeare Studies," *Shakespeare Studies* 50, no. 3 (2022): 17–23 (19–20).

3 See Laura Bates, *Shakespeare Saved My Life: Ten Years in Solitary with the Bard* (Naperville: Sourcebooks, 2013); Niels Herold, *Prison Shakespeare and the Purpose of Performance: Repentance Rituals and the Early Modern* (New York: Palgrave MacMillan, 2014); Amy Scott-Douglass, *Shakespeare Inside: The Bard Behind Bars* (London: Continuum, 2007); Jean Trounstine, *Shakespeare Behind Bars: The Power of Drama In a Women's Prison* (London: St. Martin's Press, 2001); and Helen Zelon, "The Shakespeare Redemption: Inmates in a Kentucky Prison Grapple with the Truths of Human Existence," *American Theater* 18, no. 8 (October 2001): 132–135; Sophie Ward and Roy Connolly, "The Play Is a Prison: The Discourse of Prison Shakespeare," *Studies in Theatre & Performance* 40, no. 2 (2020): 128–144.

4 Rob Pensalfini, *Prison Shakespeare: For These Deep Shames and Great Indignities* (New York: Palgrave MacMillan, 2016), 53.

5 On funding and working within institutional systems, see Pensalfini. On institutional subversion, see Ramona Wray, "The Morals of Macbeth and Peace as Process: Adapting Shakespeare in Northern Ireland's Maximum Security Prison," *Shakespeare Quarterly* 62, no. 3 (2011):

340–363 and Rowan Mackenzie, "Producing Space for Shakespeare," *Critical Survey* 31, no. 4 (2019): 65–76. On building bridges, see Sheila T. Cavanagh and Steve Rowland, "'Those Twins of Learning': Cognitive and Affective Learning in an Inclusive Shakespearean Curriculum," *Critical Survey* 31, no. 4, (2019): 54–64 and Jayme M. Yeo, "Teaching Shakespeare Inside-Out: Creating a Dialogue between Traditional and Incarcerated Students," *Teaching Social Justice through Shakespeare: Why Renaissance Literature Matters Now*, eds. Hilary Eklund and Wendy Beth Hyman (Edinburgh: Edinburgh University Press, 2021), 197–205.
6 Pensalfini, 169.
7 Jenna Dreier, "Decolonising Pedagogies in Prison Performance Programmes: Making Shakespeare Secondary," *Research in Drama Education* 26, no. 3 (2021): 477–493 (479–480). See also Pensalfini, 170–171.
8 Cavanagh and Rowland, 62–63.
9 Pensalfini, 5.
10 Herold, 2.
11 Brown, Akhimie, and Little, 18.
12 See, for instance, Thomas J. Tobin and Kirsten T. Behling, *Reach Everyone, Teach Everyone: Universal Design for Learning in Higher Education* (Morgantown: West Virginia University Press, 2018).
13 Isis Artze-Vega, et al., *The Norton Guide to Equity-Minded Teaching* (New York: Norton, 2023), 5.
14 Artze-Vega, 5.
15 See David Sterling Brown, "(Early) Modern Literature: Crossing the Color-Line," *Radical Teacher* 105 (2016): 69–77.
16 Marin Shakespeare Company, "Racial Equity Action Plan," https://www.marinshakespeare.org/wp-content/uploads/2021/06/Racial-Equity-Action-Plan-Policies-%E2%80%93-Final-6-1-21.pdf, 8–11.
17 Dreier, 484.
18 Wray, 340–341.
19 Scott-Douglass, 62–69.
20 Dreier, 484–485.
21 Ayanna Thompson and Laura Turchi, *Teaching Shakespeare with Purpose: A Student-Centered Approach* (London: Bloomsbury, 2016), 77.
22 Farah Karim-Cooper, *The Great White Bard: How to Love Shakespeare While Talking About Race* (London: Viking, 2023), 5.

Shakespeare at Auburn: Reflections on Teaching and Learning in the Prison Classroom

Julio C. Iglesias, Stephen K. Kim, and Chester "Al" Wood

Six

INTRODUCTION

In Fall 2021, the Cornell Prison Education Program (CPEP) and Cayuga Community College (CCC) offered a course on Shakespeare for incarcerated students in Auburn Correctional Facility, a men's maximum-security prison located in Auburn, NY. Many of the students in our class came in skeptics and left, as they identified themselves, "Shakespeare nerds." We wish to serve other instructors and students who will study Shakespeare in prison classrooms by communicating what made Shakespeare so compelling to us.

This essay is also a writing experiment. First, it is an experiment in form. Many reflections on the prison classroom are authored either by a single student or an instructor. We are hoping to describe more capaciously the impact of teaching and learning Shakespeare in the prison classroom through a collaborative piece, co-authored by two students (Julio and Al) and the instructor (Stephen). It includes both jointly written sections and individual vignettes. It is also an experiment in process. This contribution is the result of a pilot program proposed by CPEP to allow incarcerated students to co-author publications with their CPEP instructors. Our process involved a combination of in-person meetings in the prison and correspondence.

DOI: 10.4324/9781003451662-9

As the individual vignettes will illustrate, what we especially enjoyed about reading Shakespeare together was a mix of familiarity and unfamiliarity with the course material. For example, one form of resistance that initially came up was with early modern English. It was difficult to understand, seemingly convoluted. But, working together to understand it became a source of joy and illumination. We discovered together how the unfamiliar words and cadences could also put words to ideas of our own, those which were so familiar that they seemed inexpressible. Like James Baldwin, we learned to cherish the salient features of Shakespearean language: "its candor, its irony, its density, and its beat."[1] Al remarked that working through Shakespeare's English gave him agency and voice in his own writing, to write in ways that imbued language with meaning and beauty. Julio described that reading Shakespeare was like "looking in from another world" and "an opportunity to encounter something new." What worked best was highlighting both the familiar and the unfamiliar as we read the plays and poems, as it was the tension between the two that sparked invigorating ideas.

Immersing ourselves in Shakespeare's world also helped us to better understand our worlds and ourselves. One student mentioned how "Shakespeare was a way to make sense of broader systems." Shakespeare's works helped exercise a kind of ethical and political imagination that put individual actions and circumstances into a structural context. Students used the plays and poems to think through pressing issues of inequity. *Twelfth Night* and the sonnets served as a vehicle to think about gender and sexuality in ways that posited connections between queerness and pleasure. *The Tempest* and *Othello* sparked conversations on institutional racism and the ways our histories of colonialism still hold us in thrall today.

In Al's case, *Othello* offered self-forgiveness, allowing him to accept life's situational ambiguities as the distorting features of his previous decisions. Similarly, encountering the Ghost in *Hamlet* revealed for Julio his relationship to gang violence and allowed him to overcome the specter of that past. Our collective process of reading and meaning-making also clarified new ways of understanding Shakespeare for Stephen, who provides one example of how teaching on the inside changed his reading of a key scene in *The Tempest*. Most importantly, this course encouraged us to recognize our humanity, rekindle a sense of wonder, and reaffirm the importance of connecting with one another through a communal reckoning with language.

CHESTER "AL" WOOD: FORGIVENESS THROUGH *OTHELLO*

While reading William Shakespeare's *Othello*, I not only engaged with the character, but I also found his predicaments most relatable to my own life. I, like Othello, was young and had my whole life ahead of me, and, somehow, we were both driven to extreme acts of carnage. At the end of the play, Othello speaks eloquently after he murders Desdemona:

> Soft you; a word or two before you go.
> I have done the state some service, and they know't.
> No more of that. I pray you, in your letters,
> When you shall these unlucky deeds relate,
> Speak of me as I am; nothing extenuate,
> Nor set down aught in malice: then must you speak
> Of one that loved not wisely but too well;
> Of one not easily jealous, but being wrought
> Perplex'd in the extreme; of one whose hand,
> Like the base Judean, threw a pearl away

> Richer than all his tribe; of one whose subdued eyes,
> Albeit unused to the melting mood,
> Drop tears as fast as the Arabian trees
> Their medicinal gum. Set you down this;
> And say besides, that in Aleppo once,
> Where a malignant and a turban'd Turk
> Beat a Venetian and traduced the state,
> I took by the throat the circumcised dog,
> And smote him, thus.
>
> (5.2.331–349)[2]

My reading of Othello's final words felt like the speech I gave to the judge at sentencing. I, like Othello, took a person's life, and I wounded another person. I had an extreme sense of shame for myself, and my family and friends. Othello ironically states that he will, "Unlucky deeds relate" (5.2.334). His act of killing his wife was a very unfortunate act. Here, Othello realized what he did was wrong. It brought him to the lowest point in his life, as it did in mine. He takes full responsibility for his actions, as do I. We both insist, "nothing extenuate" when our stories are told (5.2.335).

After Othello killed his wife, he learns that she was an innocent woman, and during his last words he reaches a moment of psychological and emotional clarity: "Like the base Judean, threw a pearl away / Richer than all his tribe" (5.2.340–341). Othello not only killed the one that loved him the most, but threw away all of his honor and possessions as well. For me, I lost so much from a 30-second tragic act that I know I will never fully recover from. I had a good job, a loving wife, a recently mortgaged home, and a new-born son. Like Othello, I did not know what I had till it was thrown away.

As I was delivering my final words at sentencing, I remembered having "subdued eyes;" my heart was full of guilt and remorse and this was expressed through my tearful words (5.2.341). I believe (after re-reading Othello's final words) that he had a profound sense of remorse.

I still remember how sad and sorry I was for taking another person's life and severely wounding another. It was hard for me to even fathom that I could commit such an act. Even after being arrested and informed of what I did, I still could not believe it. At my sentencing, I apologized to my victims, my victims' family, as well as my family for what I did. However, no amount of hurt and pain I felt could turn back the hands of time and bring the person I killed back to life, or fully heal the person I wounded. In reality, I wounded everyone that knew and loved my victims. And I wounded all of my family and friends, for they all would have to live with what I did for the rest of their lives. For the past 23 years, I have been suffering with the pain and carnage that I caused. In a way, I was killing myself daily for not being able to forgive Chester "Al" Wood, for what he did. I still "drop tears as fast as the Arabian trees" just thinking about what I have done (5.2.343).

The victim that I wounded forgave me years ago, and some of my victim's family have forgiven me and some have not. The same is true for the family and friends of the one I killed. However, I could not come to terms with forgiving myself for what I did. Reading *Othello* helped me find forgiveness for myself. Somehow during my reading of Othello's last words, I was able to turn my tears of sadness and remorse into a "medicinal gum" to find forgiveness within myself (5.2.344).

Whether Othello gave a good justification for his actions or not, he still took his own life in the end: "I took by the throat the circumcised dog / And smote him, thus" (5.2.348–349). I think Othello wanted to be remembered (or spoken of) as a fool that was in love. However, Othello was intelligent enough to know that others might speak ill of him. He entreats the audience that when speaking of him, we "set down aught in malice" (5.2.336). No matter what, he could not live with himself knowing what he had done.

When I was sentenced to 40 years to life, I had thoughts of suicide—thankfully I chose to live. Now after being in prison for over 23 years, I have reached a point of forgiveness within myself. This is very hard to do. I wonder if Othello could have ever forgiven himself, or endured decades in a prison cell.

JULIO C. IGLESIAS: THE TRAUMA OF THE GHOST AND THE CARCERAL CONDITION

"*Hic et ubique?*" is the stern question demanding absolute secrecy in reference to the Ghost's encounter (1.5.159). "Here and everywhere?" Hamlet asks his accompanying watchmen, as in "swear by my sword that you won't speak of what you have seen tonight!"

In the ordinary classroom setting, the Ghost provokes discussions concerning the secret later revealed to Hamlet. In a way, these conversations lean favorably towards unraveling what is, by Hamlet's demand, forbidden; a breach of that secrecy is implied the moment it's spoken of, and suddenly the prospect of danger looms with possibility. It is the danger of realizing the meaning to my confinement that the Ghost has exposed me to. By aligning my reading of the text with the dark proportions that the carceral condition represents—chief among them, solitude, violence, and despair—I realize that without incarceration I would've been dead by now. Granted, literature has liberated me from the haunting traumas that led me here, but the irony of the matter is that I've also been able to notice the creeping shadow of regret alongside me, symbolizing how a completed education could've altogether avoided the malediction of a life sentence.

I'm now left questioning the practicality that reading Shakespeare serves, asking myself whether the knowledge gained has become tantamount to the empty and lifeless figuration of the Ghost. *Is this what the Ghost wanted me to see and accept? If so, should I, like Hamlet, give in to the rage that blinded him?* It's discoveries like these, I think, that warn against digging into our former selves where the memories of trauma and fears lie buried, and is perhaps why the dangers of confronting those specters can summon the cautionary events foretold by the Ghost in *Hamlet*:

> But that I am forbid
> To tell the secrets of my prison house,
> I could a tale unfold whose lightest word
> Would harrow up thy soul, freeze thy young blood,
> Make thy two eyes, like stars, start from their spheres,
> Thy knotted and combined locks to part
> And each particular hair to stand on end,
> Like quills upon the fearful porcupine:
> But this eternal blazon must not be
> To ears of flesh and blood.
>
> (1.5.10–22)

In other words, to uncover the secret to our underlying trauma means to willingly unravel the blazon of blows that will come to the mind and body. *Could that eternal blazon be relived and even survived?* I've grappled with the difficulty of survival in order to understand my life of violence as a youth; I was not prepared, nor equipped, to wrestle with death early in life—and so violence stemmed, primarily, from the spectral trauma of family loss.

Through Shakespeare, this traumatic revelation eventually told me something more: that suppressed emotions cannot contain the ghost of my haunted past. And so this entity forced me to confront the new reality of prison with the possibility of dying unremembered, unless I channel its destructivity into the productive act of writing. I became even more curious about who or what the Ghost now represented. *Where did this new meaning come from?* I wanted to answer this last question, for I believed that the experience of incarceration granted me a perspective that most scholars do not, and could not, have. But most importantly, I wanted to liberate myself from the fate of the Ghost.

Upon descending into the existential origins of the Ghost, alone, I remember the scenes of gang violence unfolding a bleak reality. In my youth, I could only defend myself with more violence. But with the company of the Ghost, combined with the solitude of my carceral condition, that dreaded past acquired a new meaning, interpolating the person I once was into the writer I am today. My past became the prime source for transformation.

This journey into the self must be done alone, which might explain why Hamlet elects to meet with the Ghost in private, allowing him to interact with the specter of his dead father under the solitary conditions. Suddenly, it started making sense why Hamlet surrendered to that same brutal violence. His father was murdered. He murders in return. As Gregory Orr claims, questions of meaning and purpose tend not to push survivors of trauma forward, but backwards, into the dismal places where our violent demons reside.[3] It all depends on how we react to it.

Orr claims—and I agree—that the confrontation with trauma could be what nevertheless turns this demon, or Ghost, into the angel of rebirth and transformation.[4] Indeed, when fear and trauma is overcome, the demon tends to cough up the gift reminiscent of Federico Garcia Lorca's concept of the *duende*: an inner demonic being that, when wrestled with, hands over the angelic ability to versify words that are capable of changing the soul through, say, a poem.[5] Reading a poem, for instance, may turn out to be a wonderful reading experience, but without the Ghost of Shakespeare—that is, without *duende*—the poem may nonetheless fall short of reinventing the most crucial aspect of our humanity: ourselves. This is to say, without literature, without Shakespeare, whom I encountered while incarcerated, I would have not envisioned a healing process by which, through writing, the self can be recreated.

STEPHEN K. KIM: RECONSIDERING CALIBAN AND MIRANDA

Early on, *The Tempest* presents a thorny confrontation between Miranda and Caliban that escalates the ethical and political stakes of the play. Miranda speaks eloquently about Caliban's attempted sexual assault and condemns him for it:

> Abhorrèd slave,
> Which any print of goodness wilt not take,
> Being capable of all ill! I pitied thee,
> Took pains to make thee speak, taught thee each hour
> One thing or other. When thou didst not, savage,
> Know thine own meaning, but wouldst gabble like
> A thing most brutish, I endowed thy purposes
> With words that made them known. But thy vile race,
> Though thou didst learn, had that in 't which
>   good natures
> Could not abide to be with. Therefore wast thou
> Deservedly confined into this rock,
> Who hadst deserved more than a prison.
>
> (1.2.421–436)

As Patricia Parker has noted, women who used language publicly and eloquently were often deemed promiscuous and unchaste, a way to exercise patriarchal control over women.[6] But, Miranda's public and eloquent redress of her sexual assault lends her authority and reaffirms her chastity. Still, Miranda's speech (as Caliban's rebuttal to it emphasizes) is also one of the clearest articulations of racism and arguments for colonialism in the play.[7]

When teaching *The Tempest* at Auburn, many of the students (perhaps unsurprisingly) were sympathetic to Caliban. I remember trying to get my students to see the situation from Miranda's perspective, and it's the first time I felt my students were resistant to my encouragement to view the situation in a different light. Many students were repeatedly shifting the attention from Miranda back to Caliban, and I was unsure why this was happening.[8] I remember feeling frustrated because yet again, a group of men seemed unwilling to explore the perspective of a woman character, but of course, the situation was not that simple. Miranda asks for a retributive response to attempted rape. She also justifies Caliban's imprisonment through essentializing Caliban based on his race. Even in a traditional classroom, this perspective-taking exercise would be challenging, and the stakes were even more fraught in prison. I was not prepared to unpack how this moment might bring up challenging past experiences that questioned my students' humanity. I remember feeling shame at this realization, and I am also grateful that my students were willing to look past my failure of empathy.

This experience made me more sympathetic to Caliban. His "isle is full of noises" speech hits with deeper heartbreak; for me, it's now permeated by my students' memories of loneliness in prison (3.2.130–138). I have also grown more sympathetic to Miranda. I wonder how much pain she endured to wish something like imprisonment upon someone whom she once viewed as a student. I still admire her courage and self-advocacy. To borrow from Ariel, my affections towards the characters have become more tender. Like Ariel chastises Prospero to remember his humanity, my students at Auburn reminded me that these plays are not just intellectual exercises. Especially in the prison setting, where institutional power differentials feel especially salient, I'm reminded to honor the ways differing life experiences impact the ways we read.

In addition to offering this pedagogical correction, my students pushed me to explore the carceral layer of this confrontation between Miranda and Caliban. Miranda traffics here in a logic of carceral justice: Caliban has committed a crime and therefore is "deservedly confined." But, in advocating for justice for herself, Miranda participates in discourse that dehumanizes incarcerated individuals. If we read Caliban as a stand-in for incarcerated people, the adjectives used to describe him resemble the stereotypes of incarcerated people today: "savage," "brutish," "vile." I still wonder how we can take these connections even further, as others have started to do. What happens to our readings of *The Tempest* when we consider that the Isle itself resembles a prison, a likeness that informs Margaret Atwood's rewriting of the play?[9] How can we better understand *The Tempest*'s reliance on carceral metaphors in its language and its plot through dialogue with justice-impacted people, as Amy-Scott Douglass does by interviewing incarcerated individuals?[10] While pursuing these questions is outside of the scope of this short contribution, my hope is that scholars, teachers, artists, and students (both on the inside and outside) will continue exploring together *The Tempest*'s uneasy entanglement with incarceration.

CONCLUSION

We hope these vignettes motivate you to consider supporting Shakespeare, and more broadly, college in prison. At the end of our collaborative writing experiment, we are left with the importance of recognizing the myriad motivations that drive people to a Shakespeare classroom on the inside. For some, it can help imagine life outside prison walls, to read about the lives of others. For others, it's a way to do something productive and meaningful with their time, to have something to show to themselves and others. And, as is the case with many college courses, a few are there because it completes a requirement.

We found remaining open to these varied motivations difficult because of the strong expectation that prison Shakespeare must be "rehabilitative," that Shakespeare holds the answer to becoming a "better" person. Constantly looking for the ways that Shakespeare makes incarcerated students "better people" often occludes the many other kinds of impact a Shakespeare course can have. For example, representing Shakespeare as a path to individual self-betterment would eclipse what we found most valuable from the course: our community. Shakespeare courses in prisons can create space for dialogue that incarcerated students feel is necessary because it is not ordinarily available. Julio and Al both described the Shakespeare classroom as a site for collaborative meaning-making, both for the text and their own lives. Commitment to our learning community pushed us to craft more incisive critiques of ourselves, the plays, and our society.

We close with a brief note about Shakespeare's position in the canon. Shakespeare is a lightning rod for conversation about the reification of whiteness and patriarchy in curricula. We didn't reach a firm conclusion on this issue (nor did we expect to). Rather, we recognized that the stakes of the canon are different for incarcerated students. As Julio and Al articulated, the expectation is that incarcerated students would not possess any fluency with Shakespeare. Knowing his work is, unfortunately, still a potent means for disrupting the assumptions of incarcerated people as lazy, unlearned, and inarticulate. Though we work towards a world without the stereotypical associations between the canon and intelligence, it also seems extreme to stop teaching Shakespeare in prisons now when that is not yet the world we inhabit. We hope that other instructors and students will continue engaging with Shakespeare to expand our understanding about the Bard's works. But, more importantly, we hope that others will discover how Shakespeare in the prison classroom reminded us that recognizing each other's humanity means studying both the familiar and the unfamiliar with openness and curiosity.

NOTES

1 James Baldwin, "Why I Stopped Hating Shakespeare," in *The Cross of Redemption: Uncollected Writings*, ed. Randall Kenan (New York: Pantheon, 2010), 55.
2 William Shakespeare, *The Norton Shakespeare: The Essential Plays/The Sonnets* (New York: Norton, 2015). All lines from Shakespeare's work in this chapter refer to this edition.
3 Gregory Orr, *Poetry as Survival* (Athens: University of Georgia Press, 2002), 118.
4 Orr, 118.
5 Orr, 118.

6 Patricia A. Parker, *Literary Fat Ladies: Rhetoric, Gender, Property* (London: Methuen, 1987), 26–27.
7 Kim F. Hall, *Things of Darkness: Economies of Race and Gender in Early Modern England* (Ithaca: Cornell University Press, 1995), 143–145.
8 Al wonders if part of the explanation could be that I was teaching in a men's prison as opposed to a women's prison.
9 Margaret Atwood, *Hag-Seed: The Tempest Retold* (London: Hogarth, 2016).
10 Amy Scott-Douglass, *Shakespeare Inside: The Bard Behind Bars* (London: Continuum, 2007).

"Prisoners of Our Actions": Teaching *Hamlet* on Rikers Island

Brian Chalk

Seven

In 2017, I began regularly co-teaching in Manhattan College's Engaging, Educating, and Empowering Means Change Program (E3MC), created by Andrew Skotnicki, a professor of Religious Studies.[1] The program forms learning communities following the "Inside-Out" teaching model, with roughly equal numbers of Manhattan College students and inside students at Rikers Island or the Westchester Correctional Facilities with the hope that the inside students will continue on to pursue a college degree at Manhattan College after they are released. Regardless of whether this longer-term objective is met, we aim to instill in our students "agency-related benefits," or "a set of related constructs" such as the "ability to self-advocate, general self-esteem," and "hope for the future" that will prove useful to them both pre- and post-release.[2]

Our course, "Shakespeare, Prison, and God," combines discussion of Shakespeare's plays with a selection of theological readings on topics such as violence, the ethics of incarceration, and the possibility of redemption. Andrew and I chose thematically appropriate plays: *Romeo and Juliet*, exploring causes and consequences of youthful violence; *Othello*, dealing with intersections of violence and race. However, it's *Hamlet* that consistently proves most popular. For contemporary relevance, I suggested we include an episode of the popular podcast *This American Life*. "Act V" follows a group of

DOI: 10.4324/9781003451662-10

incarcerated men in a high-security prison who gain new insight into Shakespeare's most famous play by rehearsing and staging its final act. Taking my initial experience teaching "Act V" as a representative example, this chapter considers how the pedagogical missteps and successes I experienced teaching this podcast encapsulate my experience teaching Shakespeare in prison. In this course, we link Shakespeare with topics germane to the experience of the inside students such as violence and incarceration to invite reflection without inadvertently imprisoning them within that aspect of their identities. As my colleague and I gradually discovered, however, and as the "Act V" experience made clear, sometimes both results are possible within the same class meeting.

"The inside-out model," Jayme M. Yeo observes, by emphasizing "dialogue and equal participation," has the potential to "overcome pre-conceptions regarding out-groups—students from both populations as well as faculty."[3] At the same time, Andrew and I are mindful that the experiences outside students have before they enter the classroom inevitably complicate this process. Students from Manhattan College's campus must attend training sessions required by the prison. These include policies about boundaries and consent that are useful to the extent that they protect the incarcerated students. The majority of the training, however, warns students of dangers endemic to a prison environment in a manner that reinforces stereotypes our course seeks to counter. Incarcerated people, according to the introductory videos, are expert grifters, tirelessly devoted to discovering advantages to exploit, especially easy "marks" like college students and teachers. One of the Rikers videos, in fact, describes incarcerated people as "PhDs in grifting."[4] These experiences can increase the imbalance the outside students feel with the inside students but, rather than ignoring it, Andrew and I acknowledge and embrace that the unique setting in which the class takes place will inevitably be the most valuable aspect of the course for all of the students. We encourage the outside students to be vigilant but remind them that their classmates are more likely to be intimidated by the class than they are. One guideline that we establish in our first session, moreover, is that no two inside or outside students may sit next to each other, physically eliminating the distance between the two groups in the hope of doing the same to the psychological barriers between them.

Our approach draws on what Katherine Boutry describes as "Creativity Studies," which "encourages students to uncover their own life themes and to decide what gives their own lives meaning [...] Shakespeare's power for them is that even in the face of the deepest tragedies…there is a lesson to be told and a lesson to be learned through which painful experiences are made meaningful."[5] We often have the students create and enact scenarios that explore the dynamics of that week's play. Given that we integrate Shakespeare and Religious Studies materials that engage with ethics and the causes of violence, the didactic experiences Boutry describes come up naturally in our group discussions. For example, in our final class on *Romeo and Juliet*, we use James Gilligan's *Preventing Violence*, a study that considers how excavating the roots of violence helps to reduce and eradicate it, to analyze the final three acts of the play, which feature the deaths of four young people. We assign each of the discussion groups a character, and ask them to imagine the sort of life that character might lead if he or she grew up in a modern context. We then ask students to stage the death of their character in a manner that reflects their interpretation of the scene (who shoulders the most blame, who initiates the violence, etc.). The skits they put together must make use of what they have learned of Shakespeare's staging conventions. We have found that the best way to encourage student empowerment is through discussion, with an emphasis on group work that allows students to share their perspectives with one another. Our goal in introducing these subjects in conjunction with Shakespeare is to inspire the class to reflect on issues involving prison without making the inside students feel as if they themselves are objects of study. In other words, to borrow Robert Scott's phrase, our pedagogy emphasizes that "teaching must not be something done *to* the incarcerated student, nor misconstrued as something done *for* the incarcerated student, but *with* them."[6]

Much like this classroom work, the "Act V" podcast explores Shakespeare's cultural value as it considers how his text translates to the stage. Early in the episode, the reporter, Jack Hitt, confesses that he had not anticipated having a transformative experience with the play itself. He remarks, somewhat pompously, that he's "seen *Hamlet* a dozen times," including notable productions starring Kevin Kline at the Public Theater, "the famous Diane Venora version three nights in a row" and even "Ingmar Bergman's production done in Brooklyn, performed entirely in Swedish." "What else," he wonders, "is there to learn from watching another *Hamlet*?"[7] Over the course of his time at the prison, Hitt continues, "After hanging out with this group of convicted actors for six months, I did discover something. I didn't know anything about *Hamlet*."[8] In the drama of the episode itself, Hitt's revelatory experience parallels those of the cast members, with the latter serving as unexpected instructors to the former.

My first impression of the podcast was that it provided a readymade lesson plan for our course. The central question the narrator poses in the introduction, "Why does *Hamlet* prove particularly resonant and meaningful when performed in incarcerated contexts?" was one that I was eager to introduce to the students. My enthusiasm only grew when the podcast transitioned to the section I thought would be most helpful to the class: testimonials from the performers themselves. The first of these interviews is with the actor playing Horatio, Derrick "Big Hutch" Hutchinson. As his nickname suggests, Big Hutch not only looms large over his fellow cast members but, we hear, over the prison population as a whole. He compares the social hierarchy of a prison to an ocean, explaining, "you've got the minnows, and you've got the killer whales. Minnow being the lowest, killer whale the highest." Big Hutch himself, he quickly points out, transcends these categories. Instead, he is a "blue whale," capable of controlling even the fiercest of the killers. Big Hutch admits that he considers his castmates "minnows" with whom he normally wouldn't associate. As he continues, he extends this criticism to his own character, Horatio:

> Yeah, I think he a chump. I mean, he supposed to be cool with Hamlet. And they're best friends. But I think Horatio is just somebody—a sounding board for Hamlet. I mean, the majority of his lines is, "eh, my lord, yes, my lord." I mean, if we're friends, we're going to communicate better than that. I mean, you're going to tell me your deepest secrets. So I want to know what you and Ophelia did last night.[9]

Big Hutch's deft comedic touch never fails to amuse students. From his perspective, Hamlet's famous devotion to opacity is irritating, even unacceptable, rather than fascinating. Even more striking, however, is the insightful window into the play that his irreverence toward the text produces. Although we have more access to Hamlet than any other character in the play, Big Hutch points out that the experience of playing his "best friend" highlights Hamlet's limitations as well as his strengths. In this way, Big Hutch's engagement with the text and confidence in the validity of his perspective exemplifies the interpretive method we try to instill in our students from our first session.

Despite his keen insights, our students often point out that Big Hutch does not reflect on his willingness to play the role of a minnow; his relationship to Horatio emerges from the stark contrast with his character. Nor does Big Hutch consider the way in which the larger framework of the prison inevitably subsumes the social hierarchy he describes, and subordinates even "Blue Whales" to the rules and structure of the institution. Other members of the cast in the "Act V" episode, however, construct direct bridges between themselves and their characters. Danny Waller, the actor depicting the Ghost, for example, admits he feels as if he is speaking from the perspective of a man he killed. He interprets Claudius's soliloquy, in which he attempts to reconcile his desire for forgiveness with his inability to repent, as an apology to his wife and children for his failure to be there for them. Lines which convey a deeply human desire for renewal, "Help, angels! Make assay— / Bow, stubborn knees, and heart with strings of steel, / Be soft as sinews of the newborn babe," become particularly resonant in this context (3.3.69–71).[10] In both the play and the podcast, the sympathy the lines inspire is for an individual normally written off as a "criminal."

The episode's primary example of this practice is James Word, who plays Laertes. Word, even Big Hutch concedes with a combination of admiration and jealousy, is "a natural." The soundbites of his line readings bring Shakespeare's language to life in commanding fashion. Unlike Big Hutch, moreover, Word feels that his understanding of the role provides a window into his own psyche:

> Laertes, he falls into the manipulation. And he becomes a bad guy for a little while because he's being deceitful now. You know, I never really looked at it, and it's somewhat cowardly. And I can relate that to my past life as a criminal. To put a gun in somebody's face, that's an unfair advantage. You know, and that's a cowardly act. That's what criminals are. We're cowards. You know, when we're criminals, we are cowards.[11]

To Word, the overlap between Laertes's behavior and his own is unmistakable; his description slides seamlessly from Laertes's encounter with Claudius, who "becomes a bad guy" for more than a "little while," to his own experiences in his "past life." When Hitt asks Word to consolidate this connection, to confirm that he's able to play the part so brilliantly because "so much of Laertes is inside James Word," Word's response collapses the difference completely: "I am Laertes. I am. I am."[12]

As Andrew and I hoped they would, the students found the testimonies of the actors illuminating and empowering. The candor of Big Hutch and the emotional bravery of James Word were helpful both to our in-class discussions and the students' reflection papers. The testimonials from the podcast encouraged the students to return to the text with renewed energy and confidence. Based on the introductory section of the podcast at least, the narrator's role in many ways seemed to mirror our quest to be what Scott calls "critical teachers" who make "advocating" for incarcerated students central to their pedagogy.[13]

As the episode continues, however, Hitt insinuates himself into the narrative in a way opposite to the aims of our "radical classroom." As the performance draws near, despite his growing fondness for the cast members, Hitt finds himself "playing a constant guessing game" about what crimes caused his "new friends" imprisonment, a line of questioning that is strictly off limits in our classroom. Eventually, his curiosity overwhelms him; he visits a records depository and begins "reading old case files." The results, in Hitt's words, are "more horrible than I thought":

> One guy I particularly liked shot a man in the head twice at point-blank range. Another of my new friends raped his pubescent daughter, impregnating her. Later, there was an abortion. Another friend grabbed a man getting out of a car, put a gun to his chest during a robbery, and pulled the trigger. Others had sodomized children—younger children, the age of my own children.[14]

The clash between Hitt's growing sense of friendship and his discovery of their crimes, we might notice, reverses how cast members such as James Word relate to their respective parts. Whereas the actors use the play as an impetus to move forward in time, Hitt moves backwards. Whereas the actors in many cases seek to reinvent themselves through their performances, to come to terms with or attempt to atone for their past actions, Hitt's insistence on learning of their crimes and then confronting them places them in the past or, to use a theatrical metaphor, recasts them in their former roles.

Before he tells the actors he has looked up their crimes, Hitt reflects on his predicament in revealing fashion: "Someone I knew and liked was a murderer. I wanted to talk to the cast about this, but I was anxious. I know this sounds crazy, but I was afraid it might hurt their feelings. I felt like they had betrayed me. But strangely, I felt that I had betrayed them too."[15]

When I vetted the podcast prior to the semester, I experienced this moment as an unsurprising and even interesting narrative direction. In the context of the classroom, I felt the full force of the irony to which Hitt seemingly has no access. I agreed that betrayal had taken place, but I now realized that it was completely one-sided in nature. The men Hitt befriends are in prison for the crimes the case files describe; falsifying their identities is, in a real sense, impossible. Adding to this irony is Hitt's profound sense of the relevance of the play's thematic preoccupations for the actors. When made aware of his newfound knowledge of their crimes, Hitt observes, "They all said the same thing. But I'm this guy now, I'm not that guy. Are we forever the prisoner of our actions? It's a good question. It was Hamlet's question, and it's the unresolvable conflict in our penal system."[16] Given his insistence on confronting these men with the actions of the past, how could his answer to Hamlet's question be anything but yes?

As I played this section of the podcast on Rikers Island in 2017, I immediately realized I had made a serious pedagogical mistake. I somehow underestimated the potential of Hitt's decision to undermine what I hoped would be a positive and affirming session. Once in the actual classroom, the contradictory nature of the episode became obvious. Identifying with the cast members quickly became demoralizing rather than empowering. One student who was nearly eligible for parole said that listening to this excerpt made her feel as if she belonged in prison, and that she was certain to return after being discharged. Another left the room crying soon after the recording ended. In addition to upsetting these students, the situation also divided inside and outside students in ways that were hurtful rather than instructive. Several of the students from campus quickly and emphatically objected to Hitt's behavior. Nevertheless, the effects on both sets of students was unsettling. Just as Hitt's betrayal transformed the castmates from talented actors to dangerous criminals in his eyes, I seemed to have turned the inside students back into incarcerated individuals. The formerly lively discussion became stagnant; I feared I had undone the progress we had made in the weeks prior to that session.

In fairness, Hitt is not an educator and the cast members included in the episode are not students. Nor does the episode market itself as a teaching tool. I assign the blame for my predicament to myself rather than Hitt: I was oblivious to the insensitivities of his behavior until I introduced them to actual incarcerated students.[17] The popularity of This American Life amplifies the complexity: despite our class's objections to his process, Hitt's work brought national attention to director Agnes Wilcox's Prison Performing Arts program.[18] Despite the ethical questions it raises about journalistic practice, the episode's listeners get to hear the voices of a segment of the population normally doomed to social silence.

Since my first experience teaching the podcast in Rikers Island, I have refined my lesson plan in a manner that, I hope, encourages both the inside and outside students to think critically and productively about the potentially troubling aspects of Hitt's engagement with his subjects. When I foreground these moments, the incarcerated students are often more sympathetic with Hitt's decision to investigate the crimes of the actors than the outside ones are. The potentially unpleasant experience of encountering Hitt's reaction does not negate the positive experience of hearing from the actors themselves. To shape my lesson plans, I have also relied on scholars such as Niels Herold, who sees theatrical performances in prisons as "repentance rituals," or events that allow "inmate actors" the opportunity "to assemble into a community of reforming rogue players, a company of self-redeemers who are transforming the punishing purpose of penitentiary life into a spiritual force-field for repentance and forgiveness."[19] Nevertheless, my experience teaching has generated more questions than answers. How can instructors who teach in prison environments avoid the kind of negative reinforcement this podcast includes? How can course content that reflects societal antipathy toward incarcerated people be taught in a prison classroom? How best, in other words, to be a radical teacher who has intense experiences with the students rather than at their expense?

NOTES

1. The ethos that underlies the E3MC program and that I allude to throughout this chapter was developed entirely by Andrew Skotnicki. In addition to his tireless, inspirational, and deeply humane efforts to educate incarcerated individuals as an instructor, Andrew has produced a large body of scholarship articulating and defending his positions. Most recently, see Andrew Skotnicki, *Conversion and the Rehabilitation of the Penal System* (Oxford: Oxford University Press, 2019).
2. Sarah Moore and Tanya Erzen, "The Relationship Between Liberal Arts Classroom Experiences and the Development of Agency-related Wellbeing for Incarcerated Students," *Journal of Higher Education in Prison* 1, no. 1 (2021): 32.
3. Jayme M. Yeo, "Teaching Shakespeare Inside-Out: Creating a Dialogue Between Traditional and Incarcerated Students," in *Teaching Social Justice Through Shakespeare: Why Renaissance Literature Matters Now*, eds. Hilary Eklund and Wendy Beth Hyman (Edinburgh University Press, 2019), 202.
4. These samples are from notes that I took during the introductory sessions described above. I should add that the staff at both institutions has been almost uniformly welcoming and supportive, despite the challenges inherent in their positions.
5. Katherine Boutry, "Creativity Studies and Shakespeare at the Urban Community College," in *Shakespeare and the 99%: Literary Studies, the Profession, and the Production of Inequity*, eds. Sharon O'Dair and Timothy Francisco (Cham: Palgrave Macmillan, 2019), 133. "*King Lear*," for example, "provides a useful test case for teaching Shakespeare through the lens of Creativity Studies. Lear's lack of creative vision causes his kingdom to stagnate while it allows other characters to demonstrate their own creative responses to adversity. This all starts from nothing; or more precisely, Lear's fear of nothing" (134).

6 Robert Scott, "Distinguishing Radical Teaching from Merely Having Intense Experiences While Teaching in Prison," *The Radical Teacher* 95 (2013): 28.

7 All quotes from the podcast are from the transcript provided at the following: Ira Glass and Jack Hitt, hosts. "Act V" *This American Life* (podcast), August 9, 2002, https://www.thisamericanlife.org/218/act-v.

8 Glass and Hitt.

9 Glass and Hitt.

10 Quotes from *Hamlet* are taken from William Shakespeare, *The Norton Shakespeare: Third Edition*, eds. Stephen Greenblatt, et al. (New York: Norton, 2015).

11 Glass and Hitt.

12 Glass and Hitt.

13 Scott, 23.

14 Glass and Hitt.

15 Glass and Hitt.

16 Glass and Hitt.

17 Although I teach the course with Andrew Skotnicki, I am responsible for the aspects of the lesson plan involving Shakespeare.

18 See Amy Scott-Douglass, *Shakespeare Inside: The Bard Behind Bars* (London: Continuum, 2007), 62.

19 Niels Herold, *Prison Shakespeare and the Purpose of Performance: Repentance Rituals and the Early Modern* (London: Palgrave Macmillan, 2014), 8. Kirsten N. Mendoza's essay on how trigger warnings have the potential to inspire rather than stifle class discussion has also been helpful. See "Sexual Violence, Trigger Warnings, and the Early Modern Classroom," in *Teaching Social Justice Through Shakespeare: Why Renaissance Literature Matters Now*, eds. Hilary Eklund and Wendy Beth Hyman (Edinburgh: Edinburgh University Press, 2019), 97–105.

Playing Many Parts: The Challenges of
Representing Incarcerated Shakespeares

Grace Duffy, John S. Garrison, and Anthony Rhodd

Eight

This chapter captures a dialogue between a Professor of English at Grinnell College (JG), a recent graduate of the college (GD), and a currently incarcerated student (AR), as they reflect on their experience participating in the class "Introduction to Shakespeare," taught at Newton Correctional Facility during the spring of 2022 through Grinnell's Liberal Arts in Prison Program (LAPP). The discussion centers on several facets of how representation operates in the prison classroom: that of canonical literature, of the instructor, of the students. This discussion also showcases how the available depictions of incarcerated Shakespeare instruction might influence expectations surrounding the experience of teaching or learning in prison.

JG: **You've both seen or read depictions of Shakespeare in prisons (for example, the documentary *Shakespeare Behind Bars*).**[1] **How did this match up with your own experiences of teaching or studying Shakespeare?**

GD: One difference between our class and a lot of the depictions I've seen was its structure: students attended two class sessions with Dr. Garrison per week and one optional peer mentor session with me where they could bring up questions, clarify assignment prompts,

DOI: 10.4324/9781003451662-11

and further discuss class content. The small-group allowed for an environment even more casual than the discussion-based course, which may have helped add variety to the traditional class format and student-professor roles.

In 2021, Dr. Garrison and I also designed a course taught on Grinnell's campus that focused on different depictions of Shakespeare taught in carceral settings. The students spent time trying to understand the experience of learning Shakespeare in prison through these narratives, but ultimately felt like the documentaries and essays by and about prison education fell short of communicating how the incarcerated students actually felt. In part, the accounts are usually told from the perspective of the educator, but also because they relied on stereotypes of incarcerated individuals to craft a compelling narrative, leaning into tropes of reform and rehabilitation.

AR: Where the incarcerated subjects of the documentary *Shakespeare Behind Bars* depict the struggles and joy of playacting in prison, our class analyzed Shakespearean themes such as love and war, community, character, and my personal favorite: remembrance. In analyzing the relationship between memory and identity in desolate environments, our class discussed several plays, including *Hamlet*. After exploring Hamlet's obligation to harbor the memory of his slain father, we read *Station Eleven*, Emily St. John Mandel's novel of retaining art, humanity, and hope in a post-apocalyptic world. Where Hamlet held his father's memory, and Mandel's "Traveling Symphony" held the memory of

Shakespeare, our class identified with loss and how remembering remains a precursor to redemption.

The oppressive structural components of mass incarceration typify the detachment from normalcy depicted in apocalyptic literature. Like the characters in *Station Eleven*, incarcerated persons struggle with the absence of luxury, normalcy, and the intimacy of their lives pre-incarceration. Naturally, our discussions with on-campus students focused on aspects of prison life which disassociate incarcerated persons from their former identities. So we remembered. We spoke about movies, books, and music. We spoke about Shakespeare. Despite oppression and the stigmas associated with incarceration, we claimed our humanity by connecting, by analyzing, and by remembering. Ultimately, Hamlet's own relationship between memory and identity allowed us to analyze our own pasts through a Shakespearean lens.

The incarcerated subjects of the documentary *Shakespeare Beyond Bars* tapped into this same highway of memory, albeit in different ways. The incarcerated actors transcended the hopeless environment of their prison by performing Shakespeare. Through performance, they remembered their humanity. Where they performed, we analyzed. Both are acts of remembering, and each is essential to experiencing Shakespeare in carceral settings.

AR: I realize now, Grace, that a significant difference between our course and the *Shakespeare Behind Bars* documentary was your feminine presence in the classroom. While LAPP students brought diverse lived experiences, none had experience as a female student. What was that like? Did you feel open and free to contribute to class discussions despite the carceral environment, and the overwhelmingly masculine presence?

GD: That was a dynamic I definitely thought about while tutoring at the prison. In the classroom, I always felt welcomed and respected. Rather than limit my participation, my status as the only woman in the room was a chance to share observations about the text that were not as readily noticed by the men. For example, encouraging discussion about the perspective of female characters when this was lacking, like the trope of madness and femininity with Ophelia in Hamlet. It was an environment of mutual curiosity and openness that allowed for this type of trust. Outside of the classroom, too, the majority of prison staff were men. Passing through security to enter class made me wonder how the roles that educators, students, and staff play are not only impacted by the status of incarceration, but also gender.

AR: Mass incarceration perpetuates the belief that prisons are necessary, but more, that society's often negative view of incarcerated persons justifies its necessity. What were your beliefs about incarcerated persons prior to entering the prison? How did these beliefs change? What does the world need to know about prisoners?

GD: Part of the way I prepared for the experience of being a teaching assistant for the course was to read existing depictions of teaching Shakespeare in prisons. In the book Prison Shakespeare, Rob Pensalfini highlights how schools and prisons both foster a dependence on extrinsic motivation—reward and punishment—in a way that's harmful to self-worth. Going into the class, I thought a lot about the ways that students' perception of their own capabilities might be impacted by this, plus the general belief that Shakespeare is challenging to read and to understand. I'd volunteered for the prison program before this class and knew that the students were highly capable, but I still wondered how these internalized expectations would shape their willingness to engage with such canonical—and such canonically difficult—material.

Pensalfini writes that someone who is intrinsically motivated "typically displays traits such as empathy and compassion, and a desire to understand and be understood, to belong to a community."[2] I found this description to resonate perfectly with our class. What I observed in class was not low self-esteem, but impressive resilience and creativity when engaging with the texts.

JG: One big thing that was occurring for me when I first started teaching in the prison was the question of how to build trust. I was aware of the fact that I was coming in as an outsider, both in the sense of not being part of the group who see each other all the time and the reality of being able to walk out of the building at the end of the session. Early on, I tried to communicate just how curious I am about Shakespeare's work and how many questions I have about the plays and the poems… questions I'm still asking about them, even though I've been studying and teaching the author for almost two decades. Given that I was the instructor, I knew I needed to play the role of expert, but it was equally important for me to play the role of interlocutor. I genuinely wanted to talk to the incarcerated students about Shakespeare to hear what they were thinking, not even necessarily as folks in prison but also because the students comprised such a diverse group.

AR: **In one of our final class discussions with you, Dr. Garrison, we each chose which Shakespearean character we most identified with. Were you surprised by our answers? What values did you find the students most identifying with? What do characters like Coriolanus, Hamlet, Henry V, and Richard II teach incarcerated students about identity?**

JG: It was interesting to me that many of the incarcerated students identified with characters who were faced with impossible odds and still moved forward. But they also connected with those characters who were very aware of how they represented themselves to the world in the face of pressure to present themselves in a certain way. I'm thinking here of Hal in *Henry IV* specifically and Hamlet, too. They're both people who are very aware of what the world expects from them and what's been handed down to them as they struggle to figure out how to carve their own niche in the world.

GD: **Engaging with Shakespeare in a prison setting can shed light on aspects of the text that would go unnoticed in other contexts. You've both already mentioned some readings that were unique to our class, but I'm wondering: What is something that you took away from this experience that caused you to re-think what you already knew about Shakespeare?**

JG: I have always loved *Coriolanus*, especially for all its questions about honor, heroism, loyalty, and comradeship.

However, it's been a difficult text for my undergraduate students in traditional settings to grapple with. I tried it once years ago and thought "never again," but then I decided to give it a go at the prison. The language is especially difficult. The protagonist can seem cold. The world itself is full of trauma and choices that promise no good outcome. However, I was so impressed by the way that the incarcerated students really took to the text, bringing it up throughout the semester and pointing out ways that it tied to the histories, poems, and even comedies. In fact, it not only was a hit among the students in the class, but it was also read widely outside of the class, as students talked it up amongst others throughout the prison.

AR: Prior to the start of class, the other incarcerated students and I discussed our limited knowledge of Shakespeare's work. We felt familiar with plays such as Romeo and Juliet, but as a class, our lack of experience left much to be desired. Most of us were raised in unconventional homes such as foster care, detention centers, or with abusive parents; the priorities of our caretakers did not always align with education. As such, we didn't know much about Shakespeare.

Early in the course, the professor introduced excerpts from a Neil Gaiman graphic novel highlighting works such as A Midsummer Night's Dream. I didn't understand the language. I felt distanced from the thematic elements of love and relationships. The characters seemed odd, flamboyant, and exaggerated. However, when introduced to Coriolanus, Shakespeare's focus on character transformation allowed me to rethink my approach to analyzing the texts. Once invested, I realized the complicated language clarified and corresponded to the protagonist's fall from grace. This I could grasp. As an example, Coriolanus's unintended transformation from hero to villain mirrors the experience I feel as an incarcerated person when inheriting labels contrary to my actual character.

Despite stereotypes which portray prisoners as socially inept, incarcerated students resist such mischaracterization through disciplined commitments to academia. While the class empathized with Coriolanus's banishment, we also identified with his fight for redemption, an analysis likely to go unnoticed in other contexts. Analyzing Shakespeare in a carceral setting provides students the opportunity to re-think character and redemption in refreshing ways. But this isn't the only takeaway. Shakespeare also teaches the "outside" world how stigma and ostracism result in emotional and social trauma.

Although I knew little about Shakespeare prior to the beginning of class, this experience taught me that there's a lot to learn about the world, and, more importantly, that the world has a lot to learn about me.

GD: **Dr. Garrison, earlier you mentioned how your curiosity with the students' perspectives focused less on their incarceration and more on the fact that the nature of mass incarceration meant that the class was very diverse. How did that play out in the classroom. Also, A. Rhodd, as a student, how did you participate in these discourses?**

JG: It's funny because a lot of the existing stuff out there about Shakespeare in prison programs talks about how transformative it can be for incarcerated folks to reflect on their own wrongdoing through those of the characters. However, I found that something very different was happening in our classrooms in the prison. There was some of this, for example, in discussions of Richard II's speech when he is incarcerated and imagines trying to claw his way out of his cell or imagining an entire world to keep him company in solitary confinement. That scene is central to the experience of incarcerated people in Laura Bates' *Shakespeare Saved My Life*.[3] However, it speaks to the diversity of prison Shakespeare experiences that this scene did not resonate as strongly with our students. Rather, it was the scenes of heroism that did. Although our students certainly spoke openly about the experience of being imprisoned or labeled as criminals, these issues were not at the heart of our conversations.

AR: Our class included students of various ages, race, gender, sexual identity, and socioeconomic backgrounds. As students, our educational backgrounds ranged from high school and junior high dropouts, to collegiate graduates. Our racial composition included persons of Latinx, Native-American, African-American, and Caucasian descent. Some students had spent decades behind prison walls, some had spent less than a year. We engaged intellectually with "on-campus" students seemingly unaccustomed to social hardship, but well versed in the academic language and class structures found in traditional higher education. Each class member's breadth of lived experience breathed energy into the daunting task of studying Shakespeare.

My experience as an incarcerated student, Native-American, and punk rocker offered unique cultural, historical, and social context to class diversity. During discussions, I spoke on a personal level about Prince Hal's youthful rejection of expectation in Henry IV, Part 1.

Further, my final course project involved writing a scene employing Shakespearean tone and style, and including characters we studied in class. Drawing upon my Indigenous heritage, my scene found Sir John Falstaff, alone and banished, in a new land after enduring five years of solitude. He encounters a tribal leader and explains his version of events surrounding the banishment. Where Falstaff ultimately seeks battlefield glory and respect amongst his peers, he finds redemption and honor amongst a Tribal community that values the oral tradition. This unique analysis of Shakespeare derives from my diverse lived experience, but also, exemplifies Shakespeare's ability to bridge dichotomous cultural structures, both in carceral settings and the free world.

JG: **How do you feel your individual identity (e.g., gender, race, class, culture) contributed to your understanding of Shakespeare or what you contributed to class discussion? Did it present any barriers, lead to a unique perspective, or change how you relate to your identity?**

AR: I am a Native-American male raised in a middle-class Iowa home. In prison, however, I am merely an incarcerated person. Prison officials restrict the clothes I wear, the books I read, my religious participation, the music I listen to, the shows I watch, and the things I say. Like everyone else in prison, I make less than 50 cents an hour. Upon entering the prison system, a state identification number replaced my name. Because of the restrictive nature of prison, there's not much space for identity, and prison officials tend to target any public displays of individuality. This all changed the moment I walked into a college-in-prison classroom. The academic expectations of higher education demanded that I reject the de-individualization of prison life and reclaim my identity as a human being. After 15 years of incarceration, this was not easy.

My whole life I resisted what I believed to be the status quo. In junior high, I loved books such as *The Outsiders* by S. E. Hinton and *One Flew Over the Cuckoo's Nest* by Ken Kesey. However, my analysis of plot, character, and themes did not always align with the teachers' assessments of the same books. I felt weird sometimes. I felt like my answers had no value. By the time I was in ninth grade, I stopped answering and dropped out. For the majority of my life, my drive to question almost everything maintained the cornerstones of my individual identity. I didn't accept things at face value. I thought outside the box. Prison nearly killed this part of me. Then I met Shakespeare.

Where prison restrictions dampen individuality, Shakespeare implored me to explore, to question, to analyze, resist, and contribute. In this space, the analytical characteristics of my identity flourished. I felt free. I felt challenged. More than anything, I felt worth. As the class progressed, my drive to question contributed unique perspectives on sexuality, comradery, and the significance of hope in environments of desperation. Studying Shakespeare encouraged my identity as a thinker. The class discussions rejuvenated my drive to question, to analyze. For several hours a week, I was not a prisoner devoid of identity. I was a student studying Shakespeare.

GD: I like what A. Rhodd says about his developing identity as a student and a thinker. Teaching in that setting, I was reminded constantly how lucky I've been to have access to uninterrupted, quality education my whole life. The way that the students in the class practiced what A. Rhodd talks about—questioning, curiosity, connection—challenged how I engaged as a learner in my own studies. The level of humility and reflection that the men exemplified was something I'd never seen in my own classes, and it pushed me to be less self-conscious in the classroom.

Going back to the structure of our course, my perspective also allowed me to bring an aspect of on-campus life to the class, demonstrating how discussion of course content outside of designated class time can enrich learning and create a sense of community. Not only was I able to share my tips about writing a strong essay or understanding iambic pentameter, but students asked about my experiences reading Shakespeare for the first time and we commiserated over the frustration of feeling confused by difficult passages. While much about our lives differed greatly, we connected over our shared experience as students studying Shakespeare.

AR: **This edited volume is about mass incarceration. If all the world's a stage, what's the role of incarcerated students? Where and how do our voices fit in? What do incarcerated students need to learn about the world, and what role does Shakespeare play in teaching us? What does the world need to learn about incarcerated students? Where mass incarceration**

devalues its victims, what values did the incarcerated students exude, and how do these values differ from those of the "on-campus" students?

JG: Wow. Your question helps me see something I have seen before in Jaques' speech in *As You Like It*. Those "Seven Ages" are supposed to capture the stages all men go through in their lives: the infant, the schoolboy, the soldier, the lover, and so on. But there's no stage called "the prisoner." When we see what and who is left out of the speech, it reminds us who's left out of the conversation so frequently. I do believe that "Shakespeare is for everyone," with the caveat that not everyone has to read or like his work. One really powerful thing I heard from incarcerated students was that knowing about Shakespeare and studying his work in depth helped create their own little world outside of the correctional officers. The students possessed specialized knowledge, a tailored vocabulary, and access to a broader world that those who imprisoned them did not. And it wasn't said naively—as if books can set people free—but it nonetheless was a really powerful statement about how literature and a liberal education can build community and help us all feel like we're part of something larger than ourselves and our immediate world.

NOTES

1 Before the class began, the students all watched the documentary *Shakespeare Behind Bars*, directed by Hank Rogerson (Philomath Films, 2006).

2 Rob Pensalfini, *Prison Shakespeare: For These Deep Shames and Great Indignities* (New York: Palgrave Macmillian, 2016), 110.

3 Laura Bates, *Shakespeare Saved My Life: Ten Years in Solitary with the Bard* (Naperville: Source Books, 2013).

Michael Chekhov Technique: A Trauma-Responsive Practice in Shakespeare in Prison

Frannie Shepherd-Bates

Nine

A BRIEF OVERVIEW OF SHAKESPEARE IN PRISON

Shakespeare in Prison (SiP) at Detroit Public Theatre uses theater as a catalyst for empowerment, community, and hope with incarcerated and formerly incarcerated people. Founded in 2012 at Michigan's only prison for women under the auspices of Magenta Giraffe Theatre Company, SiP moved to Detroit Public Theatre in 2015. During my time as director (2012–2023), the program worked with more than 300 people behind bars and continued working with SiP alumni after their release, providing mentorship, professional opportunities, and connections with resources in the free world.

SiP is centered on the needs, ideas, and lived experience of its participants, rather than the production of a play. SiP's primary outcome, identified through a case study of the 2016–2017 season with the women's ensemble, is the positive development of each participant's narrative identity—how they define who they are based on their interpretation and telling of their life stories: past, present, and future.[1] SiP's 2020 follow-up report, based on interviews with women's ensemble alumni, found that the long-term benefits of SiP involvement are an enhanced sense of self-efficacy, empathy, and community.[2]

Prior to the COVID-19 pandemic, an SiP season comprised roughly 40 weeks divided into three phases: (1) Discussing and analyzing the text; building trust in the ensemble;

DOI: 10.4324/9781003451662-12

exploring the play with movement; (2) Going through the play again after adding new members; continuing to build trust; (3) Casting, rehearsing, and performing the play.

SiP incorporated exercises from Theatre of the Oppressed, Chekhov Technique, and others, according to each ensemble's needs. SiP's staff did not include a therapist; nevertheless, Justin Greenlaw, an SiP alum, maintains that our role was to facilitate "therapeutic energy" and a space that was, for many, therapeutic.[3]

MEMORY, TRAUMA, AND THE POTENTIAL DANGERS OF MAINSTREAM ACTING TECHNIQUES

SiP strove to avoid retraumatizing participants by using acting exercises that rely on imagination and physicality, rather than those that focus on recalling memories—especially traumatic ones. While mainstream American acting techniques are based in part on the recollection of specific events from the actor's past, SiP took its cues from a school of acting that explicitly rejects this reliance on personal memory: Michael Chekhov Technique.

Memory is at the heart both of traumatic response and of many mainstream acting exercises, creating a risk for incarcerated actors. In his 2014 best-selling book, *The Body Keeps the Score*, former president of the International Society for Traumatic Stress Studies, Bessel van der Kolk writes, "If elements of the trauma are replayed again and again, the accompanying stress hormones engrave those memories ever more deeply in the mind."[4] In prison, the vast majority of people report a history of trauma prior to incarceration (which is compounded by the trauma of incarceration itself).[5] This makes them especially vulnerable to the adverse effects of reliving traumatic memories, whether voluntarily or involuntarily.

Memories, though, are the core of most modern acting techniques. Konstantin Stanislavski, the "father of modern acting," was dissatisfied with the highly stylized theatrical performances prevalent in Russia at the turn of the 20th century. In response, he developed a naturalistic style of acting, which he called the "System," that provided the foundation for nearly all acting techniques that are still used in Western theater. The System evolved over time, but Stanislavski's early work centered on his assertion that the authenticity of an actor's performance flowed from the inside, "where the mind and imagination create the thoughts and feelings of the character," to the outside, "where the body expresses and communicates what is going on inside."[6] Crucially, Stanislavski wrote of the importance of an acting technique which "can bring back feelings you have already experienced"[7] that "have been smelted in the furnace of your emotion memory." Often called "sense memory" or "affective memory," he wrote that this "is the best and only true material for inner creativeness."[8]

Stanislavski's System birthed countless variations all over the Western world. Most famously, Lee Strasberg developed The Method, which has been practiced by celebrities such as James Dean and Marlon Brando. Method acting is based almost entirely on intensive use of affective memory (a person who has been sexually assaulted, for example, would relive their experience of that attack and its aftermath to portray a character who has been raped). Phoebe Brand, who studied with Strasberg, said "Lee insisted on working each little moment of affective memory; we were always going backwards into our own lives. It was painful to dig back…Lee crippled a lot of people."[9] Midway through his career, Stanislavski renounced affective memory in favor of a method of physical actions:

"how starting from the outside, from creating the outer line of a role, planning it in terms of a series of actions, would take you inside a character's mind."[10] Strasberg rejected this shift, holding fast to his own technique, which was based entirely on Stanislavski's early work and remains controversial even in professional circles. While I am not aware of any prison theater practitioners who explicitly use The Method in a carceral setting, its principles and exercises threaten to creep into any practitioner's work in prison because of its ubiquity and cultural power. Though it has largely fallen out of favor in traditional acting training programs, The Method remains entrenched in popular culture due to its use by high-profile, critically acclaimed artists like Daniel Day-Lewis and the late Heath Ledger.

Sanford Meisner's approach to acting, another descendant of Stanislavski's System, is the most widely taught and practiced technique in the United States today, and it also carries risks for incarcerated theater participants. Meisner Technique was developed for use by acting students and professional actors learning the craft of acting and preparing for performances. Meisner rejected Strasberg's insistence on actors needing to relive the specific experiences of their characters, but he still wanted actors to find a memory from their past that could stand in for the experience of the character (for example, an actor might recall the memory of being cold, alone, and lost as a child to portray a character who has been sexually assaulted). This approach of finding an analogous feeling in one's own experience is often called the "as if." While not as obviously fraught as The Method for facilitators working with incarcerated individuals, any acting technique that calls for digging into personal memories carries significant risks to vulnerable people.

Meisner taught that the reason for doing something onstage "has to have a consuming reality for" the actor to be believable.[11] To that end, his technique includes exercises in which actors repeat lines of text over and over until they stop thinking and respond impulsively. In Meisner's words, "If I repeat what I hear you saying, my head is not working. I'm listening, and there is an absolute elimination of the brain."[12] But this focus on "bringing the actor back to his emotional impulses and to acting that is firmly rooted in the instinctive"[13] poses its own problems; "traumatized people," van der Kolk writes, "are afraid to experience their emotions, because emotions lead to loss of control."[14] And, importantly, mastering Meisner Technique requires a structured progression that is all but impossible in the inherently unpredictable carceral environment.

IMAGINATION AND MICHAEL CHEKHOV'S TECHNIQUE

In SiP, I avoided using Meisner Technique for the reasons noted above. Instead, I focused on the approach developed by one of Stanslavski's students, Michael Chekhov. Chekhov's technique firmly rejects reliance on personal experience and emphasizes energy and imagination. It also deemphasizes words and analysis in favor of exercises that explore the mind-body connection to inspire universal emotions and impulses.

Chekhov Technique is older than either The Method or Meisner Technique, and it evolved separately. Michael Chekhov (nephew of playwright Anton Chekhov) started studying with Stanislavski in 1915 and soon became one of his star pupils. Almost immediately, Chekhov began making his own modifications to the System. He believed that Stanislavski's use of affective memory led to performances that were artificial and psychologically harmful for actors. If the actor relies on their personal experiences and emotions to create a realistic performance, Chekhov said, they will not truly connect with their character and give a truthful performance. Furthermore, in repeatedly revisiting traumatic experiences, the actor risks reactivating that trauma, blurring the line between their own life and that of the character. Chekhov Technique helps participants maintain balance by making the demarcation between memory and creative expression clear, providing a means by which they can stay present while exploring emotions objectively; "When I am very tortured by someone or something, I am not objective about it—it is me, me, me. When I forget it, the same pain becomes richer and I am objective about it."[15]

Through physical and imaginative exercises, including those outlined below, Chekhov Technique provides a means of deep engagement with the creative process that can be used in any environment—even a prison. Chekhov believed that the key to embodying a character came not through intellectual analysis ("that is just what psychologists do," he wrote, "but it is wrong for the actor") but through physical exercises designed to fire the imagination.[16] In this way, he presaged modern psychology. van der Kolk writes that "imagination gives us the opportunity to envision new possibilities...Without imagination there is no hope, no chance to envision a better future, no place to go, no goal to reach."[17]

Unlike many acting teachers, Chekhov decentralized words in preparing for a role. Instead, he focused on images, movement, energy, and sensations. "Our psychology [is] incorporated in our whole body," he wrote.[18] This approach, too, is well-suited for work with incarcerated people. Meisner Technique's reliance on analyzing and expressing emotions in words—which trauma survivors may not be able to do—could trigger responses that prison theater practitioners are unequipped to handle. According to van der Kolk, "traumatic events are almost impossible to put into words,"[19] but the antidote may be "the capacity of art, music, and dance to circumvent the speechlessness that comes with terror."[20] Chekhov Technique allows participants to remain in control and safely explore their characters' experiences, even if those experiences might otherwise reactivate traumatic memories.

Chekhov Technique's use in a carceral setting is best illustrated with specific examples, which follow. It is a "grab bag" unto itself, with many exercises well-suited for adaptation. I sometimes refer to what we did in SiP as "fast food" Chekhov Technique because it was necessary to complete each exercise in one two-hour session to make it relatively easy for absent participants to catch up; in fact, we never explored psychological gesture—the technique's core principle—due to its need for structure and consistent attendance. Nonetheless, participants reaped profound benefits from the exercises we employed.

SIX DIRECTIONS

SiP participants used the Six Directions to warm up their bodies, center themselves, and find the focus and energy that are often difficult to muster in the carceral environment. Participants close their eyes, place one hand on their sternum and the other between their shoulders, and imagine that the space between—what Chekhov called the "ideal center"—is filled with bright, pulsing light and energy. They use their whole bodies to radiate that inner energy outward through movement in a sequence of six directions: right, left, up, down, forward, and back. This is repeated several times, alternately in short, snappy "staccato" fashion and in long, flowing "legato" fashion.

This exercise has utility beyond a theater program. A women's ensemble member who was on the verge of getting in a physical altercation reported that she chose instead to use the Six Directions to calm and center herself, thus avoiding actions that could have resulted in solitary confinement. This is precisely the sort of body work van der Kolk recommends for trauma survivors to help with emotional regulation and impulse control.

SENSATIONS

Chekhov Technique emphasizes the imaginative use of sensations to call up truthful—but not personal—emotions. "Remember different moments in your life when you were in a heavy, gloomy, or light and gay mood," Chekhov wrote. "Compare them, and you will realize that heaviness or lightness lived in your limbs as well as in your psychology."[21]

For example, in preparing for Macbeth's "Tomorrow and tomorrow and tomorrow" speech, an ensemble member recalled the sensation she felt during her first night in jail—not the actual memory, just the physical sensation—in which her entire body felt "heavy, like a brick."[22] The embodiment of that feeling provided everything she needed to produce a powerful rendition of the speech, without the need for her to relive her trauma. That memory was relegated to the past, where it belongs.

One can also use a specific image to inspire a sensation. The woman who played Lady Macbeth in 2018 had personal experiences similar to the character's that could have reactivated trauma during the character's famous sleepwalking scene. After some discussion, she and I "agreed to try the scene as if she were underwater, moving slowly, weighed down, and seeing things around her distorted. We decided that there also should be [...] some sort of shivering or vibrating object in her ideal center (chest) to help her experience the character's anxiety without having to call up her own emotions or experiences."[23]

ATMOSPHERES

Chekhov Technique includes the creation of imaginary atmospheres. Chekhov taught that actors can "imagine the atmosphere [...] objectively as being in the actual air around us. But not yet in us. [...] [W]e can imagine that the air is filled with sorrow. It is just as easy as to imagine it filled with smoke. The mistake would be to try to feel that you have to be sorry. No, sorrow is everywhere around you and yet you are free from it."[24]

Several women who worked on *Twelfth Night* had survived trauma that mirrored some of the play's themes and situations. To keep those memories at bay, we went through a series of personal atmospheres: "bubbles" of space around each person. These included tastes (sweet, bitter, sour, salty), bubbles, cactus spines, and tears. We created imaginary thresholds to separate each atmosphere and provide a quick exit if painful memories began to surface. One woman reflected, "When we did the tears, there was a heaviness in the air because everyone was so down. When I stepped over [the threshold], I almost felt a wall come up...As soon as I stepped over that line, I left it behind."[25]

The exercise provided insight, connection, and relief even for women who observed but did not participate. One woman wrote, "Imagine the bubble filled with tears...this really kinda made me feel better because I've felt tears all day but couldn't cry...and the act of shaking it off helps me let this feeling of helplessness & lonely all day go."[26] Another participant said the technique would "really help," because "sometimes my atmosphere gets mixed up with my character's."[27]

CENTERS: THINKING, FEELING, WILLING (STICK, VEIL, BALL)

Chekhov taught that human behavior is driven by three functions: thinking, feeling, and willing. Only one of these can be experienced in a given moment, and each is centered in a specific place in the body: thinking, in one's head; feeling, in one's chest; willing, in one's groin. Each center corresponds with an image: thinking, a stick (probing, examining, linear); feeling, a veil (influenced by outside forces); willing, a ball (always in motion). By imagining these images and incorporating them into movement, participants find creative ways of gaining insight into their characters—and often gain personal insight along the way.

The SiP men's ensemble that worked with *King Lear* asked for techniques to help get out of their heads and achieve depth and relaxation in performance, and the Stick/Veil/Ball exercise proved extremely effective. One person reflected, "'I was able to access the subconscious of my own personality.' He said that he'd curled up in a ball when in his feeling center, which reminded him of when he was very shy as a kid. 'As I became more comfortable, I opened up,' he said, describing how he'd spread his veil. 'I was more confident in the will area…in a way that was very surprising to me.' His 'old self' wouldn't have been."[28]

The man who played Edmund used the technique to avoid reactivating a traumatic memory. Edmund, he said, was hurt—his motives came from his feeling center—but his actions, fueled by anger, came from his willing center. He performed Edmund's first soliloquy, and it was extremely powerful. "'I was Edmund. I was Edmund,' he said. 'The feelings were my feelings, but they were coming through the character.'"[29]

IMAGINARY BODIES

In the Imaginary Bodies exercise, individuals imagine their character's body—or a part of the body—as something invisible in the space that they can "put on" like a costume. "This assumption of the character's imaginary physical form influences your psychology ten times more strongly than any garment!" Chekhov wrote. "The imaginary body stands, as it were, *between* your real body and your psychology, influencing both of them with equal force."[30]

Imaginary Bodies emphasizes the actor's agency over their character. The exercise, in which they literally mold the character's form with their hands, helped the woman cast as Clarence in *Richard III*, who suffered from stage fright, to "know that when I go on stage I can be this Clarence who I've created."[31] The concept was also useful for the woman who played Malvolio in *Twelfth Night*, who envisioned her body as "a giant walking stick;" all she needed to get into character was "a second to get sticky."[32]

CONCLUSION

Throughout my time as director of Shakespeare in Prison, we safely and effectively utilized Michael Chekhov Technique to aid participants in deep exploration of the emotional lives of their characters—and themselves. My observations indicate that the technique is aligned with neuroscience's current understanding of trauma and the value of body-based treatment; however, as my background is in theater, my ability to thoroughly examine the connection is limited. The technique's emphasis on mind-body connection provided a means for participants to reconnect with their bodies and emotions in ways that benefited them far beyond their experience in the program; this merits further examination by trauma experts and more widespread use by prison theater practitioners. As Ashley Hoath, a former SiP participant, told me: "Chekhov's Technique is a huge steppingstone toward the true healing that needs to take place for one to overcome their trauma and the side effects from it."[33]

NOTES

My thanks to Matthew Van Meter and James Luse for their readership of and support for this project.

1. Kyle Fisher-Grant, Frannie Shepherd-Bates, and Matthew Van Meter, *Shakespeare in Prison Case Study Report* (Detroit: Detroit Public Theatre, 2019).
2. Kyle Fisher-Grant, Frannie Shepherd-Bates, and Matthew Van Meter, *Self-Efficacy, Empathy, and Community: The Long-Term Benefits of Shakespeare in Prison Involvement* (Detroit: Detroit Public Theatre, 2021).
3. Justin Greenlaw, interview by Frannie Shepherd-Bates and Ashley Poulin, August 7, 2023, video, 00:49:20.
4. Bessel van der Kolk, *The Body Keeps the Score* (New York: Penguin, 2014), 66–67.
5. Rachel Lee and Lisa Callahan, *Trauma-Informed Approaches Across the Sequential Intercept Model* (New York: The Council of State Governments Justice Center, 2022.)
6. Jean Benedetti, *Stanislavski & the Actor* (London: Methuen, 1998), 13.
7. Konstantin Stanislavski, *An Actor Prepares* (New York: Routledge, 2003), 182.
8. Stanislavski, 192.
9. Foster Hirsch, *A Method to Their Madness: A History of the Actor's Studio* (Cambridge, MA: Da Capo, 2002), 77.
10. Hirsch, 78.
11. Sanford Meisner and Dennis Longwell, *Sanford Meisner on Acting* (New York: Random House, 1987), 40.
12. Meisner and Longwell, 36.
13. Meisner and Longwell, 37.

14 van der Kolk, 337.
15 Michael Chekhov, *Lessons for the Professional Actor* (New York: Performing Arts Journal Publications, 1985), 101–102.
16 Chekhov, 114.
17 van der Kolk, 17.
18 Chekhov, 24.
19 van der Kolk, 233.
20 van der Kolk, 245.
21 Michael Chekhov, *On the Technique of Acting* (New York: Harper Collins, 1991), 8.
22 "Season Seven: Week 25," Shakespeare in Prison blog, Detroit Public Theatre, January 23, 2019, http://www.detroitpublictheatre.org/blog/2019/1/23/season-eight-week-20.
23 "Season Eight: Week 20," Shakespeare in Prison blog, Detroit Public Theatre, February 27, 2018, https://www.detroitpublictheatre.org/blog/2018/2/27/season-seven-week-25.
24 Chekhov, *Lessons*, 30.
25 "Season Eight: Week 20," Shakespeare in Prison blog.
26 SiP Ensemble Member, Shakespeare in Prison session notes, January 23, 2019.
27 "Season Eight: Week 20," Shakespeare in Prison blog.
28 "Season Two: Week 23," Shakespeare in Prison blog, Detroit Public Theatre, December 5, 2018, https://www.detroitpublictheatre.org/2018/12/5/season-two-week-23.
29 "Season Two: Week 23," Shakespeare in Prison blog.
30 Michael Chekhov, *To the Actor* (Abington: Routledge, 2002), 78–79.
31 "Session Six: Week 18," Shakespeare in Prison blog, Detroit Public Theatre, January 3, 2017, https://www.detroitpublictheatre.org/2017/1/3/session-six-week-18.
32 "Season Eight: Week 22," Shakespeare in Prison blog, Detroit Public Theatre, February 14, 2019, https://www.detroitpublictheatre.org/blog/2019/2/14/season-eight-week-22.
33 Ashley Hoath, Jpay message to author, January 25, 2024.

Practices

"Presume Not That I Am the Thing I Was": Collaborative Theater Companies in English Prisons

Rowan Mackenzie, Pheelix Obun, and Ian West

Ten

Incarceration often alters or shatters the identity of those who experience it, impacting their life irrevocably, especially for those convicted of particular crimes or serving long sentences. Within the UK penal system there is a stigma attached to men convicted of sexual offenses (MCoSOs), with these people serving their sentence isolated from the main prison population to prevent harm from other prisoners. This separation is facilitated through their being held in specialized MCoSO prisons or being segregated from the main prisoner population in Vulnerable Prisoner Units (VPUs). Emergency Shakespeare is a democratic theater company in a medium-security prison for MCoSOs. The company is co-owned by 15 prisoners and the facilitator, who work on productions of Shakespeare and form a supportive community within the prison, having a far-reaching impact on those involved. This chapter is a collaboration of three people whose perspectives are usually assumed to be diametrically opposed: an academic/practitioner, a serving prisoner, and a prison governor, who have been united by the existence of Emergency Shakespeare. It combines the voices of the three authors because we are writing as three equals, invested in the theater company and the way in which it brings commonality and shared understanding to otherwise different perspectives.

DOI: 10.4324/9781003451662-14

Establishing a theater company in such an environment, we encountered numerous challenges, some of which were resolved, others which continue to occur. The attitudes of prisoners and staff were initially often hostile; the prison regime has adverse impacts on rehearsals; adaptations to scenes, props, and set design are often required due to the prison environment, and countless other obstacles have to be addressed. However, Rowan Mackenzie's belief that this initiative would be beneficial quickly spread to founding members including Pheelix Obun.[1] It is the combined commitment and tenacity of the group and the support of successive Governors such as Ian West which has enabled Emergency Shakespeare to grow over the last five years.

In 2019 the Governing Governor asked Mackenzie to bring her theater company model to the prison as part of the prison's Rehabilitative Culture focus which aims to "return citizens not offenders to communities."[2] Such a venture was rare in English prisons and demonstrated the Governor's willingness for innovation, which always carries an element of risk in carceral settings. Prison is an environment which encourages displays of what R.W. Connell described as "hegemonic masculinity" focusing on power, dominance, ambivalence towards femininity, and emotional avoidance.[3] While this focus on dominance may be less evident within a prison for MCoSOs than in the wider prison population, there is still a definite sense that prisoners do not wish to show their vulnerability. Yet, to act in a theater company is asking for someone to share a part of themselves with others, to make mistakes, receive feedback, and open themselves up to a position of vulnerability. While these men are segregated from "mains" prisoners and deemed vulnerable within the criminal justice system, theatrical vulnerability is of a more personal nature—sharing yourself at some level.[4] So, the very concept of asking a dozen men who barely knew each other to do just that was a challenging one.

Prison strips individuals of their autonomy and infantilizes them over a period of time as they are unable to make even the smallest decisions for themselves. Ben Crewe, et al.'s recent article on relational ambiguities and dynamics notes that "infantilization is embedded within wider disciplinary practices, notably the intensive surveillance and regulation to which imprisoned women are routinely subjected" and while their study focused on women's experiences in prison the same applies to incarcerated men too.[5] Jason Warr, Thomas Ugelvik, and Simon Scott have all studied the impact of imprisonment on self-identity and the infantilization that male prisoners experience.[6] The impact of being arrested, tried, and convicted of a sexual offense is in itself damaging to an individual's sense of identity and purpose. Timothy explained, "it was like a mirror being shattered, my identity was in tiny pieces and everything I thought I knew about myself was no more."[7]

That first session, in March 2019, the attendees were rather less willing *volunteers* and rather more prevailed upon by a zealous Custodial Manager to attend. Some of the men decided they really enjoyed exploring their creativity through theater while others chose not to engage going forward. Establishing a prison theater company is challenging: initial recruitment is difficult and attendance sporadic as prisoners will attend some weeks but other weeks decide not to, have alternative commitments, or the prison regime will not enable their presence. Prisoners tend to be apathetic towards activities and unwilling to take themselves outside their comfort zone. Furthermore, while purposeful activity is widely accepted as being beneficial to mental wellbeing, reintegration into the community, and successful desistance, it is regularly identified as lacking in availability and has worsened since COVID-19 with few prisons returning to pre-pandemic levels of activities and time out of cells. Charlie Taylor, Chief Inspector of Prisons for England and Wales, summarized that "purposeful activity was judged to be poor or not sufficiently good in all but one of the adult male prisons we inspected this year and 34% of our priority concerns this year were in this area" in the *Annual Report 2022–2023*.[8]

The other notable issue when beginning this type of work is staff attitudes as many are initially quite hostile. Initiatives to support prisoners with desistance are widespread, designed with the best of intentions and the belief that they bring intrinsic value through improving individuals or developing tools and options to desist from the causes of offending. However, the reality of such initiatives often falls short of these ideals and this creates a cynicism amongst staff of all grades. Operational staff are often dismissive of activities and in this prison particularly there was a high-level of resentment from many of them about the idea of offering enrichment opportunities to MCoSOs. The prison had re-rolled from a general population into one specifically for those convicted of sexual offenses six years prior and it was evident that many staff felt a dislike for this population.[9] Nicholas Blagden et al.'s research in a recently re-rolled prison identified "ambivalent and conflicted prisoner-staff dynamics" where prisoners felt staff judged them for their offenses more than in a main prisoner population and this tallied with some staff in this prison.[10] Ievins research in HMP Stafford following the re-rolling of this prison to MCoSOs in 2013 identified a "static view of the sexuality of those convicted of sexual offenses" with one officer quoted as saying "ninety per cent of the people in here, you're not going to cure" and evidence that they saw their role as to enforce discipline, not aid rehabilitative activities.[11] This manifested itself in Mackenzie being told she was placing herself at risk of sexual assault, officers teasing men who joined the group and being unhelpful when it came to facilitating the men's release from wings. Fritzi Horstman writes "a prison officer invariably comes face to face with everything they've been taught to despise—not only on a societal level but within themselves" and this leads to many of them experiencing compassion fatigue towards those in their care.[12] However, Mackenzie's tenacity and positivity in speaking to prisoners and staff about the sessions and overcoming resistance saw the formation of a core group of actors over the first few months.

The intention with all of MacKenzie's Shakespeare UnBard's projects is to offer participants an opportunity to experience "positive autonomy" within the confines of the prison regime: having their voices heard, a chance to influence decisions, and an opportunity to be treated as an equal within the theater company.[13] Emergency Shakespeare began with the same premise as Mackenzie's other theater initiatives: encouraging the actors to explore their own identity, develop self-confidence, and take responsibility for their contribution to the work within the rehearsal room. Many prisoners have had negative educational experiences of Shakespeare during school, literacy levels amongst prisoners are low, many lack a feeling of self-worth given their conviction, and staff and peers frequently ridicule initiatives such as Emergency Shakespeare. These factors combine to suggest that interweaving Shakespeare and MCoSOs should not work, yet it does, helping to reverse some of the infantilization and loss of autonomy imposed by prison-life. In addition to Emergency Shakespeare (the theater company), Mackenzie, Obun, and another Peer Mentor also facilitate 12-week Creative Workshop programs, to widen access within the prison. These workshops offer an introduction to Shakespeare and theater through exploration of ten plays selected by the participants and culminate in a sharing of creative pieces, including artworks (see Figure 10.1). Many Creative Workshop participants go on to join Emergency Shakespeare.

In the first seven months of the formation of Emergency Shakespeare, a disparate group of individuals coalesced around an adapted script of *Macbeth* and, in September 2019, the first performances took place.[14] The men came together and supported each other to perform in front of their peers and families, overcoming their individual fears as a collective group. The actors chose to set the play in a theater company where the character playing Macbeth was understudy to Duncan in a production of the Scottish play; Macbeth wanted the opportunity to perform so put something in Duncan's drink with the intention of making him ill for a few days but he suffered a fatal heart attack. Macbeth initially intended only to remove Duncan from the stage for opening night and his reaction to the news of the death was hysteria and panic. It was only after the first death had occurred that he began to devise ways to remove other perceived enemies to his position as leading man, until the play culminated in his arrest and imprisonment. The witches were the Stage Manager, Director, and Producer who reflected on the events unfolding, often breaking the fourth wall to speak directly to the audience. The actors chose to adapt the story in this way to account for the unfinished nature of our performance space and also as many of them felt uncomfortable with the idea of Macbeth

Figure 10.1 *Othello* program cover image, Emergency Shakespeare, 2021. Image courtesy of Pheelix Obun.

intentionally setting out to commit murder. Given the hierarchy within prisons which sees MCoSOs as being the most vilified, this abhorrence of the concept of murder was one which seemed incongruous, but which was respected. They felt unable to imagine plotting to take a life despite the fact that many convicted of murder would argue sexual offenses to be worse than murder.

Since that inaugural production, the company has gone on to rehearse The Merry Wives of Windsor (production cancelled due to COVID-19), Othello, The Tempest, Julius Caesar, and King Lear and are currently working on Henry IV, Part 1.[15] Since 2019, over 50 men have been part of the theater company, with the majority leaving only due to transfers to other prisons or their release into the community. A number of them have left prison seeking a community theater which will allow them to continue to explore their creative talents (although it is acknowledged that many such organizations will be unlikely to accept them due to required disclosures of their offenses). The impact on individuals has been significant with actors documenting the way in which the community of Emergency Shakespeare has supported their mental health, helped them to deal with issues of identity, self-confidence, family traumas, and deaths. They have the opportunity to discuss issues without fear of judgement and to model pro-social behaviors such as empathy, compassion, and respect for each other. One participant, Wade, told the group that "this has been a lifeline for me, I would not be here today without Rowan and the guys; you've been there for me through every hurdle."[16]

The company provides a safe space where an individual's strengths are recognized and encouraged but people are also given the opportunity to identify their own shortcomings and to work on them if they choose to do so. From its formation it has been a disparate group of men from various ethnic backgrounds; extroverts and introverts, young and old, able-bodied and disabled. The talented take time and effort to support those less talented, the extroverts encourage and support the introverts to grow in self-confidence, with the team working where its strengths are, and working together to achieve the group aspirations. Through the process of working on a production these groups merge into strong, supportive teams who develop emotional resilience and "positive autonomy."[17] For example, Max, a member of Emergency Shakespeare throughout his sentence and who had a psychological breakdown, became a greatly respected mentor to newer recruits in latter times. The co-ownership of something they care about counters the issues of loss of self-identity and infantilization endemic in prison life and as one actor, Bob, explained "it's given [me] a purpose in life I never had before."[18]

Many of the men who have been actors in Emergency Shakespeare identify "empathy and the ability to see other's perspectives" as a key element of their personal progression within the group.[19] As a rehabilitative and self-enrichment exercise this can lead to an examination of how an individual interacts with others and how they have previously treated others and encourage a positive impact in the context of future interactions. Using empathy in learning about a character, even those parts which aren't easily relatable, enables individuals to open their minds to the feelings and thoughts of others. The various topics tackled during productions engage the company in discussions not just around themes and plot elements, but deeper meaning and difficult issues which need to be addressed before a production can be staged. Portraying scenes which can incorporate aspects of an individual's own experiences and potentially their crime (or that of members of the audience) requires an honest, respectful, and reflective approach which the group achieves through their openness with each other.

For many of the men, including Obun, Emergency Shakespeare has become a fundamental part of prison life, an immersive activity which pervades every part of their incarceration. The group offers participants opportunities for involvement in visual arts (set design, costumes, props and program illustrations [see Figure 10.2]), writing (editing scripts, rehearsal diaries, journals, activity packs and program content), acting, line learning, and forming a supportive community in which these activities flourish. Obun describes the work as his prison vocation: filling days and nights, occupying his mind through good times and challenging ones. Obun had never shown an inclination for the arts prior to his incarceration but this has become a fundamental part of his life now, which he intends to continue to develop when he is released. In comparison to the rest of prison life and other interventions, he asserts that nothing else incorporates so much of his identity, passion, ambition (which was previously absent), and personal aspirations as Emergency Shakespeare does. This is attributed to the way in which the plays enable self-reflection through "dramatic distancing"[20] of the characters and also from the "positive autonomy" offered through having his voice heard in a democratic community.[21] The empowering nature of realizing self-identity through having co-ownership of the company, supporting his peers, and moving forward in a liberated, positive mindset to become the man he wants to be has been closely entwined with his Shakespeare journey. Whether asking the question "to be or not to be?" or rewriting Richard II's prison soliloquy into a self-reflective piece about his

Figure 10.2 *Othello* program synopsis image, Emergency Shakespeare, 2021. Image courtesy of Pheelix Obun.

own experiences, there have been multiple elements within Shakespeare which have allowed Obun to externalize internal conflicts which have long caused him significant anxiety and distress.[22] Being able to work through such issues using the plays as a way into dealing with his own trauma has enabled him to address his own flaws.

Playing monstrous characters can be therapeutic. For example, the misogyny, violence, and malevolence of Iago both fascinated and repelled Obun. He felt that the role would allow him to see elements of himself which led to his offense and whether any of those were present in the mosaic of his new identity he was forming from the pieces of the "shattered mirror." The journey through this character was an enlightening one, albeit intensely challenging and one which enabled Obun to:

> acknowledge that he [...] committed a monstrous act and that in the moment of that he was every bit the monster which he now loathes to look upon but he also knows that he was not born or raised a monster.[23]

Another example was the domestic abuse in *The Taming of the Shrew* (a play chosen by one Creative Workshops cohort). Mackenzie's Activity Pack for this session included an academic analysis of the gender dynamics within the play.[24] During the explanation of the plot it became apparent that for a number of the participants the issues within this play resonated on a deeply personal level. One such man, Craig, spoke to the group about his experiences both as victim and perpetrator of such abuse. He spoke of early experiences of domestic abuse and how he had then gone on to display coercive and controlling behavior in a subsequent relationship but that he had not realized the extent of his behavior until confronted with recorded evidence of it. The group was respectful of his admission and others also chose to share their own experiences as people who perpetrated such abuse and their subsequent remorse. A number of them said they were surprised that they had chosen to share this as usually they would have resisted being encouraged to examine their own negative behavioral traits but that the "dramatic distancing" Sue Jennings describes and the safe space created as a group enabled them to feel confident to do so. They chose to share their vulnerability within the group and to discuss their emotions, something many struggle to do.

Within Emergency Shakespeare, the process of editing, casting, rehearsing, and staging a production is one which encourages the men to take ownership and responsibility for a co-operative endeavor, work closely with peers, and contribute positively to the group. They form strong bonds with each other and Mackenzie, supporting each other in preparing the play and also in coping with the challenges of prison life. Navigating the complexities of family relationships, mental wellbeing, friendships, and the resilience needed to return to society after a custodial sentence is daunting. The performances give them an opportunity to showcase their talents but also the magic which is woven through the theater company, in terms of the emotional sustenance it enables. They allow themselves to be vulnerable in performance because they have developed resilience and autonomy which gives them the confidence to do so. Bob, who joined the company at the insistence of a friend and who lacked self-confidence as he began a long sentence, describes Emergency Shakespeare as "the greatest gift I could hope for in my time here" and he's developed skills such as public speaking, group interaction, and line-learning as he has taken on increasingly large roles.[25] He delights in sharing his work with his family to whom he remains close. For most of the men involved it is the only thing they have been able to share in real-time with their families since they were arrested. Family days, which allow them the opportunity to share a meal with their loved ones, perform the production, and then spend quality time together, are an endorsement of the work they put in and for many are the highlight of their year and a source of pride. Some have no family connection and it is important to be mindful of the emotional challenges posed by witnessing others enjoying what they cannot. However, the company supports each other in this too, introducing their fellow-actors to family, ensuring no one eats alone and demonstrating emotional intelligence in their interactions on the day and afterwards.

Emergency Shakespeare aims to support the wellbeing of those involved, encourage "positive autonomy" and emotional resilience, support family connections where appropriate, and enable people to develop a positive identity for their future.[26] Belonging to a community which is non-judgmental, supports every member, and encourages authenticity and social-emotional growth enables this to happen. The community within the theater company is a supportive one and can act in the same way as "pulling a helium balloon back down to earth [to make] me feel there was still a place available for me on earth."[27] The work also serves to encourage positive prisoner/staff relationships and affirm the shared humanity between them with one Supervising Officer commenting, "this makes me realize why I joined the service—to help change lives."[28] Seeing the commitment and pride the actors take in their work often encourages staff to move beyond the "othering" which is common within the criminal justice system.[29] Shakespeare is the catalyst for these opportunities to transform but it is the way in which it is interwoven with lived experience, shared emotions, and the reality of incarceration which give Emergency Shakespeare the power it has to offer hope at the darkest of times.

NOTES

1 Throughout the chapter, names are anonymized in line with His Majesty's Prison and Probation Services (HMPPS) requirements but pseudonyms are used to signify their humanity in a way in which a number or "Prisoner A" denies.
2 Rehabilitative Culture vision, displayed throughout the prison and on documents shared with staff and prisoners.
3 R. W. Connell, *Masculinities* (Cambridge, UK: Polity, 1995).
4 English prisoners within the adult male estate are divided into "mains" and "vulnerable" prisoners. "Mains" prisoners are those on remand or sentenced for a range of offenses, excluding sexual offenses or offenses which the criminal justice system deems to make them "vulnerable" to violence or threats from other prisoners.
5 Ben Crewe, Anna Schliehe, and Daria Aleksandra Przybylska, "'It Causes a Lot of Problems': Relational Ambiguities and Dynamics between Prisoners and Staff in a Women's Prison," *European Journal of Criminology* 20, no. 3 (2022): 925–946 (927).
6 Jason Warr, "The Prisoner: Inside and Out," *Handbook on Prisons: Second Edition*, eds. Yvonne Jewkes, Jamie Bennett, and Ben Crewe (Abingdon: Routledge, 2016), 586–604; Thomas Ugelvik, *Power and Resistance in Prison: Doing Time, Doing Freedom* (Cham: Palgrave Macmillan, 2014); Simon Scott, "Go in Young, Come out Old: The Challenges Facing People Serving Life Sentences," Clinks Blog, June 2023, https://www.clinks.org/community/blog-posts/go-young-come-out-old-challenges-facing-people-serving-life-sentences.
7 Timothy, Actor in Beyond the Walls (Mackenzie's community theater company for those with lived experience of the criminal justice system) who received a conviction for sexual offenses, speaking to Mackenzie (2020).
8 Charlie Taylor, *HM Chief Inspector of Prisons for England and Wales Annual Report 2022–2023* (July 2023) London: Crown Copyright. https://assets.publishing.service.gov.uk/government/uploads/system/uploads/attachment_data/file/1167739/hmip-annual-report-2022-23.pdf.
9 "Re-rolling" is the term used to describe the transition of an English prison from one population to another, ie from a young offenders institution to an adult male prison or from a prison for all types of offenses to one specifically for men convicted of sexual offenses.

10 Nicholas Blagden, Jake Jones, and Kirsten Wilson, "'It Doesn't Matter What You've Done You're Accepted Here': A Multi-Site Qualitative Exploration of the Experiences of Being Incarcerated in Prisons for Individuals with Sexual Convictions," *Sexual Crime and the Experience of Imprisonment*, eds. Nicholas Blagden, Belinda Winder, et al. (Cham: Palgrave Macmillan, 2019), 109–141 (126).
11 A. Ievins, "Prison Officers, Professionalism and Moral Judgement" *Sexual Crime and the Experience of Imprisonment*, eds. Nicholas Blagden, Belinda Winder, et al. (Cham: Palgrave Macmillan, 2019), 85–108 (92).
12 Fritzi Horstman, "Afterword," *The Good Prison Officer: Inside Perspectives*, ed. Andi Brierley (London: Routledge, 2023), 132–134 (132).
13 Rowan Mackenzie, *Creating Space for Shakespeare: Working with Marginalized Communities* (London: Bloomsbury, 2023), 7.
14 Mackenzie has written extensively about Emergency Shakespeare's *Macbeth* in *Creating Space for Shakespeare* but it is relevant to include some details in this chapter also.
15 Emergency Shakespeare works on a production cycle of six to eight months and each production includes four performances: three for their peers and staff and one for their families and loved ones.
16 Wade, Emergency Shakespeare actor speaking to the group, December 2023.
17 Mackenzie, 7.
18 Bob, Emergency Shakespeare actor speaking to Mackenzie, January 2024.
19 Written feedback during the debrief following the production of *Othello* (2021).
20 Sue Jennings, *Dramatherapy: Theory and Practice Volume 2* (London: Routledge), 17.
21 Mackenzie, 7.
22 William Shakespeare, *Hamlet*, ed. Harold Jenkins (London: Bloomsbury, 1982), 3.1.56.
23 Rowan Mackenzie, Pheelix Obun, and Ralph Lubkowski, "'If To Do Were as Easy as to Know What Were Good to Do': The Rehabilitative Potential of Collaborative Theatre Companies in English Prisons," *Advances in Preventing and Treating Violence and Aggression*, ed. Madhumita Pandey (London: Springer, 2023), 209–226.

24 Rachel De Wachter, "Power and Gender in *The Taming of the Shrew*," British Library (2016), https://www.bl.uk/shakespeare/articles/power-and-gender-in-the-taming-of-the-shrew.
25 Bob, Emergency Shakespeare, written feedback after performing *The Tempest* (2022).
26 Mackenzie, 7.
27 Bernard, quoted in *Othello* program (unpublished, 2021), 12.
28 Supervising Officer, HMP Stafford, verbal comment, (2021).
29 Gayatri Chakravorty Spivak, "The Rani of Sirmur: An Essay in Reading the Archives" *History and Theory* 24, no. 3 (1985): 247–272.

"Like Bright Metal on a Sullen Ground": The First Six Months of a Prison Shakespeare Program

Kate Powers

Eleven

June 2017. I walk into a prison multi-purpose room, a place with all the fluorescent charm of a shuttered DMV. 110 miles north of Minneapolis, 100 feet inside the secure perimeter, I arrange a circle of chairs. A few men help me; more trickle in, 28 in all. The men are polite, curious, vigilant, ranging from mid-20s to mid-60s; they are Black, Indigenous, white. I have been doing this work in New York state prisons since 2009; I recognize the questions on their fortified faces.

When I arrived in Minnesota, there were no performing arts programs in which incarcerated people could participate. Conducting an informal analysis of several established programs, I created The Redeeming Time Project (RTP), shamelessly borrowing from and building on their successes. I consulted with Shakespeare Behind Bars founder Curt L. Tofteland and Queensland Shakespeare Ensemble's Rob Pensalfini. Grounding our work in Shakespeare, I include texts by contemporary BIPOC authors so all our ensemble members can see themselves in the texts we choose. RTP holds space for voices we have heard less frequently and troubles the "great man" narrative around Shakespeare, even as we leverage what he offers. In this chapter, I chronicle our first workshop at Moose Lake Correctional Facility, a medium-security prison for men who have largely earned that status after years in maximum-security. I look at the impact of the

DOI: 10.4324/9781003451662-15

work within a new program, and engage with the question of "Why, specifically, is Shakespeare so compelling within a correctional environment?"

FORSOOTH!

In the little prison in the North Woods, the men are sizing me up: *What does this woman want? Why did she drive all this way to see us?* One man bursts dramatically into the room, proclaiming, "Forsooth!" Shaheed will go on to become one of the thought leaders in our circle, playing Becker from *Jitney* and *Othello* in the first year.

In this preliminary session, I introduce myself and the practice of using theater as a tool for communication, critical thinking, self-reflection, and play. I invite everyone to stand and take a breath. *O, God, what is she going to make me do?* I ask the men to close their eyes if that is comfortable for them, or soften their focus, to observe where they might be holding tension in their bodies, to imagine sending breath there. It is, as Curt told me, "always an invitation, never a demand" to join the circle, the exercise, the scene.[1] Incarcerated humans have had most of their agency revoked; RTP will offer, but never force, the experience. The men should have as much ownership of our shared work as circumstances will allow. If someone is uncertain and all he can do is stay in the room, that might be a victory.

I introduce the check-in which will begin our sessions: "Based on how you are feeling and what you are thinking, what body of water might you be right now? When you have said what you need to say, hand the focus off to the person next to you through eye contact and breath." We often employ a metaphor during check-in to lubricate our imaginations, create critical distance, and keep the check-in succinct. I learned this, as, indeed, so much else, from Kevin Coleman at Shakespeare & Company: the act of checking in is a way to leave the worst of the day behind, to share good news. Every person gets to be heard; every person gets to listen. In a place where there is no guarantee of connection, this is a tiny revolution.

We play a game. You turn to the person next to you, take a breath, make eye contact, and clap simultaneously. It's harder than it sounds to clap simultaneously, and in prison, eye contact is scarce. The game cultivates connection, presence, breath, all in the guise of play. When, inevitably and very quickly, the clap is out of sync or someone forgets to breathe, I invite the room to celebrate the failure. Really cheer and applaud. This feels ridiculous, subversive, joyful; we're starting to collectively destigmatize failure. Emma Marie Heard et al. note that "fear, anxiety, loneliness, trauma, depression, powerlessness, and violence can all be a part of life in prison."[2] Along with these other oppressive aspects of incarceration, shame may inform an incarcerated individual's choices, causing him to retreat, make himself smaller, or, alternatively, inspire him to lash out in order to prove that the shame is unjustified. But failure is also part of how we learn. If we can start to make it safe to take a risk, everyone in the room gets a little braver for the next ask, and the next.

The circle grows in comfort, enthusiasm, speed. Except for one gentleman directly across from me. Slight of build, in his early 60s, Bob looks harried, flushed to the point of mortification; when it is his turn to make eye contact and clap with a partner, he cannot do it. Every time the clap comes his way, the rhythm falters. He and the guy next to him have to try twice, three times to clap together. The circle slowly picks up momentum…until it arrives back at Bob. I am certain

I will never see this man again; he cannot flee this room fast enough.

ó

25 men show up for the first class session, including, to my surprise, Bob! Travis, my teaching artist, perceives the men immediately leaning into the work. Psychiatrist James Gilligan writes about shame as a root cause of violence, contending that "a humane environment is an absolute prerequisite for the healing of violent men;" we strive to cultivate that.[3] Everyone is welcome in this circle. We never ask about anyone's conviction; we are building a relationship with the individual in front of us, not the worst day he ever had.

Our two extraordinary staff advocates throw themselves into every exercise with zeal; while I've experienced tolerance and support from Department of Corrections employees, I've never seen a staff member participate in any theatrical activity. Laraine and Candy, each with more than 20 years in corrections, have managed to retain their optimism and sense of possibility, ability to see each of these men as individuals, and heartfelt desire to bring them new opportunities.

We check in, doing a breath exercise from Patsy Rodenberg's book, *Presence*; we introduce ourselves and create a set of agreements about how we want to treat one another.[4] As we complete the *Presence* exercise, we strike a pose that evokes DaVinci's Vitruvian man; we imagine strength, knowledge, confidence. One of the men names this gesture "imaginary puissance;" before long, we hear men call out to one another through the corridors, "Puissance!" In his essay, "The Prisoner's Voice," Joe White talks about the power of quoting lines to other men in the yard: it "gave us the chance to demonstrate and delight in our secret world."[5]

We play "Zip! Zap! Zop!" (this will become a joyfully competitive part of many sessions), and we do an initial Globetrotters-like text lay-up drill, with Brother Bones' rendition of "Sweet Georgia Brown" as accompaniment. As the men ease into the exercise, their movement, which begins as mimetic basketball dribbling, passing, and running, transforms into dancing, strutting, swimming, and cruising easily down the highway. That "trip down the court" ends with one partner feeding short bits of Shakespeare to the other and having them speak the text aloud. Just like that, the men are speaking, and embodying, Shakespeare.

We talk about "Ó." It is a gift that Shakespeare gives us: an "Ó" (think "O for a muse of fire" or "O that this too, too sullied flesh would melt") is Shakespeare's way of telling us that the character is experiencing an emotion which defies language. He's not telling us which one, but it is no place for a modern, mumbled "oh." We explore alternative vocal, physical, and emotional choices for "Ó."

The second-to-last thing we do is check out. This is a way to reinforce the worth of the work, the time spent. It helps the group to share gratitude, discoveries, and next steps. At the end of our first three hours, I ask, "what do you want to reinforce? What will you take away?" The men want to reinforce:

> Breath.
> Playfulness.
> Listening.
> Risk-taking.
> Joy.

Then we laugh. (I tip my grateful hat to Sabra Williams, formerly of the Actors' Gang Prison Project, for this exercise.)

I say, "I don't know how we're going to do it. We're going to fake it 'til we make it, and we're going to laugh for forty seconds." The Mayo Clinic says that laughter "enhances your intake of oxygen-rich air, stimulates your heart, lungs and muscles, and increases the endorphins that are released by your brain," and that it "activates and relieves your stress response."[6] Sometimes 40 seconds feels like a season to me, sometimes it is over in an instant. By the middle of our first workshop, the men report, "Laughing is great medicine."

FOR A MUSE OF FIRE

In our second class session, I introduce the Chorus' "O for a muse of fire" soliloquy from *Henry V*, because it teaches us what theater is, even as it invites us to engage with the lift of the language. We define vocabulary: *muse, monarch, Mars, leash'd in, crouch*. The men split into small groups. Each group gets a line of text, but the individual words are on separate cards, in no particular order. The men arrange them. They speak their chosen word order, then create a tableaux. They rearrange the words into new sequences, sharing their favorite versions. Travis called this "Muse of Fire mad libs." The men perform an entire section of Shakespearean text as the first part of the prologue travels around the room, line by line, group by group, with increasing confidence. There is a moment of delicious theatrical silence after "affright the air at Agincourt" as we all take in what we've heard. "Can we do that one more time?" We can; we do. As we debrief the exercise, reinforcing our ownership of the words, I ask "what does it mean, taken together?" Leon says, quietly, "It's like—after all these stories, will Harry live up to the hype?"

THAT WOULD ASCEND

In week three, we distribute speeches from Shakespeare, August Wilson, and James Baldwin. I have cut some to just a few lines; I have included Brutus' entire "It must be by his death." Each ensemble member can take as big or as small a bite of the textual apple as he's ready to chew.

Bob never misses class. He participates in every exercise, activity, and discussion; he laments regularly that this will be the death of him. He selects Hamlet's "O that this too, too solid flesh would melt" soliloquy. Three weeks in, he reports that his visits with his wife are improving, because "she says I am more willing to talk about my feelings," and that he has commissioned her to do some dramaturgical research.

Enthusiastic and curious, Feeney wants to work on a piece that isn't in the packet. He remembers, from childhood, the feeling it evoked when a neighbor performed it on Christmas Eve. He doesn't know if he'll be released from prison before his elderly father passes, and he would like to perform it for him. He doesn't recall the name of the play or the character. I ask, "Do you remember who the character is talking to? Or what he is talking about?" Feeney says, "He's a king." That does not narrow it down a bunch. "I think he's talking to the troops." Ah. I bring him the St. Crispin's Day speech from Henry V, and he gets to work.

The men share a very real worry about Getting Shakespeare Wrong. They feel the power in the words; they don't want to mess it up. Montea asks, "Why doesn't Shakespeare just say what he means?" Dennis says, "Man, Shakespeare could BRING it." The men perceive the Cultural Church of Shakespeare as hallowed ground. Travis and I invite them to the Shakespeare block party instead, to meet the heightened language on their own terms, to trust that they absolutely have the capacity to harness this power. Part of Shakespeare's value behind the walls lies in this perceived difficulty. Many of the men have been told their whole lives that they're stupid; once Shakespeare belongs to them, their relationship to world culture, education, themselves as thoughtful and smart humans, changes. Their possibilities expand.

I am ever-mindful of how much of their time has been wasted—in schools that wrote them off, on street corners, inside these walls. I want everything we offer to be worthy of their thoughts, trust, time. Leon perceives changes:

> I've watched this class transform the lives of the men who've chosen to participate. Those involved have opened up and showed some other sides of themselves. In prison, you're basically only allowed to be offenders, and this project has brought humanity back, and hope for the future.

Bob reports, "You can teach an old con new tricks." I know enough about this ecosystem to know that we'll experience setbacks, heartbreaks; sometimes men stop showing up, are sent to solitary, or get transferred without warning. But at the end of week four, we chip away at institutionalization; we begin to redeem the time.

THE BRIGHTEST HEAVEN OF INVENTION

In week five, one man asks what theater has to do with restorative justice (RJ). Travis and I mostly hold the room while the men debate, discuss, and teach one another. RJ perceives crime not just as a violation of the law, but as a harm to individuals, relationships, and communities. An RJ conference or circle creates an opportunity to connect with those one has harmed and to work for transformation. The men talk about opportunities to practice empathy, engaging with one another and with us as human beings, how that is practice for reentry.

I offer that, together, we practice critical thinking skills as we engage with challenging material; we cultivate connection and risk vulnerability. As we check out, Matthew says he's been thinking all week about my stated goal not to waste the ensemble members' time: "Every volunteer who comes in here to teach acts as if what they have to offer is great just because it is from outside, and we're in here, so we should be grateful. But you have come in with humility, with respect for us as people."

The middle weeks of the workshop are filled with focus, growing trust, curiosity. It is impossible for Travis and me to be everywhere at once, but we have been building a scaffold. They ask one another questions, offering constructive, supportive feedback. They become actively-listening scene partners as others rehearse. Montea now makes proud uncle sounds as other men work; he turns Sonnet 29 into a conversation with his God. When we explore iambic pentameter, through discussion and embodied exercises, Montea says, "You mean to tell me Shakespeare wrote my heartbeat into every line? That's cold."

The men are gentle with differences in ability while also holding one another accountable; they start meeting on Sundays to rehearse. The whole circle leans in, practically willing each actor to find the word, the impulse, the moment. If they feel impatience, they keep that to themselves; they protect this experience for one another. In our group work on "O for a muse of fire," they debate whether to conjure up the spirit of the muse with that initial "Ó" or to make a discovery that the muse is waiting for them; they are collectively on the hunt of whether the emotion that "Ó" signifies is muscular, magical, curious, or cosmological.

A KINGDOM FOR A STAGE, PRINCES TO ACT

After 12 weeks of classes, we return to the industrial stylings of the multipurpose room to perform for 100 of their peers, as well as staff and correctional officers. As we gather in our circle before the performance, I ask each man to share three words: "Excited. Anxious. Proud."; "Bring. It. On."; "Let's get busy." Micah, who dropped out a couple weeks earlier, has resurfaced: "Missed you guys." The ensemble asks him to give the introductory remarks; he talks about the web of community, reflection, and accountability. The men perform their ensemble "O for a muse of fire" and then their individual monologues, culminating in Feeney's "we few, we happy few." Every man remains upstage, a supportive semi-circle, as the others perform. Feeney makes his way through the Crispin's Day speech. As each man is persuaded to go into battle with this king, he stands, cheers, or puts an arm around another in this band of brothers.

Even when they falter, the men regain their footing. Remember Bob, who was sure the workshop would kill him? He forgets a word in his soliloquy, but he holds the rhythm of the verse. Instead of "How weary, stale, flat and unprofitable seem to me all the uses of this world," we hear "How weary, stale, flat and uncomfortable." Afterwards, he approaches me, his eyes moist, to tell me that the workshop has changed his life: "People keep asking me what happened to the grumpy old man." Bob has begun to tend the unweeded garden which was slowly going to seed behind the prison walls.

The men in the audience talk about their pride in their brothers, their gratitude that this opportunity is available in the facility. The men of Redeeming Time are discovering what it feels like to be part of a team and to be held in higher esteem by both their peers and the prison administration. They are experiencing hope.

MONARCHS TO BEHOLD THE SWELLING SCENE

Just before Christmas, we perform for family and friends. Five of the men have never had a visit. One father's shame has kept him away for five years; today he is coming to see his son perform Shakespeare. We check in, warm up, wait. When family members finally come through the door, the men leap to their feet. I am struck by how happy the men without visitors are for those who have guests.

The men are on their game, wrestling with the dilemmas at the core of their texts. Gone is the early fear that "there's a right way to do Shakespeare." One spectator told me later that when they dove into their ensemble "O for a muse of fire," he felt a rustle of energy through the audience: "We weren't expecting to hear all their voices raised as one. Everyone leaned forward." Department of Corrections Commissioner Tom Roy tells the men he wanted to put humanity back into Corrections, and "you've reaffirmed that."

Wives, friends, disconnected fathers, discover a new reason to be proud of their incarcerated loved one—perhaps after decades of disappointment—when they see them tackle Brutus, Becker, or Prince Hal. This may be the first time that they see others recognizing that their loved one is talented, intelligent, and determined. After the performance, we drink juice, eat cookies, chat. Like people. This is restorative on its own, practicing being human. Rob Pensalfini identifies an additional, subversive-in-the-best-way, ingredient in a prison performance, an "inverted power relationship between prisoners and the free when there is a general audience for prison theater. The actors speak, the audience listens."[7] This is agency temporarily restored. Bob's wife tells me it's the best Christmas since he's been incarcerated.

GENTLY TO HEAR, KINDLY TO JUDGE

In processing this first workshop and performance experience, Matthew wrote, "I have become a better communicator. I am less intimidated in front of people, and I have learned solid teamwork skills. This program has given me purpose here. In the 15 years I have been in prison, this is the most impactful, beneficial, and meaningful program I have been part of."

Prison theater creates a space apart from the grind of doing time. Many participants develop a sense of accountability and connection through an endeavor which lifts everyone. The men are cognizant that the wider world thinks of them—if it thinks of them at all—as animals, as monsters, as something less than human. They strive in an undertaking borne not of shame, despair, and anger, but of possibilities, self-expression, and shared commitment. Prison theater programs lift the communitas any of us might experience in a college or a professional production and weaves it into a true community within a deliberately isolating and oppressive environment.

Shakespeare asks fundamental moral questions without serving up answers. The characters feel what they feel and think what they think intensely. Shakespeare's text demands a particular commitment, a willingness to engage with complexity, a specificity of thought. In *Violence*, James Gilligan talks about the therapeutic work he does with violent men, "trying to facilitate their ability to think about and talk about their thoughts and feelings before, and instead of, committing impulsive, unreasoned, unthinkable acts of violence."[8] How can one possibly "to thine own self be true" if one cannot see who one is, under the weight and anonymity of an inmate number and a monotonous stack of gray incarcerated years? Shakespeare's text can be a lens which offers critical distance as well as emotional magnification through which to consider alternate pathways. One of our ensemble members wrote at the end of this first workshop, "I have locked away so many elements of myself, but this space at RTP, working with others, have (sic) help me find the place where I put my creativity and my fun, and helped me reconnect with it, so I would go forward living in my whole self and not just part of me." It is time redeemed.

NOTES

1 Curt L. Tofteland, Conversation with author. January 6, 2013 and several times thereafter.
2 Emma Marie Heard, et al., "Shakespeare in Prison: Affecting Health and Wellbeing." *International Journal of Prisoner Health*, 9, no. 3 (2013): 111.
3 James Gilligan, *Violence: Reflections on a National Epidemic* (New York: Vintage Books, 1996), 51.
4 Patsy Rodenburg, *Presence: How to Use Positive Energy for Success in Every Situation* (New York: Penguin Books, 2009).
5 Qtd. in James Thompson, ed., *Prison Theatre: Perspectives and Practices* (London: Jessica Kingsley, 1998), 192.
6 Mayo Clinic Staff, "Stress Relief from Laughter? It's No Joke," https://www.mayoclinic.org/healthy-lifestyle/stress-management/in-depth/stress-relief/art-20044456.
7 Rob Pensalfini, *Prison Shakespeare: For These Deep Shames and Great Indignities* (London: Palgrave Macmillan, 2016), 159.
8 Gilligan, 57–58.

Wasps and Falcons: Figurative Language
and Teaching Shakespeare's Women

Karrah Davidson and Amanda Kellogg

Twelve

During a summer reading group that we co-hosted for the women's population of a regional jail, we read a selection of stories by Flannery O'Connor. In what ended up being an incredibly fruitful session, we talked at length about using language to label people and the ethics of teaching texts with offensive and racially denigrating language. We discussed how the terms "lady" and "ladylike" are often used to communicate expectations about women's behavior. We felt the conversation had gone incredibly well. As we were ending the three-hour block, the Assistant Superintendent asked to address the group. She thanked us for bringing such a fascinating set of stories to class, and she expressed her gratitude that we had such an in-depth conversation about why it is important to act like a lady. Acting like a lady, she said, means that you do not "ride high"—sitting on top of the tables in the jail—which is discouraged behavior. And, acting like a lady means choosing to marry a man who will respect you. She told a story about her grandmother, who used to remind her that she should never enter into a relationship with a man who did not hold the car door open for her, because doing so would indicate that she did not respect herself. She concluded by thanking us for giving the group an opportunity to think about what it means to be a lady and reminded the women that good behavior is rewarded at the jail.

DOI: 10.4324/9781003451662-16

While our partner at the jail may have inadvertently undermined the work of the class, it was also an instance of the principles we had been discussing in action: she followed up the abstractions of our literary analysis with a concrete example, one designed to reinforce expectations for cisgender, heteronormative expressions of desire, for the sanctity and value of the institution of marriage, and, crucially, for behavior in the jail: here, she might have said, we must control people's behavior, and one method of exerting that control is by identifying helpful societal norms and applying them.

Expectations about "ladylike" behavior and other gender stereotypes have powerful impacts on women involved in the United States justice system, from sentencing through their lives after release.[1] Given our passion for supporting incarcerated women, we began the process described in this paper adamant that we would work exclusively with incarcerated women; however, our subsequent work with incarcerated men has helped us understand the value of engaging with men on the subject of representations of women. In our experiences working with incarcerated men and women, it has become clear that a sustained focus on how meaning is made about women can encourage individuals both to advocate for themselves and to alter their interactions with and descriptions of others. Because as an instructor, Amanda believes strongly that a study of Shakespeare's women provides opportunities for students to engage with questions about how language and gender interact, she offered a course titled "Shakespeare and Justice" at a jail near the university where she taught. Enrolled in the course were nine students from the university student population and ten students from the jail's population; one of the authors of this article, Karrah, took the course as an undergraduate from Amanda's university. In a previous semester, Karrah had participated in a traditional Inside-Out course through Radford University's Criminal Justice Department.[2] The course covered an array of topics from the War on Drugs to mandatory minimum sentencing and provided meaningful insight into the complexities of the criminal justice system. Having studied a curriculum directly focused on criminal justice topics, Karrah was interested in seeing how other disciplines might negotiate the process of carceral teaching. It became apparent through her participation in Amanda's course that English departments can create opportunities to discuss societal issues in a broader context, encouraging students to see varying perspectives, gain confidence in their abilities to write and speak, and enter into new discourse communities.

"Shakespeare and Justice" provided a unique experience for Amanda, Karrah, and the other students in the class; anticipating that they would be working with a group of incarcerated students from the women's population—and having enrolled a group at her home institution comprised almost entirely of women—Amanda decided that a class of mostly women might be the opportune environment for reading *The Taming of the Shrew.* Two days before the class began, however, Amanda learned that the jail's administration had changed their minds: the incarcerated students were coming from the men's wing of the jail. Since all materials were submitted well in advance, it was too late to make changes, so Amanda prepared to teach a class, composed of roughly equal numbers of individuals identifying as men and as women, that still offered a rich context for thinking about gendered expectations.

The content and practices of the course were designed not only to encourage an examination of representations of women, but also discussions and reflections related to the theme of justice. Using Shakespeare's plays as hypothetical case studies, students could consider how class, gender, and race affect individuals' experiences of justice and incarceration, and how social norms are communicated to women. In what follows, we offer some ideas, grounded in theory and praxis, in support of teaching incarcerated populations to use Shakespeare to examine the construct of gender in their social and cultural contexts.

Because both the university-enrolled and incarcerated students were mostly not English majors with relatively little experience reading Shakespeare, Amanda spent much of the first few weeks reviewing language, literary devices, and historical context. Students completed increasingly challenging assignments requiring them to find evidence related to particular topics in each play. For instance, the response to *The Taming of the Shrew* built off of a "translation" exercise, where students updated the language from a passage in *Richard II*.[3] For the *Shrew* response, the assignment began with the exchange about Petruchio's "taming school":

> TRANIO: Faith, he is gone unto the taming school.
> BIANCA: The taming school? What, is there such a place?
> TRANIO: Ay, mistress, and Petruchio is the master,
>   That teacheth tricks eleven and twenty long
>   To tame a shrew and charm her chattering tongue.
>   (4.2.56–60)

Students received the following explanation and instructions:

> In *The Taming of the Shrew*, Tranio suggests, facetiously, that Petruchio is giving lessons on how to tame shrews at "the taming school."...Building on the translation work you did for

> Assignment 1, Assignment 2 asks that you use your dictionary, textbook, and notes in order to put the language of the play in a contemporary context; however, this time, you will have to go searching for the evidence yourself, reviewing all five acts from the play in order to submit the strongest possible response. Drawing exclusively on evidence from the play (not your own opinions about marriage or women), create a Taming School Handbook, which lists 8–12 principles/strategies deployed by Petruchio in order to tame Katherine. Each of your strategies should be accompanied by a specific quotation that illustrates the strategy at work.

Students were subsequently invited to imagine this project as an actual book, including illustrations, graphs, or other features that might clarify or enhance their readers' understanding. Because this assignment was designed for students in the women's population, Amanda felt quite uneasy in the days before introducing it. She worried that students might experience the work not as an opportunity to reflect on cultural practices used against them, as it was originally conceived, but as an opportunity to make light of or fetishize those practices.

Ultimately, however, the assignment created space for reflection both on the personal abuses experienced or deployed by individuals in the class and on the systemic forms of control used by jails and prisons. One strategy that many students listed in their handbook involved controlling what the "shrew" wears. The students drew on Petruchio's exchanges with the haberdasher and tailor, particularly Petruchio's admonishment to Katherine's objection that the hat the haberdasher has made is just the sort gentlewomen are wearing: "when you are gentle, you shall have one too, / And not till then" (4.3.75–76). Clothing, we noted, can be a crucial component of self-expression, and efforts to limit or control the clothing of others are often tied to efforts at broader suppression and disenfranchisement. In class, we examined some examples of this phenomenon in the early modern period, particularly the connection between fashion and social class in Elizabethan sumptuary laws. We also noted this theme more broadly in *Shrew*, where Christopher Sly describes how his identity is shaped by his clothes (Prologue 2.8–11). Sly initially disbelieves the suggestion that he is a lord based upon his memories of wearing the other Sly's clothing. He is also convinced of his lordly status, in part, because he is granted access to rich robes. Through the experiences of Sly and Katherine, Shakespeare demonstrates clothing's potential almost immediately to redefine the individual.

While for people everywhere, clothing constitutes an important way of communicating about themselves and asserting power, different kinds of meaning derive from clothing in the context of a jail or prison. For incarcerated students and the individuals who work with them, clothing is both a means of organizing information and a form of systematic punishment or reward. From color codes that indicate the level of security risk the incarcerated individual is perceived to pose, to using access to certain clothing options (such as blue jeans) as an outcome for good behavior, jails and prisons have developed elaborate systems for uniforms. "When you are gentle," we might imagine a guard saying, "you shall have denim, too."

Near the end of the conversation about clothing in *Shrew* and in carceral settings, one of the men mentioned his own attempts to control what clothing a former girlfriend wore. He described never explicitly telling her what to wear, but, instead, buying her clothes and then making her feel bad if she chose to wear something else. As a class, we noted similarities between the strategy he had used with his girlfriend and Petruchio's efforts to reframe his abuse with a language of care (Petruchio suggests, for instance, that he will "kill a wife with kindness" [4.1.208]). Students noted that while such actions are often represented as an expression of love they are hurtful to the individuals who may be controlled by them.

It is, as the students noted, damaging to have one's capacity to decide about clothing stripped away—even dehumanizing. While clothing regulation may be regarded as a necessity in carceral settings, Petruchio's sartorial approach to taming gave the students an opportunity to examine how the criminal justice system might be dehumanizing in other ways as well. What, for instance, might compel jail officials to refer to the students in the class as "offenders" rather than "people" or "men"? How might making the decision to refer to them as "students" communicate something essential about the persistence of their humanity and about their capacity to learn?

Petruchio is a reliable model for practices one might compare to the strategies of the criminal justice system. His falconry speech points to several methods for controlling Katherine's behavior, including regulating her sleep and food. Moreover, he draws on metaphors that describe her as an animal. The explanation he delivers to the audience makes clear his imaginative potential:

> Thus have I politically begun my reign,
> And 'tis my hope to end successfully.
> My falcon now is sharp and passing empty,
> And, till she stoop, she must not be full-gorged,
> For then she never looks upon her lure.
>
> (4.1.188–192)

Petruchio describes himself as a sovereign at the start of his "reign." Meanwhile, he imagines his wife not only as his subject, but also a domesticated falcon kept for sport. His strategies for bringing Katherine to heel are, he reveals, drawn from his knowledge of taming falcons: in order to bring a falcon to the "lure," it is necessary to starve it to the point of capitulation, and, as Petruchio's speech further intimates, to keep it from sleep (4.1.198).

Part of the difficulty that the men and women of this play face is rooted in the language they use to describe each other and their relationships. Even as the title indicates, men in the play are inclined to imagine women as non-human. Katherine is a shrew, a falcon, and a turtle dove (2.1). Meanwhile, Bianca is a treasure and a jewel locked away in Baptista's house (1.2.119–120). Karen Newman has noted that, in likening the taming of a curst wife to the breaking of an animal, Shakespeare aligns with a long tradition: "In both popular and elite materials on marriage and education, taming or educating a wife is likened to the training or domestication of animals—unbroken horses, intractable cats, untamed hawks, even wild beasts."[4] The men of Shrew take actions that align with their understanding of women as non-human.

To make choices that reflect the reality one's language constructs, as the characters in Shrew do, is human nature. For instance, recent research by Paul H. Thibodeau and Lera Borodisky demonstrates how metaphors affect people's responses to crime.[5] The researchers provided subjects with two descriptions of urban crime, but altered the metaphors so that some subjects read about crime described as a wild beast, while others read about crime described as a virus. Beyond this shift in the figurative language, all other aspects of the stories were identical. Readers of the beast metaphors adopted a more aggressive, punitive response to crime, while readers of the illness metaphors were more willing to recommend supportive and preventative responses.

The metaphorical registers individuals use to understand the world can have tangible effects on their reactions to them, as Shakespeare clearly understood. In the context of the "Shakespeare and Justice" class, Amanda encouraged students to use this knowledge to recognize how the language they use may indicate value judgments that subtly shape their decisions. She encouraged them to take control of how they talk about themselves as much as possible, pointing to Katherine as a potential model. Even as she surrenders to Petruchio's whims, her language reflects a careful fashioning of her own identity. Petruchio famously insists on calling her Kate though she asserts in their first meeting, "They call me Katherine that do talk of me," but—despite Petruchio's aggressive use of "Kate" throughout the play—Katherine continues to think of herself as Katherine (2.1.192). In response to Petruchio's insistence that she agree with him that the sun is actually the moon, Katherine says:

> Then God be blest, it is the blessed sun.
> But sun it is not, when you say it is not,
> And the moon changes even as your mind.
> What you will have it named, even that it is,
> And so it shall be so for Katherine.
>
> (4.5.21)

The language "what you will have it named, even that it is" sounds like an utter admission of defeat, but she concludes with a reassertion that her name is Katherine. Though Petruchio "will have [his wife] named" Kate, as he vehemently emphasizes in their first meeting, Katherine chooses a name for herself even in a moment of capitulation (2.1.193–198).

Another compelling facet of the "Shakespeare and Justice" discussion was Katherine's final speech, which students tended to interpret ironically, given how much it diverged from Katherine's earlier behavior. Evidence that Petruchio has "tamed" Katherine has been open to opposing interpretations, and scholars have long debated the effects of Katherine's speech on the play's representations of marriage and women's agency. To be sure, the speech offers much both to reinforce and to undermine the arguments delivered on its surface. Phyllis Rackin, for instance, maintains that the context of the speech matters for thinking through its meaning. Rackin, recalling that the lines were initially delivered by a boy dressed as a woman, argues that the cross-dressing plot of the induction would undermine Katherine's affirmations of "the authority of patriarchy."[6] Rackin, too, suggests that, if the play were staged as a farce, the meaning and import of the final speech would shift dramatically (55).[7] Natalie K. Eschenbaum, meanwhile, argues that "the extreme nature of Petruchio's actions indicates its artificiality."[8] In the same way, the exaggerated nature of Katherine's final speech suggests artificiality. Recent readings from Amy Smith and Laura Kolb, too, argue that the extreme submission demonstrates the complex and negotiated nature of marriage, which is both commented upon and shaped by Katherin's speech and by the varying performances of it through time.[9] This new bent in criticism of the play reminds readers that marriage is not a static concept to be accepted or rejected.

In reviewing this scene with the class, we considered that Katherine now knows how to perform and navigate the patriarchal society most strikingly represented by Petruchio, partly because she is attuned to the ways in which that system uses language as a means of control. Katherine explains to the wives that "Thy husband is thy lord, thy life, thy keeper" (5.2.162). She goes on to say: "I am ashamed that women are so simple

/ to offer war where they should kneel for peace...when they are bound to serve, love and obey" (5.2.177–180). When students are able to note the violence of the image of the bound wife, or to detect the potential use of irony by Katherine in describing the hard work of husbands, they practice skills of rhetorical analysis that may help them navigate their cultural context. Our discussion of Petruchio's taming strategies and Katherine's potential moments of resistance complicated the students' understandings of the play and encouraged them to see a version of Shrew in which Katherine's resilience and wit allow her to resist succumbing to the identity prescribed to her by the men who attempt to overpower her. Providing students with a framework to discuss the implications of a patriarchal society empowers all students to enter into the conversation with confidence and curiosity.

Although Amanda's "Shakespeare and Justice" course was originally designed with a female incarcerated population in mind, teaching The Taming of the Shrew to a men's population allowed for examination of how a patriarchal system can be harmful for its members, regardless of gender. Shrew both enforces and challenges antifeminist norms. Katherine can be represented as a woman who navigates the constraints of a patriarchal society and, by virtue of her wit and her capacity to understand the importance of naming, does not lose herself. Instead, she deploys tactics of self-preservation to survive in the cultural moment she inhabits. A similar approach may be available to the women with whom we read Flannery O'Connor. By honing their abilities to recognize how language—especially ideologically gendered language like "lady" and "ladylike"—is deployed (and to what ends) by those working within the criminal justice system, they cannot remove themselves entirely from their cultural moment, but they are, at least, in a better position to recognize and respond to the language that is used by and about them. Katherine's speech depicts, very powerfully, how language used against women can erase their agency; Katherine describes a married woman, for instance, as a kept thing, beholden to her husband and totally subject to his demands. It is perhaps easier for modern readers to see, in Katherine's radical submission, the harm that language can do. After our work with *The Taming of the Shrew* in the Shakespeare and Justice course, we believe that students were better equipped to appreciate the potential for their own language to have tangible effects on the people around them, and we know that the two of us have developed a richer appreciation for the play and for incarcerated men's capacity to work with it in deep and meaningful ways.

NOTES

1 Even the experience of carceral education programs differs widely for men and women. As Belknap notes, "Historically, women's prisons have led programs in cosmetology, office skills, typing, sewing, hairdressing, and homemaking, but few train women in skills to help them become financially independent upon release." Men's carceral education, on the other hand, often includes "access to programs in welding, electronics, construction, tailoring, computers, plumbing, and college programs." Joanne Belknap, *The Invisible Woman: Gender, Crime and Justice*, 4th ed. (Los Angeles: SAGE Publications, 2015), 240.

2 "Founded in 1997, the Inside-Out Prison Exchange Program weds community-based learning and prison education, bringing college or university students and people in prison together as classmates for a semester of shared experiential learning." Simone Weil Davis and Barbara Sherr Roswell, *Turning Teaching Inside Out: A Pedagogy of Transformation for Community-Based Education* (London: Palgrave Macmillan, 2013), 1.

3 Students responded positively to this assignment, which asked them to translate the "Music do I hear" speech: 5.5.41–61. Feel free to email Amanda for a complete copy of this or any assignment.

4 Karen Newman, "*The Taming of the Shrew*: A Modern Perspective," in *The Taming of the Shrew*, eds. Barbara A. Mowat and Paul Werstine (New York: Simon & Schuster, 2014), 250.
5 Paul H. Thibodeau and Lera Boroditsky, "Metaphors We Think With: The Role of Metaphor in Reasoning," *PLoS One* 6, no. 2 (2011): 1–11.
6 Phyllis Rackin, *Shakespeare and Women* (Oxford: Oxford University Press, 2005), 55.
7 Rackin, *Shakespeare and Women*, 55.
8 Natalie K. Eschenbaum, "Modernising Misogyny in Shakespeare's Shrew," *Critical Survey* 33, no. 2 (2021), 32.
9 Amy L. Smith, "Performing Marriage with a Difference: Wooing, Wedding, and Bedding in 'The Taming of the Shrew,'" *Comparative Drama* 36, no. 3/4 (2002–2003); Laura Kolb, "Feminine Performance in *The Taming of the Shrew*: Finale Speech and Missing Soliloquy," *Renaissance Drama* 50, no.2 (2022). Smith argues that the play's "particular reiteration of marriage enacts a series of negotiations for power, none of which results in a marriage based on simple domination and submission or perfect egalitarianism" (290). Similarly, Kolb suggests that "a performance of feminine obedience (directed specifically at a father or husband) within a multi-person scene (populated by other men and women besides father or husband) might seamlessly contribute to that scene's 'surface agreement.' Taken to extremes, however, performances of obedience threaten or disrupt the mutual production of shared reality…rather than confirming their sense of things" (138).

Counter-Readings: Reimagining
Shakespeare in Prison Libraries

Kevin Windhauser

Thirteen

In late 2016, Texas prisons briefly made headlines by barring prison libraries from keeping a copy of Shakespeare's *Sonnets*. Condemnation was vigorous, but also vague; commentators either decried the decision by way of comparison to obviously odious texts that were not banned ("Shakespeare's Sonnets Are Banned from Texas Prisons, but Hitler's *Mein Kampf* Is Allowed" read one representative headline) while others gestured toward general benefits of reading for incarcerated people ("Books Have the Power to Rehabilitate. But Prisons Are Blocking Access to Them").[1] Neither of these responses, however, makes a positive case for the value of keeping Shakespearean texts on prison library shelves; if the standard for prison library books amounts to "books not written by Hitler" then the copious legal textbooks found in every American prison library thanks to *Bounds v. Smith* or the oft-haphazard collections of donated novels and magazines that make up underfunded prison libraries in the United States should suffice just fine as is.

If this feels instinctively wrong to most Shakespeareans, it is nonetheless a surprisingly difficult challenge to describe just what makes having Shakespearean texts in a prison library beneficial.[2] A growing body of scholarly work and public writing examines the impact of Shakespearean encounters for

DOI: 10.4324/9781003451662-17

incarcerated performers and students, but almost exclusively in communal forms: performance, classroom study, discussion groups, and other forms of structured interaction with Shakespeare's work. Indeed, those who found, run, and study programs dedicated to using Shakespeare in prison education often emphasize a sense of community and communal learning as key to their success.[3] Undirected, unsupervised reading of Shakespeare's work—the sort of thing one can do by finding Shakespeare in the library, for instance—remains largely outside the scope of most prison education scholarship, relegated mostly to a small number of case studies made notable by the subsequent fame of a given Shakespearean reader, such as the Robben Island Shakespeare shared by Nelson Mandela and others, or the experience of Anwar Ibrahim, a diligent Shakespeare reader during his time in solitary confinement in Malaysia.[4] When it does appear in contemporary scholarship, the prison library is often seen as an impediment to the liberatory work of Shakespearean performance; one article on a Shakespeare performance group held in a British prison facility laments being consigned to "a tiny library where there were interruptions by people wanting to loan or return books. There was little doubt that this was a functional part of the prison and not somewhere where the imagination could soar and the confines be forgotten."[5]

If the COVID-19 pandemic, in largely shutting down in-person prison teaching, made clear how valuable having instructional materials in prison libraries is, it bears remembering that for the great majority of incarcerated people in the United States, this is essentially status quo. Ways of measuring the number of incarcerated students able to access education programs vary, but a Vera Institute for Justice report found that only 9% of theoretically eligible incarcerated students in the United States were able to enroll in educational programming in 2019.[6] The library, open to all readers by legal decree, will remain many prison students' only connection to Shakespeare in the near future, despite the urgent efforts of many to increase formal educational offerings. In Georgia, to take but one example, a 2019 *Atlanta Journal-Constitution* survey found Shakespeare's works available in the libraries of all of the state's correctional facilities, and noted that "several carry dozens of his works," while formal higher education programming is limited to nine of the state's 34 adult facilities.[7] Considering the potential affordances of having Shakespearean texts in a prison library is therefore more than a theoretical question, worthy of more detailed attention than it has received in the academic literature of both Shakespeare studies and prison pedagogy to date.

Examining and analyzing the experiences of incarcerated readers encountering, without the aid of a formalized arts or education program, Shakespearean texts in prison libraries may demonstrate that a perceived weakness of independent reading of library texts can actually be at times a strength. Reading Shakespeare's work independently by discovering it in a library setting, while presenting a host of basic pedagogical challenges related to reading comprehension, can also create space for independent, reader-driven responses to the text. Research by librarians and scholars of information science has already shown that incarcerated individuals view the library as a unique space in its enabling of independent decision making and time structuring; unlike most prison classrooms, and certainly unlike the vast majority of the prison experience, a library is designed to enable visitors to make active choices about what to read and which texts they wish to encounter.[8] Two case studies—one from one of the 20th century's most famous and prolific prison library patrons, Malcolm X, another from a far less famous incarcerated reader encountering Shakespeare in a makeshift prison library in solitary confinement in a juvenile prison— help us to ask how reading Shakespeare, specifically, contributes to and enhances practices of agential, independent reading. Shakespeare's uber-canonical status gives special significance for incarcerated individuals pulling his work from library shelves. In their independent, undirected reading of his work, students challenge, redefine, and respond to the Shakespearean canon in ways that cannot happen in the classroom. A prison classroom, no matter the efforts made by an instructor invested in liberatory and radical theories of pedagogy, recreates the regulation of time, space, and movement that the prison imposes upon the incarcerated: students typically must read Shakespeare according to a syllabus guideline, discuss Shakespeare at an appointed time in an appointed classroom, and respond to Shakespeare within a given timeframe for assignment submissions. The library, by contrast, while presenting perhaps the most challenging setting in which to encounter Shakespeare, also presents potentially the most radical opportunities for incarcerated students to read Shakespeare's work on their own terms, making it a uniquely valuable setting for incarcerated readers.

At a time when the potential independent reading in prisons is simultaneously growing and contracting in different parts of the United States, the question of the value of encountering Shakespeare's works in a prison library is one that demands study and action all at once.[9] On one hand, the experiences of incarcerated readers examining Shakespearean works through independent reading remain largely hidden;

while this essay outlines two important case studies, a great deal of scholarly work remains to be done to widen the canon of such writings. On the other hand, even a limited examination of the unique impacts of reading Shakespeare independently in prison settings makes clear that librarians, activists, and educators cannot wait for a larger body of scholarly work to emerge before considering how ongoing efforts to expand formal Shakespeare-focused programming in prisons can coexist with, rather than obviate, the practice of independent discovery and reading of Shakespeare. In demonstrating the distinct value of these reading practices in what follows, this chapter attempts to foreground the urgency of preserving, expanding, and critically examining independent Shakespearean reading in American prisons.

The *Autobiography of Malcolm X* details Malcolm X's extensive prison reading, centering on the large prison library at Norfolk Prison Colony, which Malcolm describes as something "any college library would have been lucky to get."[10] In describing his reading, Malcolm is careful to emphasize the language of discovery and awakening, a series of initially accidental discoveries made wandering the libraries, which led to the eventual creation of a personal library reading program: "at Norfolk, we could actually go into the library, with permission—walk up and down the shelves, pick books. There were hundreds of old volumes, some of them probably quite rare. I read aimlessly, until I learned to read selectively, with a purpose [...] I found books like Will Durant's *Story of Civilization* [...] I discovered philosophy [...] the ability to read awoke inside me some long dormant craving to be mentally alive."[11] Out of this culture of reading, according to Malcolm, came a prison debating club, in which groups of incarcerated men debated issues among themselves. It is in a retelling of these debates that Malcolm reveals where his reading of Shakespeare in prison has led him:

> Another hot debate I remember I was in had to do with the identity of Shakespeare. No color was involved there; I just got intrigued over the Shakespearean dilemma. The King James translation of the Bible is considered the greatest piece of literature in English. Its language supposedly represents the ultimate in using the King's English. Well, Shakespeare's language and the Bible's language are one and the same. They say that from 1604 to 1611, King James got poets to translate, to write the Bible. Well, if Shakespeare existed, he was then the top poet around. But Shakespeare is nowhere reported connected with the Bible. If he existed, why didn't King James use him? And if he did use him, why is it one of the world's best kept secrets?
>
> I know that many say that Francis Bacon was Shakespeare. If that is true, why would Bacon have kept it secret? Bacon wasn't royalty, when royalty sometimes used the *nom de plume* because it was "improper" for royalty to be artistic or theatrical. What would Bacon have had to lose? Bacon, in fact, would have had everything to gain.
>
> In the prison debates I argued for the theory that King James himself was the real poet who used the *nom de plume* Shakespeare. King James was brilliant. He was the greatest king who ever sat on the British throne. Who else among royalty, in his time, would have had the giant talent to write Shakespeare's works? It was he who poetically "fixed" the Bible -which in itself and its present King James version has enslaved the world.[12]

In this debate, Malcolm coined what the *Oxford Companion to Shakespeare* calls the "James I Theory," an idea it describes as "one of the less widely published lunacies of the Authorship Controversy…first made, for no obvious reason, by Malcolm Little, later known as Malcolm X, during a debate in the Norfolk Prison Colony in Massachusetts."[13] This reaction, however, largely misses the context in which Malcolm X encountered and read Shakespeare (and Bacon and the King James Bible, for that matter), pulling them out of the unpacked "boxes and crates" sitting in the library building. A closer examination of Malcolm X's experience encountering Shakespeare in a prison library offers one potential answer to the "no obvious reason" behind his creation of the "James I Theory."

The Autobiography of Malcolm X is explicit in positioning the classroom and the library as ideologically opposed. Malcolm makes clear that Norfolk offered what he calls "educational rehabilitation programs" taught by faculty from "Harvard, Boston University, and other educational institutions," but the Autobiography omits any mention of Malcolm's participation in formal coursework, and generally denigrates formal university education throughout. As Jed B. Tucker has shown, however, Malcolm X did pursue a literature course offered at Norfolk, called "The Great Books," which he dropped out of before its conclusion, earning a tantalizing note on his record from his instructor: "had his own ideas but was ok."[14] The omission of his two years of formal education at Norfolk from the Autobiography, combined with his instructor's comment about Malcolm having "his own ideas" about "Great Books," hints that Malcolm felt formal, classroom study of literary texts to be intellectually restrictive (especially considering that, as Tucker notes, Malcolm passed courses in Latin and German, focused on language acquisition rather than discussion of literary texts, with "excellent marks," indicating his intellectual aptitude for formal study). In the debate group, however, Malcolm presents himself as surrounded not by products of restrictive institutional education, but by library-fueled autodidacts like himself: "There was a sizable number of well-read inmates, especially the popular debaters. Some were said by many to be practically walking encyclopedias [...] No university would ask any student to devour literature as I did when this new world opened to me, of being able to read and *understand*."[15] The prison debating society, as presented in the *Autobiography*, not only allows for an intellectual freedom not found in the university courses offered at Norfolk but also a level of learnedness that prisoners can achieve on their own that surpasses what the university ostensibly provides.

With this attitude toward the prison library in mind, we might return to Malcolm's "James I Theory" not as a curious manifestation of anti-Stratfordian conspiracy theories but as a record of the resistant reading the library allowed for: a record of Malcolm, unable to have "his own ideas" in his "Great Books" course, deploying them with library texts.[16] Malcolm's position, as he unfurls it, demonstrates the expanse of knowledge he has been able to acquire in the prison library, including an understanding of the importance of the King James Bible in the history of English literature and the evolution of the English language, knowledge of Francis Bacon's work, social status, and the Baconian theory of Shakespearean authorship, and an understanding of social conventions surrounding early modern authorship. At the same time, in his assertion that James I's King James Bible has "enslaved the world," Malcolm implicitly connects Shakespeare's work and its global expansion to the legacy of white imperialism he had uncovered in the library and that had driven him to debate in the first place: "My reading had my mind like steam under pressure. Some way, I had to start telling the white man about himself to his face. I decided I could do this by putting my name down to debate."[17] This practice of using his reading to challenge the status of canonical, white authors became a popular route for Malcolm to attack white supremacy in the prison debates, repeating a similar analysis in a debate about Homer:

> In a debate about whether or not Homer had ever existed, I threw into those white faces the theory that Homer only symbolized how white Europeans kidnapped black Africans, then blinded them so that they could never get back to their own people. (Homer and Omar and *Moor*, you see, are related terms; it's like saying Peter, Pedro, and *petra*, all three of which mean rock.) These blinded Moors the Europeans taught to sing about the Europeans' glorious accomplishments. I made it clear that was the devilish white man's idea of kicks. Aesop's *Fables*—another case in point. "Aesop" was only the Greek name for an Ethiopian.[18]

The ability to use library books to, in turn, launch a historical or philological attack on the European canon is what makes Malcolm's encounter with Shakespeare in the prison library particularly important. The ability to read widely not only in the primary texts to which he refers, but in secondary texts necessary to contextualize his argument, is what gives Malcolm the ability to craft original readings that, in their own idiosyncratic way, launch critiques of white supremacy almost certainly impossible within the classroom of "Great Books." The library functions as a type of space that the classroom cannot be; transferred to a different prison without an equivalent library for the final year of his sentence, Malcolm must resort to attending a Bible study class in order to engage in textual and historical debates with the "tall, blond, blue-eyed (a perfect 'devil') Harvard Seminary student" leading the course, an activity that excites his classmates but does little to satisfy Malcolm himself.

Malcolm X's experience of resistant reading in the prison library is important but, perhaps, idiosyncratic. Depictions of unmediated library encounters with Shakespeare by incarcerated individuals who don't go on to become world famous thinkers are substantially harder to find (a reminder that excavating narratives of incarcerated people's experiences finding Shakespeare in prison libraries is a fundamental building block of a larger project of making independent reading more viable in American prisons). Brief anecdotes mostly have come mediated through the language of journalists, often as asides in writing focused on the prison experience more generally. They can, however, give us a window into what it means for incarcerated people to engage with Shakespeare in a library setting, without the mediation of a classroom or other structured educational or rehabilitative program. The case of Steven Czifra is one such example. Featured in a 2016 New Yorker article on a group of formerly-incarcerated students at the University of California, Berkeley working together to help other formerly-incarcerated persons attend college, Czifra spent four years in solitary confinement at a California juvenile detention facility, punishment for refusing to enroll in the facility's drug rehabilitation program. Included in the harrowing depiction of Czifra's time in solitary confinement is a brief comment about the "library" there:

> The one good thing about solitary in Y.A. was a big box there containing hundreds of books. He read until all that was left was a volume of Shakespeare, with four plays in it. At first, he found the language nearly impossible to understand, but he had nothing else to do, so he kept at it. He gradually realized that it was better than anything he'd read before, and he looked for more. He decided that his favorite play was

"Richard II," because of the way it forced you to confront a disagreeable man-child who ruined his life and killed people, and yet, by the end, made you feel compassion for him.[19]

While the erasure of Czifra's own voice in this passage in favor of journalistic paraphrase is unfortunate, we can nonetheless glean something about the independent reading incarcerated individuals can engage in when encountering Shakespeare outside of an explicitly educational context, in this case in the "library" of books offered to prisoners in solitary confinement. In Czifra's encounter with Shakespeare in solitary, we see first understandable difficulties in comprehension, but also the formation of a critical sensibility that leads to a conclusion about the dramatic trajectory of *Richard II*. In a brief comment in an interview with the *Berkeley City College Voice* in 2018, Czifra looked back on his breakthrough in reading Shakespeare in solitary, one that might surprise instructors of Shakespeare who have struggled to help even the most talented undergraduates learn scansion:

I started reading it [the Shakespeare volume] and I was like… This is impossible to read. But, it was all I had, and I had to read. And so I had to read it…and I realized what was going on. Once I realized how he was writing and how he was talking, the rhyme scheme, the iambic pentameter, I didn't have any words for it.[20]

Reading Shakespeare in a prison library very different from the one Malcolm X had at hand, with little critical or contextual information available, Czifra developed a keen ear for the formal patterns of Shakespeare's verse—it is perhaps little surprise that he then chose one of the most metrical and most heavily rhymed plays in the canon as a personal favorite. In an environment of extreme sound deprivation—the solitary unit in which Czifra was confined was specifically designed to prevent those in solitary from being able to speak to each other across cells—Czifra's encounter with Shakespeare's language led him, perhaps not coincidentally, to a reading method that embraced sound and rhythm in the language of the plays.

The anecdotal evidence of Malcolm X and Steven Czifra finding Shakespeare in the prison library and reading his work in counterintuitive ways suggests that much can be gained from further exploration of the role reading Shakespeare independently plays in understanding his function within the American carceral system. The stakes are high—independent reading will likely remain the way some of the most vulnerable incarcerated people come to Shakespeare's work for at least the near future: one very painful irony of Czifra's reading of Shakespeare from a book in the makeshift solitary library, for instance, is that the facility where he endured solitary confinement for four years was simultaneously offering both a Shakespeare performance group and college-level courses in English literature to students not in solitary. If we accept—even as we work to reduce their number—that many incarcerated individuals will come to Shakespeare only by finding donated books in an underfunded library, we might begin to ask a host of questions about how to support these encounters: how can we ensure that prison libraries stock Shakespearean works? What kinds of secondary texts and aids to interpretation should live on prison library shelves? How can we create venues and spaces for readers to share their interpretations and responses to Shakespeare? As prison education and theatrical programs expand, how can we welcome them into facilities while maintaining space for independent reading of Shakespeare's work, the kind of radical and personalized encounters inadvertently created when the library is the only space Shakespeare can be found? What else can we know about how imprisoned readers find, read, and respond to Shakespeare, and how might early modernists, librarians, sociologists of incarceration, and prison reform and abolition advocates work together to bring the stories and experiences of these readers to light?

NOTES

1 Mary Papenfuss, "Shakespeare's Sonnets Are Banned in Texas Prisons. But Hitler's 'Mein Kampf' Is Allowed," *HuffPost US*, 2017; Samantha Michaels, "Books Have the Power to Rehabilitate. But Prisons Are Blocking Access to Them," *Mother Jones*, 2020.

2 I use the term "Shakespearean texts" to mean editions of the poems and plays as well as written adaptations, critical works, study guides, and other works that respond to or aid in understanding Shakespeare's work.

3 See Laura Louise Nicklin, "'Make Not Your Prisons Your Prisons': Participant-Perceived Potential Outcomes of a Shakespeare Focused Alternative to Juvenile Incarceration in the USA," *Emotional & Behavioural Difficulties* 22, no. 1 (2017): 11–14; Niels Herold, "Movers and Losers: Shakespeare in Charge and Shakespeare Behind Bars," *Native Shakespeares: Indigenous Appropriations on a Global Stage*, eds. Craig Dionne and Parmita Kapadia (Aldershot: Ashgate, 2008), 165–168.

4 David Schalkwyk, *Hamlet's Dreams: The Robben Island Shakespeare* (London: Bloomsbury, 2013).

5 Rowan Mackenzie, "Producing Space for Shakespeare," *Critical Survey* 31, no. 4 (2019): 68.

6 Ashley A. Smith, "Report Shows Benefits of Prison Education," *Inside Higher Education*, January 16, 2019.

7 Nick Thieme, "Georgia Prison Libraries Short on Books and Titles, AJC Analysis Finds," *Atlanta Journal-Constitution*, May 10, 2019. I thank Dr. Christopher Gleason, Director of Academic Programs at the Georgia Coalition for Higher Education in Prison, for the information regarding the number of higher education programs currently available in Georgia prisons.

8   Megan Sweeney, "Books as Bombs: Incendiary Reading Practices in Women's Prisons," PMLA 123, no. 3 (2008): 666–672; Jane Garner, "Almost like Freedom": Prison Libraries and Reading as Facilitators of Escape," Library Quarterly: Information, Community, Policy 90, no. 1 (2020): 5–19.

9   On the simultaneous expansion and contraction of reading possibilities in American prisons, consider the ongoing work of R. Dwayne Betts' "Freedom Reads" project, which has made over 185,000 books available to readers in 37 facilities through donated "Freedom Libraries," alongside the state of Missouri's 2023 decision to prohibit incarcerated readers from receiving books of any kind from friends, family, or outside organizations. On Freedom Reads, see www.freedomreads.org. On the Missouri decision, see Nomin Ujiyediin, "Missouri Prisons Ban Friends and Family from Sending Books to Prisoners," KCUR, August 29, 2023.

10 Malcolm X and Alex Haley, The Autobiography of Malcolm X (New York: Ballantine Books, 1992), 172, 188.

11 Malcolm X and Haley, 193–194.

12 Malcolm X and Haley, 200–201.

13 Michael Dobson. "James I Theory," in The Oxford Companion to Shakespeare, ed. Michael Dobson (Oxford: Oxford University Press, 2015).

14 Jed B. Tucker, "Malcolm X, the Prison Years: The Relentless Pursuit of Formal Education," The Journal of African American History 101, no. 2 (2017): 205. For additional context on the impact of Malcolm X's independent reading in prison on the development of his thought, see Trevin Jones, "The Ideological and Spiritual Transformation of Malcolm X," Journal of African American Studies 24 (2020): 417–433.

15 Malcolm X and Haley, 188. Emphasis in original.

16 While a secondary question to my reading, it bears noting that the context of this debate in the Autobiography makes it difficult to tell if Malcolm is taking a debating position or expressing a genuine belief about James I's authorship of Shakespeare's work. Malcolm hints the debating society is structured in an Oxford Debate style, asking debaters to take an assigned position on a predetermined question, although he does not reveal if this is the case in the debate over Shakespearean authorship.

17 Malcolm X and Haley, 199.
18 Malcolm X and Haley, 200. Emphasis in original.
19 Larissa MacFarquhar, "Out and Up," *The New Yorker* (Dec 12, 2016): 58.
20 "Steven Czifra on Shakespeare, Solitary Confinement and Marveling at the Ordinary," *Berkeley City College Voice*, December 7, 2018, https://bccvoice.wordpress.com/2018/12/07/steven-czifra-on-shakespeare-solitary-confinement-and-marveling-at-the-ordinary/.

I Was Octavius Caesar

Reginald Sinclair Lewis
Fourteen

It was the spring of 2017. The classroom in SCI-Graterford, a dark, brooding, medieval-like structure that sat on a large swath of land in Montgomery County, Pennsylvania, was filled with prisoners. Several days earlier, an announcement was posted on the bulletin boards of every cell block inviting inmates to join a new drama class, which is where I first met director and acting coach Trevor Drake. "Life Behind the Razor Wire" was the first play Trevor directed at SCI-Graterford. We wrote our own parts and dialogue. We invited a large outside audience, families and friends of the inmate cast members-volunteers, college students, journalists, prison staff, as well as the general population. I played a character named "Poet" and opened the play with a powerful poem titled "A Sweet College Girl From Omaha." The play featured a group of reformed Lifers who met once a week to discuss their personal pain and trauma. The dialogue involved moving testimonies of redemption. Lines were written for guys who vented. Sobbed. And there were personality clashes. There was an antagonist who hurled insults and threats. In one scene, tempers flared. The bully kept taunting another guy, calling him a F—(a death sentence in prison if the straight guy took offense)—and the meeting became so disruptive violent brawls were aborted. The staged near-fight scenes were so realistic that prison guards rushed into the auditorium, wielding batons and mace. At the end

DOI: 10.4324/9781003451662-18

of the play, the audience erupted in wild applause. We took a bow. Perhaps the play enabled Trevor to capture the strengths of the characters, the tension and chaos and violent themes that dominated Shakespeare's plays.

In 2018, old Graterford prison was shut down, abandoned, uninhabitable, and the Pennsylvania Department of Corrections (DOC) contracted with members of the Corrections Emergency Response Team (CERT), to facilitate the transfer of thousands of prisoners to the massive, new, high-tech, super-maximum security prison at SCI-Phoenix. The transition was a tragedy of Shakespearean proportions. CERT was seen as a cruel, racist militia. Hordes of prisoners' valuables and property were mishandled, lost, and destroyed. Several inmates committed suicide. All programs and inmate organizations from SCI-Graterford were dismantled or suspended and most of the prison facilitators were not allowed into the new prison.

Fortunately, Trevor Drake was among the few outside volunteers finally permitted to enter the new prison. We tested the acoustics in large empty rooms in the separate squat concrete buildings. Trevor told me my big booming voice was ideal for the theater and he convinced me to read for the part of King Duncan in Shakespeare's tragedy *Macbeth*. I read for the part and he said, "You're quite kingly, Reggie." I'd always been drawn to the playwright's words and phrases, the grandeur and magnificent beauty of his poetry, and I memorized and recited King Duncan's lines with profligate ease. The role was perfect for me and it gave me a sense of power and prestige among my fellow prisoners and the staff who dropped in on the rehearsals. I was no longer some helpless, one-dimensional former death row inmate—I was a Shakespearean actor! The play made me feel as if this was preparation for something big, grand, part of some powerful, new Shakespearean Renaissance movement inside prison. The pageantry of Shakespeare gave me a real sense of, well, being secretly inducted into some royal society.

But each rehearsal was fraught with difficulty. First of all, the drama program was new. Most of us had never read such rich material of such superior quality. To be given the task of performing the historical works of a literary master was frightening and intimidating. At that point, we'd only experimented with our prisoner-written, prison-plot-driven plays with modern themes that bore little resemblance to Shakespeare's antiquated language. Some prisoners could barely read. Those who could struggled with the vocabulary and Elizabethan English. Shakespeare's work was far more challenging than anything a prisoner could ever imagine and, as a result, many prisoners dropped out. Although some people struggled with the play's difficult language, as a long time practicing Muslim, I struggled with the mandates of my faith that could not be reconciled against the ideas and themes of the play; sorcery and magic and dark prophecies made me uncomfortable. My sincerely held religious belief forbid me to call any mere mortal "Lord," "Your Majesty," or "Your Grace." Islam requires the total submission to God—and God only. Muslims don't stoop or bow to Kings or Queens. And I certainly could not and would not bow in submission before any man—nor have him bow before me. Furthermore, several of the young white male inmates were all too willing to play the parts of the female witches and even Macduff's wife and Lady Macbeth herself. In prison, perception equates to 99% reality. To me, this had the potential to expose them to ridicule, embarrassment, shame, and even sexual violence. In an alpha-male-dominated, testosterone-driven prison, the powerful prey upon the weak.

Pennsylvania's prison population is still divided by class, race, and sexual identification.

I was filled with regrets. I actually liked the compassionate King Duncan! As short as his part was—I was deeply touched by his assassination. But the roles called for the male actors portraying the women to sound effeminate—and to wear white flowers in their hair. Religious scruples aside, males portraying females is not widely embraced or encouraged. I discussed my concerns with Trevor, and he completely respected my decision, though expressed a deep disappointment that I couldn't stay—he tried in earnest to explain to me that in Shakespeare's time, it was normal for male actors to play the parts of female actresses. "But we're not in Shakespeare's time!" I shot back. "And prison is not normal."

Trevor envisioned an eclectic blend of characters to do his most ambitious project: *Julius Caesar*. This time, he brought in a partner from his theater company to assist him, fellow director and actor Dan Hodge. Trevor assured me that this particular play included a large cast of characters—several I might find appealing. He'd even brought in two gorgeous and talented female actresses to play Calpurnia, wife to Caesar, and Portia, wife to Brutus. I was stunned. The gesture meant the director had given serious thought to my private discussions that the addition of female actresses to the cast of Shakespeare plays would also give it more flavor, depth, and believability. Damn! How I wanted to play Mark Antony! I effortlessly memorized his entire eloquent speech at The Forum. But Trevor was quick to alert me to certain scenes in the play that called for Mark Antony to bow in subservience to Caesar. There was a final selection of actors chosen to play the parts. The role of Mark Antony went to another cast member, a young, gifted rapper we call "Moose." I was Octavius Caesar: the loyal nephew who swore to exact a horrible vengeance upon the traitors for the foul murder of his beloved uncle. I dropped hints to the directors that I thought fellow prisoner Larry Stromberg was an ideal Julius Caesar. He should play the part. After all, he was already an accomplished actor on stage and in films and had been a member of the Screen Actors Guild before his conviction.

Rehearsals were twice weekly. And loud. At times, there were heated arguments. I got frustrated by some actors' inability to even remember one simple line. "Yo, man, we have to get this right! How many times we gotta keep going over this with you?" I yelled at fellow cast mates. I'd even snapped at Stromberg/Caesar, who struggled with his lines, at times. I experienced a wide range of emotions, some poured through my eyes, or in the way my thick, stocky, muscular physique moved about the stage with a confident, deliberate, thuggish swagger.

I dove into my lines. I felt a gravitational pull so strong I was flung far back to the Capitol City of Rome. It was also an out-of-body experience on a winged chariot that transported me to an alternate reality. One day, prisoners passing by my cell paused mid-flight, and gave me a quizzical look as I practiced drawing my sword, perfecting Octavius's menacing stare as he confronted the traitors in Act 5, Scene 1, the meeting with the traitors at the plains of Phillippi:

> Look, I draw a sword against conspirators;
> When think you that the sword goes up again?
> Never, till Caesar's three and thirty wounds
> Be well avenged, or till another Caesar
> Have added slaughter to the words of traitors.
>
> (5.1.54–58)[1]

The hawk-eyed/ear-hustling inmates could not have known that I was in a zone; that I was psyching myself up for the final scene that would define who Octavius was. Besides being a nephew of Julius Caesar—(he was also said to be Caesar's son)—what was he made of? My eyes blazed with a murderous rage as I paced back and forth inside my cell. A rumor soon spread about the prison that "Reggie Lewis was talking to himself." In the culture of prison, the suspension of disbelief as it relates to artistic expression is a thin blurred line. The lower primal regions of their minds could not disassociate the negative label of a former death row inmate from the higher forms of the arts in which I was being trained. Nor could the wide gulf between the crime of which I was unjustly convicted be separated from the violence in Shakespeare's play. Was I planning to do something crazy? Or suffering from some kind of psychotic break? The directors had instigated the tension between Octavius and Mark Antony in the scene before the two armies clashed:

> ANTONY: Octavius, lead your battle softly on,
>   Upon the left hand of the even field.
> OCTAVIUS: Upon the right hand I; Keep thou the left.
> ANTONY: Why do you cross me in this exigent?
> OCTAVIUS: I do not cross you; but I will do so.
>
> (5.1.17–21)

"Mark Antony could be setting a trap," Dan Hodge suggested. "Remember, Reggie, Octavius doesn't trust him." Dan had a point. I was warned not to trust the playboy, who'd played everyone against each other, had laid plans for succession to the crown, and felt he was far more experienced in battle than

Octavius, who was just a boy to him. Octavius insisted on proving himself in battle by leading the charge.

From the very beginning, prison officials were often hostile to the idea of prisoners performing Shakespeare, who spoke truth to power, exposed the vicious primal nature of the human soul: avarice, lust, greed, ambitions, betrayal, evil, darkness, deceit, treachery, and murder. Even though visitors/volunteers had approval to enter the prison, there were days they were denied entry. The directors and actresses were often harassed and interrogated at the gate. A few other times, the actors were told rehearsals had been canceled when they were not—or deliberately misdirected to empty classrooms. At its core, they feared the riotous nature of the play could easily spark a rebellion among the restless captives and held the potential to threaten the authority and security of the prison. The play eerily reflected the perpetual, internal power struggle for control and dominance within the seedy bowels of the prison industrial complex—a sprawling empire. Its inhabitants are an aggrieved, restless brood. Prison officials are certainly ambitious and have greater aspirations of rising through the ranks. Julius Caesar was assassinated by those closest to him who feared his ascension to the crown would consolidate a tyrannical power and unquestionable authority over the masses. The titular head of the prison is seen as, well, "Caesar."

Oh, how we fought for our proposals—most were rejected, or stamped "DENIED." Suddenly everything was attached to "security concerns." Even requests for the shiny plastic toy swords and knives and fake blood (ketchup). Really? I'd emphasized the need for authentic costumes, arguing that, after all, William Shakespeare saw Octavius Caesar as skilled, loyal, honorable—and adorned in a costume festooned with military medallions and regalia of a Great Roman General, leading his troops (in battle gear), to victory in Phillipi. The response: "No." That a former aggrieved death row inmate was at the vanguard of a simulated battle made the officials in this particular administration, well, extremely nervous. As a last resort, an outside theater was willing to lend us Shakespearean costumes. Their response: ditto. Finally, we were approved for a nominal budget. In the end, we had to settle for white sheets, thin, flimsy red and blue capes and small, rubbery toy swords. I'd even commissioned a skilled artist to do the colorful poster for the event: THE PHOENIX THEATER PRESENTS JULIUS CAESAR. After Octavius Caesar led his army to triumphant victory in the bloody battle at Phillippi, for the final scene, I'd walk downstage, and face the audience:

> With all respect and rites of burial.
> Within my tent his bones to-night shall lie,
> Most like a soldier, order'd honourably.—
> So, call the field to rest: and let's away,
> To part the glories of this happy day.

(5.5.82–87)

One week before our first performance of *Julius Caesar*, Trevor called in sick. The play was canceled. The great tragedy of the COVID-19 pandemic struck the nation and the world. Prisons across Pennsylvania were shut down. Volunteers could no longer enter. Visits were suspended. Prisoners were dying on every cell block. The infirmary was filled with bodies. I was devastated by this cruel monstrosity, which struck so close to the opening performance. It was as if Shakespeare's Soothsayer had portended doom for our magnificent cast—victimized by some tragic conspiracy, some wicked plot, devised by traitors and enemies of the arts. A funereal gloom fell over the multitude in the prison like a dark cloud. It was all so surreal. For weeks on end I'd poured my heart and soul into every scene, every line, where Octavius Caesar was called. Two weeks before Trevor went down, the directors were so proud of us they invited an accomplished Shakespearean actress to sit in on the rehearsals. She assured us prison actors were by far better than actors she'd worked with in Broadway productions of Shakespeare. "Believe me, Shakespeare is intimidating," she said. I beamed proudly. What a compliment!

Coming all the way up from the dark, dungeon-like conditions of death row, I'd made a grand entree into the rich, exotic world of the great playwright William Shakespeare that few prisoners in America get to experience. His work provided the keys that unlocked streams of consciousness in my mind where I was unfettered, free. There was no concept of space or time or prison bars that contained my body. I can boast that I'm a proven natural Shakespearean actor who never got the opportunity to perform *Julius Caesar*. And yet, Shakespeare does, indeed, allow me to dream, to envision myself as the premiere actor among the first cast of prisoners permitted to leave the prison on tours performing Shakespeare before audiences across the country and in cities and towns around the world. I see myself…in full military regalia, on a flood-lit stage in Paris, Rome, Spain, Greece, England…and I hear the thunderous eruption of applause, at the final scene, of my performance… as Octavius Caesar, in William Shakespeare's *Julius Caesar*.

NOTE

1 William Shakespeare, *Julius Caesar*, eds. Barbara A. Mowat and Paul Werstine (Washington, DC: Folger Shakespeare Library, 2004). All subsequent citations refer to this edition.

Futures

Within and Beyond: Shakespeare Behind/BEYOND Bars

Sammie Byron and Curt L. Tofteland

Fifteen

Curt L. Tofteland founded Shakespeare Behind Bars (SBB) in 1995, making it the longest continuously running Shakespeare prison program of its kind in the United States. Long-time SBB member Sammie Byron continued to work with Tofteland upon his release in 2014 on a one-person show, *Othello's Tribunal*, which tours nationally. *Shakespeare in the Age of Mass Incarceration* editors Liz Fox and Gina Hausknecht engaged with Tofteland and Byron about the history, growth, and future of this important prison arts program.

Liz Fox (LF) and Gina Hausknecht (GH): For so many of us working with Shakespeare in Prison, whether in arts or education programs, the award-winning documentary *Shakespeare Behind Bars* **that follows your program through one production has served as the foundation for communicating what we do. You've been doing this work for over 30 years: how has SBB evolved over that time?**

Curt L. Tofteland (CT): SBB's philosophy, pedagogy, and practice continues to actively evolve as we learn from our successes and our failures. For example, on March 11, 2020, when the world-wide COVID-19 pandemic locked us out of face to face contact with our

DOI: 10.4324/9781003451662-20

participants inside prisons, we innovated and created Shakespeare BEYOND Bars virtual programs to serve returned citizens and incarcerated populations in isolated areas of the country, and offer a touring memoir production of one of our returned citizens and will soon add a second touring memoir production of another of our returned citizens.

LF & GH: What has remained constant about Shakespeare Behind Bars?

CT: Shakespeare Behind/BEYOND Bars' vision, mission, and core values have remained constant over our 30 year existence. SBB uses art, theater, the collected works of William Shakespeare, and journal writing to assist its participants with their human transformation from who they were to who they are to who they wish to become by answering four life questions: Who am I? What do I love? How will I live my life knowing I will die? What is my gift to humankind? Our program provides a consistent day of the week, time, and location, where incarcerated people, who self-select to participate, are approved by the prison administration and permitted to gather together to explore the universal question of what it means to be a human being. SBB offers the field of Arts in Correction a model for success in working with incarcerated and marginalized populations.

Sammie Byron (SB): When I was transferred from Luther Luckett and Curt's SBB program, I was sent to another prison where a Facilitator mirrored components of our SBB Program. With my joining their program, Shakespeare became a more authentic part of productions as the belief evolved from thinking Shakespeare had to be dumbed down, to realizing that if you are committed and truthful to a character, the audience will understand. When I arrived at the new Green River Correctional Complex, Shakespeare was not an option and mainly the focus was on contemporary plays, mostly comedy and this generated a nice break for the prison population. Like SBB we would do productions where civilians would come in to view our performance. The Facilitator introduced me and a brief history of SBB and my participation as a founding member. An audience member asked, "could you do some Shakespeare for me?" I asked, "what would you prefer to hear?" He said, "Henry V, Saint Crispin Speech." Yes, standing ovation! This action moved our Facilitator to expand her vision, to see "what dreams may come, / when we have shuffled off this mortal coil" (3.1.74–75).[1]

LF & GH: SBB has had a profound effect on so many lives and has influenced many other programs. What do you think is the source of this impact?

SB: The power of the epiphany that "life is about the noble attempt, not the product." The noble attempt for me is to support anyone who has the courage to do the very best they can, and to witness transformation—the exuberance of the "AHA MOMENT" when we dance as if no one else is watching. This is the truest form of art! If you go online and look up SBB you may find an image of me standing on the Rec Yard with a script in my hand coaching another SBB member. Mike could not speak without stuttering. However, when he performed Shakespeare, the stuttering went away! Mike's diction was as clear as day. That is the miracle of the Noble Attempt! Losing, winning, I couldn't care less, I thrive watching others' success, the end result means nothing to me.

CT: The program was founded to assist incarcerated people in finding their authentic voices through a deeply immersive experience with Shakespeare's original language, complex themes, and multiple meanings. Shakespeare Behind/BEYOND Bars continues to be a partner in helping to bear the burden of oppressed pain borne by society's marginalized populations, including the disenfranchised, disfavored, disinherited, and those who stand with their backs against a wall. The vision of Shakespeare Behind/BEYOND Bars is inspired by the belief that all human beings are born inherently good. Although some convicted criminals have committed heinous crimes against other human beings, their inherent goodness is not negated by their criminal deeds. That innate goodness lives deep within the individual and can be called forth by immersing participants in the sanctuary of a Circle of Truth and its creative process.

LF & GH: How do you see the effects of this process manifest?

SB: Acceptance, forgiveness, appreciation, and the brotherhood that remains alive in SBB Circle of Truth members.

These are my core values. Through them I find peace and satisfaction that I am not alone, ever! I do not seek to understand, but rather to live in the moment and enjoy the beauty and uniqueness of the world I choose to live in. I have taken a life that I can never give back and there is not a day that goes by that I don't think about my horrible act of selfishness. I never want to hurt anyone, ever again.

CT: The process has taught me how unresolved childhood trauma deeply affects how a traumatized child sees themselves: as a small, insignificant, and worthless human being who is merely taking up space, trapped in an unsafe world in which they are isolated and on their own as they attempt to navigate a violent existence. The process has taught me that we are not responsible for our trauma but that we are responsible for our healing from the trauma. SBB was created to give traumatized human beings a safe space to explore themselves and the tools they need to heal themselves. The process has reinforced my belief that art can assist "injured" human beings to heal and transform themselves into compassionate and empathetic people who move from being a taker from the world to a giver to the world. The process has reinforced my belief in the power of a Circle of Truth where our core values are accountability, acceptance, agency, authenticity, confidentiality, hope, humanity, inclusivity, kindness, listening, love, non-judgement, personal responsibility, reflection, respect, and silence, rather than stringent rules and strident regulations. Our core values govern how we will be with ourselves and each other when we sit in the Circle of Truth.

LF & GH: What has SBB and programs that follow its model made possible, for those who choose to participate?

SB: A deeper understanding of oneself through examining characters we choose to play. SBB Circle of Truth's power is embodied through acceptance fostered in a safe non-judgment environment, which creates the opportunity and motivation for personal growth. I have been fortunate to work in a field of helping others, teach young adults 16- to 24-years old these very same core values. I never tell anyone what to do, instead I share my experiences and allow them to choose. Then they will own it and appreciate it and share with others the miracle of having a Circle of Truth. No judgment.

LF & GH: And SBB also generated the show *Othello's Tribunal*, right? What are *Othello's Tribunal*'s origins?

CT: Yes, Sammie chose to play the role of Othello for the SBB 1999 annual production at the Luther Luckett Correctional Complex in LaGrange, Kentucky. After the performances concluded, Sammie felt that he was not done working on the role of Othello so we decided to continue our work together. Sammie and I created an adaptation of *Othello* in which Sammie plays Othello, Iago, and Desdemona in a 30-minute one act. After he was released, we launched the *Othello's Tribunal* "Give Back Tour" by offering free performances to incarcerated adult and juvenile populations, as well as to academic institutions, national conferences, and not-for-profit organizations that serve marginalized populations.

Today, we offer a one-hour performance of *Othello's Tribunal* followed by a post-performance talk-back with the audience. In the first 40 minutes, Sammie shares his life story, then he performs the scene from *Othello* where he plays Othello, Iago, and Desdemona, and he concludes with an epilogue where he reveals the reconnection and remarriage to his ex-wife, his new career as a youth career counselor for Goodwill Industries, and touring *Othello's Tribunal*.

SB: *Othello's Tribunal* is simply a sharing of my truth. "To thine own self be true," no excuses (1.3.84). Othello says, "Curse of marriage, / That we can call these delicate creatures ours / and not their appetites!" (3.3.309–311).[2] Before justification of any violence, there has to be a dehumanized labeling or separation. Othello called/labeled Desdemona a "Strumpet" to devalue Desdemona. For me to accept complete responsibility I had to accept the beauty and value of my victim to help me understand the harm I inflicted.

LF & GH: You've both discussed SBB members discovering themselves in Shakespeare's characters. How does *Othello's Tribunal* intersect with and respond to *Othello*?

SB: In a monologue when Othello speaks to Brabantio after the accusation that he had used witchcraft to woo Desdemona, he spoke in reference to Desdemona's admiration for him, that she often wept "when I did speak of some distressful stroke / That my youth had suffered" (1.3.181–182). Othello and my life paralleled that we had no remedy to deal with the emotional content forced because of abuse we both had suffered in our youth. At best all either of us could do was to adopt a world of black and white thinking with no gray area to take into consideration. If this equals this, then this shall be my only resort or action, because, lacking healthy emotional support and healing, both Othello and I were left to our own devices for self-protection. We were governed by adopted values which we unconsciously believed to be just; as Othello said, "I am abused, and my relief / Must be to loathe her" (3.3.308–309).

For me the conflict with my victim, "Carol," was weighing out the exact same scenario. Even though I never spoke the words, "I am abused," my conscience had adopted this belief. I went from zero to ten and I exploded and took a human being's life. My psyche was already armed through the unhealed trauma I carried and being in an unhealthy relationship fueled my insecurities in such a way that I believed that I had no choice.

CT: Working with Sammie on *Othello's Tribunal* has given me deep insights into the cyclical relationship, that unresolved childhood trauma has the potential for a traumatized victim to become the victimizer and pass their violence onto others creating more traumatized victims. As Sammie and I worked on *Othello's Tribunal*, we had deep conversations about how Sammie realized he had been a user and a taker as an adult incarcerated person who was sentenced to a life bit and would not be released from prison. However, that taker persona was not Sammie's authentic self but rather his prison persona that he created to self-protect within the violent harshness of prison culture. As time went on, Sammie realized that his authentic self was a kind, compassionate, and empathetic human being who was a giver and not a taker.

SB: Othello said, "I had rather be a toad / ... / Than keep in a corner the thing I love / for others' uses... / Tis destiny unshunnable, like death!" (3.3.311–316). This began my separation from Othello's choices and I realized that Othello was "frozen in time." The "thing I learned to love" was first myself, before I could love others authentically. I am the only one who can fix me. Through playing Othello and seeing the look of terror on Desdemona's face, I came to see the humanity of my victim, Carol. When I saw the disbelief, the fear, and the betrayal in Desdemona's eyes, my rage transformed to value life, when, at this instance, I recognized the harm I was inflicting, my thinking changed to focusing less on myself and more on others. I began to develop compassion and empathy and I changed my thinking from, "I have no choice" to "I always have a choice."

I once lived in a belief pattern that like computer programming, "if this equals this, then this shall be the answer." However, in computer programming there exists an alternative course of action, which is "the else statement," meaning, if this equals this, then this equals this, "ELSE I CAN CHOOSE A DIFFERENT REMEDY! I choose to live in the ELSE!

LF & GH: Can you say more about "the else statement"? What does it mean to you?

SB: For me, living with trauma created black and white thinking, meaning "if this conflict arises, then my only course of actions equal, this! The "ELSE Statement," provides healthy options/choices by acknowledging my darkness (trauma I carried) to recognizing and accepting (I feel hurt), which allows me to discover that the "then statement" can have healthy/positive outcomes. Essentially, the "ELSE Statement" allows for pause to fully examine all possible outcomes so I can use my discernment to make healthy choices. Before performing Othello in 1999 my greatest fear was "could I take another human's life?" In performing the death scene of Desdemona, I began to develop compassion and empathy, and acceptance that my reality is that I always have a choice.

LF & GH: Do you think Othello has a choice?

SB: Othello glosses over his trauma when referring to Desdemona, that often she wept, "when I did speak of come distressful stroke / That my youth had suffered" and later he states, "She loved me for the dangers that I had passed, / And I loved her that she did pity them" (1.3.193–194). As a warrior he does not have the capacity to show that vulnerability in detail for himself, but did so through the lens of Desdemona! For me this prompted my investigation of myself and the trauma I carried as an adult.

Othello's Tribunal continues to build itself within me, and to build me. I accept that I am a work in progress who will continue to develop until I no longer exist. Through forgiveness, I move forward. I don't live in my past, but I do live with grieving for the life that I am responsible for taking. I refuse to allow the loss of my victim's life to become dormant in my brain and perhaps resurface in a harmful way. *Othello's Tribunal* is a monument to the victim of my crime and to the sacredness of life. If I can use my abundant mistakes to help others not make the same or similar mistakes, then my life is filled with purpose and meaning. I never want to hurt anyone again. This is why examining my "root" is of the utmost importance.

In *The Tragedy of Othello*, there is no detailed back story of what leads to how Othello thinks or processes issues in his life. Othello was impulsive, governed by values cloned in black and white thinking. *Othello's Tribunal* details my back story not as an excuse, but rather as an understanding of where my "root" began and how it played out in my behavior. *Othello's Tribunal* is an examination of my root and my reconciliation, and is a pathway to healing.

LF & GH: *Othello's Tribunal* is one of many manifestations of SBB beyond prison. What do you take away from how SBB has moved beyond its original prison context?

CT: Doing the work of Shakespeare Behind/BEYOND Bars has assisted me in evolving into a more non-judgmental, compassionate, and empathetic human being.

SB: I wanted to use the tragedy of Othello to honor the tragedy of the life I took. Where I cannot compensate for the life I have taken, my hope is that through *Othello's Tribunal* I can effect change in others to choose a different path. I get the information I need by asking deeper questions. I actively work on embracing nonjudgement. There's no way for me to know what has transpired in the life of another human being and how those experiences influence how they behave. If I place significant value on others, then I will make positive choices regarding how I treat them, even when they don't act like I think they should. I don't have to agree with another's choices, but I must accept, respect, and allow them to be themselves. If I consider the "bad" behavior of those around me as their "fruit," then I can acknowledge that the problem is not so much with their behavior as it is with what causes that behavior, their "root." In *Othello's Tribunal*, I share my "root" with our audiences. How you judge me is not my decision, it's yours. It is my responsibility and creative opportunity to give back. I do that by creating space to help others realize their own potential.

I chose to take on this process [developing *Othello's Tribunal*] when I came to the realization that I might never get out of prison and, weighing the balance of that, my scale moved to the reality that "I can make prison my Prison or prison my University." My purpose became being a better human being and helping myself and others which gave my life meaning and purpose. I moved my thinking from "what I got to do" versus "what I get to do." I am very proud of the process of performing, editing, rehearsing *Othello's Tribunal*. I am constantly examining and exploring every nuance. I now have no fear of my past, present and future. I choose only to be more authentic in my life, everyday!

NOTES

1 William Shakespeare, *The Tragedy of Hamlet: Prince of Denmark*, eds. Barbara A. Mowat and Paul Werstine (Washington, DC: Folger Shakespeare Library, 2012).
2 William Shakespeare, *The Tragedy of Othello: The Moor of Venice*, eds. Barbara A. Mowat and Paul Werstine (Washington, DC: Folger Shakespeare Library, 2017).

Time Out of Joint: Taking Shakespeare
from Prisons to Schools

*Elder "Tariq" Beaudouin, Amiti Bey, Charles Hardy III,
Deena Hurwitz, Steve Rowland, Shamah ShaRize,
Mohendra Singh, and Caroline Young*

Sixteen

Time Out of Joint (TOOJ) is an educational experiment—and it is working. Unlike other programs represented in this volume, we do not teach in prisons; rather, we bring Formerly Incarcerated Teachers (FITs) to high school, college, graduate, and law school classrooms. The work gives a boost to people coming home while it provides profound experiences for students at many levels. Our ambition is to prove that people who study Shakespeare and other arts in prison should be hired nationwide to teach in various capacities.

HISTORY

The Time Out of Joint project began when educator and filmmaker Steve Rowland brought videos of the 2012 Globe-to-Globe festival into Woodbourne Correctional Facility in upstate NY. There he met Amiti Bey, a former Black Panther, who ultimately served 40 years in prison and earned a BA with an emphasis on theology and an MA in social work during that time. The workshops were taped, and Rowland made a film intended for classroom use called *Time Out of Joint: Prison Reflections on Shakespeare*. The film gives viewers an opportunity to "sit" in the back of a prison classroom as incarcerated men discuss *Othello*, *The Winter's Tale*, and *Henry IV, Part 1*,

DOI: 10.4324/9781003451662-21

bringing powerful insights to Shakespeare's themes as they are moved to reflect on their own life experiences and observations about American society. Incarcerated people often have novel insights and perspectives on Shakespeare. As Felix "Flex" Machado says in the documentary, "Iago lives down the cell block from me."[1] Comparing Macbeth's shortcut to power and wealth via murder to one's own lived experience of selling drugs or talking about the deadly brawl in *Romeo and Juliet* takes on a different flavor with men who know too well the experience of hand-to-hand combat.

Following Bey's release in 2020, he made regular Zoom visits to Rowland's interdisciplinary classes at Evergreen State College in Olympia, WA. Each discussion during Bey's visits was more powerful than the last. After seeing him in the film the students then got to speak with him directly. The impact of this experience on students was clear. According to one Evergreen sophomore:

> The video reminded me that as an individual I should express my thoughts rather than going with what everyone says. I misjudged the prisoners. Everyone has family and things that they care about. Instead of criticizing people for their differences and mistakes, people shouldn't be defined by their mistakes. In terms of Shakespeare, I was able to see how timeless Shakespeare's plays are.

Reflecting on these visits, Bey and Rowland were convinced that formerly incarcerated people who earned degrees inside could serve the world profoundly as teachers. Rowland and Bey recruited more people to create a diverse team that included other formerly incarcerated people along with two playwrights, two professors (one of U.S. and one of African American history), as well as a human rights attorney. In 2021, TOOJ formed a Steering

Committee and began to make their workshops available to classrooms across the country.

WHAT WE DO

TOOJ offers workshops via Zoom and in-person that place students and formerly incarcerated teachers and artists in conversation around Shakespeare and contemporary social issues that include racism and incarceration, as well as the overall power of education. Students prepare for the workshop beforehand by viewing the TOOJ film. Classes start with a FIT facilitating a circle of trust, leading with their own vulnerability and willingness to share their time and their life stories. This activity creates a safe space in which everyone can stay focused and present, say what is on their mind without fearing judgment, and encourage active listening. Then, we discuss the film, inviting students' observations and questions. Students are encouraged to ask anything: about prison life, education, or what landed the FIT in prison.

This initial discussion session often breaks down assumptions both about Shakespeare and formerly incarcerated people. Students often ask how long the FITs were incarcerated, how they survived violence, when they first encountered Shakespeare, and what their experience of education inside was like. But one question we receive time and again is "Why Shakespeare?" Students wonder why people of color in prison would choose to read Shakespeare when they themselves find it such a chore and so alienating. We welcome the skepticism, and the FITs are always eager to respond to this question. For many of our FITs, Shakespeare became an important way for them to step into worlds different from their own and to use that perspective to better understand their own lives. Elder "Tariq" Beaudouin wrote:

> I view Shakespeare as a revolutionary writer and thinker. I have learned that there are not separate White or Black Histories, but just one complex history of knowledge and advancement across the globe. All people should be honored. Some people use knowledge to keep people in categories. I try to use knowledge to build bridges and honor each student as a human being, no matter what their background.

Bey sometimes tells students about a moment when he was surrounded by a group of men in the prison yard who warned him to "lay off Shakespeare—it is the white man's poison." He looked them in the eyes and told them to get out of his way, telling them "Shakespeare is one of my links to humanity." Bey describes his sense of connection with "an old white dude's disaffection with the things that he lived through every day there in Elizabethan England. The brother was a genius at unraveling mysteries and motivations of the mind. I saw his depth of analysis, clean cut to the socio-psychic bone." Another FIT, Shamah ShaRize, brings an artist's perspective to the discussion, pointing out that Shakespeare created lasting stories of betrayal, love, hate, and jealousy that speak to us 400 years later. As an artist and writer himself, ShaRize tells students that he would like his writing to be timeless, to create work so great it gets passed down for ages and creates change in the process.

Following these exploratory discussions, we turn to one of our core activities: pairing texts. This method, following a model developed by the Folger Library Education Department, places Shakespeare scenes side-by-side with a modern text dealing with a similar theme. TOOJ, instead of pairing scenes from Shakespeare with published material or well-known authors, employs original texts written by our FITs. We call these texts "Prison Monologues" (for an example of a Prison Monologue, see the Appendix). Our FITs have written about solitary confinement, violence, saying farewell to family, shared dreams, love, and experiences of transformation. Pairing texts is a powerful way to get students to see Shakespeare in a new light. Traversing back and forth between past and present affords the opportunity to consider how Shakespeare reflected on his time and issues, and how contemporary writers reflect and respond today. Because the FITs are contemporary authors writing about their lives and times, students more readily grasp that Shakespeare was an artist observing his own world. We invite students to read the Prison Monologues out loud and, in doing so, step into the shoes of its author, a man telling his story from 27 or 40 years in prison. They also get to speak to that living author about his writing process as well as his understanding of Shakespeare's plays.

The discussions that follow the pairing text activity are vibrant as students often find a new entry point to engage with Shakespeare's writing. The conversations are candid, meaningful and personal, about power, racism, revenge, forgiveness, and love. For instance, we had a discussion about fatherhood centering on King Henry in *Henry IV, Part 1* wishing Hal and Hotspur had been switched at birth. The scene was paired with a Prison Monologue by Mohendra "Tony" Singh about an abusive father who drove him into the streets. Two women in the class shared that they understood both fathers because their fathers were also emotionally abusive. The conversation that ensued was moving—and while it was not all about King Henry, the entire class came away with a deeper understanding of Shakespeare, themselves, and each other. As a final step to our workshop, students do their own writing and reflection, inspired by our conversations. In these highly interactive classes, stereotypes about incarcerated people, as well as those about Shakespeare, begin to dissipate as students experience the value of critical thinking and creative writing as tools to engage with and critique the world around them.

THE IMPACT WE HAVE

The impact of this work is immediately apparent to all participants. Reading Prison Monologues sparks new sensitivities across differences and lived experiences for students. The monologues challenge students' understanding of incarceration. Reading the monologues aloud and embodying those stories and characters touch them at deep emotional levels as humans. Much like Shakespeare's work, the Prison Monologues draw on universal emotions such as shame, fear, isolation, and compassion. Students become stronger readers and writers after TOOJ workshops, but, more importantly, they become more empathetic people. As one student wrote in their reflection following the workshop, "I think that I could have benefited from hearing these stories earlier in my life. I know that I am benefiting now." Students, and college students in particular, are trying to figure themselves out as developing adults, and the wisdom they absorb from the FITs leaves a lasting impression.

The TOOJ project benefits our Formerly Incarcerated Teachers (FITs) in a variety of ways as well. Practically speaking, it puts money in the pocket. Emotionally, they are moved to hear students read their work and have the benefit of seeing their stories, experiences, and writing affecting young people in a classroom, something they could not have imagined when they were in prison. TOOJ is a space where FITs teach, learn, and produce original material and then have the privilege of hearing students from different backgrounds recite that work. "The joy from seeing your literary child born regardless of flesh or scribe is insurmountable," ShaRize has said of this experience.

Moreover, TOOJ offers an opportunity for FITs to take on an authoritative role by teaching young people to appreciate Shakespeare, self-expression, and the value of education. This authority in the classroom setting has deep significance for men who suffered in a system that sought to dehumanize them and degrade their intelligence. As Elder "Tariq" Beaudouin describes:

> We are educators, counselors, veterans of street wars who have lived seeking forgiveness for some parts of our lives. We are people who use our past experiences to help reach out to youth in need of reality talks. We share our hearts, minds, past and present joys and pains, our weaknesses and strengths. Our vulnerabilities are open to help others look at life from another's reality via our prison monologues.

The FITs are not only exceptional writers, but they are also patient and compassionate mentors. As teachers with TOOJ, formerly incarcerated people can see in real-time that another person has benefited from some knowledge or experience that they had. Singh, who was deported to Guyana after 27 years of incarceration, refers to TOOJ as "My little pebble in the pond to cause the ripple effect. It showed me how I can use my life experience to teach and help/inspire others."

OUR CORE BELIEFS

We believe that using Shakespeare and the arts in the pursuit of social justice can change lives.

1. FITs are always paid for their work. Since its inception, TOOJ has been committed to paying FITs. Early grants from The Library of Congress' "Teaching with Primary

Sources (TPS)" division, and the National Endowment for the Arts made this possible. Continuing grant funding from Humanities New York, The Library of Congress, The American Folklife Center, and small private foundations has allowed TOOJ to offer workshops without charge to schools.

2. We provide support and community for those navigating reentry. Returning home from prison poses enormous obstacles. We address some of these barriers to reintegration by offering FITs a sense of community, and an opportunity to continue processing their own lives. While incarcerated, the men had a sense of being connected to others sharing their experience inside. As they navigate society post-release, they often have fewer friends. TOOJ provides a community. Our regular meetings are places where people can connect and share resources. The FITs keep in close touch via phone and emails offering support to one another as they develop new monologues and traverse life after prison.

3. By creating a successful model for employing formerly incarcerated people as teachers, we advocate for the employment of returning citizens. We would be thrilled if this concept spread widely. Through our classroom visits and workshops, we aim to spark national conversation about employing formerly incarcerated people.

With these three core beliefs at its foundation, TOOJ has weathered its early growth and curriculum developments. Although our grant-funded workshops cost schools nothing, finding teachers who will invite us into their classrooms proved a challenge early on. We are now in the early stages of growing our program and our hope is that as we expand, we might serve as a model for other reentry programs and foster communities that believe in the value of teachers with diverse backgrounds, including people who are formerly incarcerated.

APPENDIX: A PRISON MONOLOGUE

William Shakespeare, excerpt from *Richard II*

> I have been studying how I may compare
> This prison where I live unto the world,
> And for because the world is populous
> And here is not a creature but myself,
> I cannot do it. Yet I'll hammer it out.
>
> My brain I'll prove the female to my soul,
> My soul the father, and these two beget
> A generation of still-breeding thoughts,
> And these same thoughts people this little world,
>
> ...
>
> ...Sometimes am I king.
>
> Then treasons make me wish myself a beggar,
> And so I am; then crushing penury
> Persuades me I was better when a king.
> Then am I kinged again, and by and by
> Think that I am unkinged by Bolingbroke,
> And straight am nothing. But whate'er I be,
> Nor I nor any man that but man is
> With nothing shall be pleased till he be eased
> With being nothing.
>
> (5.5.1–41)[2]

Shamah ShaRize, excerpt from "Solitary Freedom"

> The box changes u
> Makes u a stranger u

Existing without my favorite anything
Haven't experienced natural light
3 years & counting
No birds fly
No dogs bark
The walls refuse to hug
Pigeon-like meat for Sunday dinner
On the chow
On the count
On the yard that I refuse to go
I refuse to show
The emptiness
They'll never know
How much I wanna go
Away from here
I hate it here
Then I think...
Glad I made it here.

......

I did time behind time
Behind walls behind walls
In prison while in prison
My box was in a box
I walk how I talk
Not outlined in chalk
Blame no one
My fault
My decision my choices
At times I heard voices
Maybe angels on my shoulders
That chapter
In a folder
Fold
Closed

Existing without my favorite anything
Now I'm my favorite everything...

NOTES

1 *Time Out of Joint: Prison Reflections on Shakespeare*, directed by Steve Rowland (CultureWorks, 2021), https://www.tooj.org/.
2 William Shakespeare, *Richard II*, eds. Barbara A. Mowat and Paul Werstine (Washington, DC: Folger Shakespeare Library, 2005).

Marin Shakespeare Company and the Returned Citizens Theatre Troupe

Lesley Schisgall Currier

Seventeen

Anyone who has been to prison has experienced trauma and has dreamed about "going home." Yet getting out of prison comes with its own set of challenges. As I write this, this week I've tried to help a young man on parole sleeping in his car find a place to live, connected an accomplished hip hop musician who left San Quentin years ago with a massively talented musician who has been home less than two months, and commiserated with a Returned Artist dealing with a myriad of family issues, car problems, and spotty internet service. In California, you leave prison with a change of clothes, your personal property in a trash bag, and $200. If friends and family don't pick you up, you are dropped at the local bus station–and good luck getting to your parole officer in time if you need to be in a different county. Other challenges include getting an I.D., navigating modern technology, getting a job, finding a place to live, and dealing with parole officers who can be obstructive or helpful, and much more.

Marin Shakespeare Company (MSC) is a professional Shakespeare theater based in San Rafael, California, founded in 1989 by my husband Robert and me. The company presents summer plays at the Forest Meadows Amphitheatre on the campus of Dominican University in San Rafael, and more recently at the Center for Performing Arts, Education, and Social Justice in downtown San Rafael, completed in 2023,

DOI: 10.4324/9781003451662-22

a year-round venue with a 165-seat theater. In addition to performances, the company also provides arts education programming for youth and adults. Marin Shakespeare Company is just a few miles from California's oldest and most storied prison, San Quentin.

In 2003, I was inspired by Curt L. Tofteland's Shakespeare Behind Bars and several of our Board members to try to offer a Shakespeare class at San Quentin. Two years later, I hired Shakespearean actor and Drama Therapist Suraya Keating to teach at San Quentin; Suraya brought a wealth of knowledge about trauma-informed teaching and healing through the arts. We began calling this new program Shakespeare for Social Justice (SSJ). As SSJ grew, we created a Drama Therapy-inspired curriculum that focuses on self-reflection, self-expression, emotional intelligence building, problem-solving, teamwork, and appreciations. Groups rehearse and perform a Shakespeare play or adaptation, as well as Parallel Plays, where participants use themes from Shakespeare to inspire their own original work that includes short plays, spoken word, songs, and sometimes dances. As of 2024, SSJ has performed 22 different Shakespeare plays and 11 years of Parallel Plays at San Quentin. SSJ later inspired MSC's Acting for Veterans program, which supports veterans and others telling stories about military service through theater. A rich video archive on YouTube preserves the work of both programs.

Starting in 2014, SSJ expanded to other state prisons when funding became available through the California Arts Council's Arts-in-Corrections and California Department of Corrections and Rehabilitation's Innovative Grants programs. Prior to this, we facilitated classes at San Quentin for over a decade with basically no funding, except a few small grants and some private donations. State funding allowed our program to eventually serve 14 state prisons, five of which have now permanently closed, as California's prison system has reorganized—and, happily, shrunk.

As the SSJ program expanded to more prisons, participants started being released from prisons, as California elected Democratic governors which greatly increased parole possibilities for people with life sentences. With new possibilities for parole came a new possibility for MSC. Some of our participants wanted to continue the work of SSJ which had become so valuable to their well-being while inside. Reflecting on his time inside, actor Pharoah Brooks recalls, "The Shakespeare group helped me, because it allowed me to express different emotions, and create together as a team. I was encouraged to be funny, be deeply emotional, write, make music, and to help lead others in making each production a success." For some men and women, SSJ was an important part of their lives; it had become a family, as well as an essential support network for dropping out of gangs and/or living a pro-social life. While inside, many participants dreamed of seeing Marin Shakespeare Company's professional productions, and, one day, being part of the company.

With no clear funding source, but the adamant belief that a good idea is worth trying, MSC created the Returned Citizens Theatre Troupe (RCTT). We paid members $20/hour (now $25/hour) to rehearse and perform, using theater as a tool to tell important stories and share them with the community, sparking rich dialogue. After the first year, an individual donor gave us $5,000 to continue RCTT for a second year. Following the demonstrable successes of the program, we secured grants to continue the program.

RCTT began with mostly men from San Quentin, who were already experienced creating Parallel Plays. Under the guidance of Suraya Keating, they quickly decided that they wanted to tell stories about their lives in prison, how they got to prison, how they got out of prison, and how they were coping with the challenges of living on the outside. Notable stories have included what it is like to spend a year in solitary confinement, getting sober behind bars, the bus ride from juvenile detention to San Quentin, and the expectation vs. the reality of reuniting with family post-incarceration. Suraya and I supported the choice to share experiences of incarceration and its lasting effects rather than continue to center Shakespeare's plays. There are many reasons to perform Shakespeare inside that don't necessarily continue outside. For example, inside we have large groups and wait lists, so we need to perform material that accommodates large casts. Outside, we have much smaller groups of men and women—typically five to eight per cast. Inside, we believe Shakespeare helps actors to access big emotions, complex personal relationships, and heightened language. RCTT participants had already benefited from engaging with and learning from Shakespeare but were ready to tell more contemporary stories. The group believes that sharing personal narratives builds empathy, fosters understanding, and underscores communication. Shakespeare continues to inspire, continues to be a jumping off place for these artists—yet their most urgent stories are about their own lives and futures.

One of the greatest barriers to reentry for people who are justice-impacted is finding a job and MSC is committed to offering paid opportunities for participants in our programs. Since 2015, MSC has hired over 25 Returned Artists and created 12 original theater pieces, providing income which, one participant told us, "has been crucial in stabilizing my financial situation post-incarceration." During the pandemic in 2021, we hired Returned Artists to perform and record writing from people who were currently incarcerated. Since MSC was unable to teach in-person in prisons, we provided "Alternative Programming" packets which gave participants opportunities to explore themselves through writing and other prompts. MSC has hired Returned Artists for our professional productions, most notably Dameion Brown who played Othello, Benedick in "Much Ado About Nothing," Pericles, Oberon in "A Midsummer Night's Dream," and Macbeth with MSC, and who became a full-time salaried Artist in Residence for several years. In 2024, MSC hired Returned Artists for our Shakespeare for Student Audiences production of "Julius Caesar Twisted," an adaptation in which men in a prison are watching a TV show about the history of Julius Caesar that shows scenes from Shakespeare's play—meanwhile the action inside the fictional prison mirrors the story of a leader grown too ambitious, who is taken down by foes and friends. MSC has also hired members of RCTT to perform their Solo Shows for public audiences at our new theater, and for system-impacted youth at Marin Juvenile Hall, and other locations. We have hired Returned Artists as Teaching Artists for system-impacted youth at Youth Correctional Facilities, as trainers for Teaching Artists who work in prisons, and to create the Prison Primer found on our website, along with other training materials. Additionally, the permanent collection of artwork that hangs at our new theater feature pieces that were commissioned and/or bought from Returned Artists.

Another barrier to reentry is community. People coming home following their incarceration often feel isolated from their friends and families. RCTT has created a peer support network, with shoulders to cry on and people who can offer concrete information about overcoming the challenges of life after prison. It has offered creative outlets, allowed artists to connect to other creative opportunities, and provided artists a platform to tell their own stories, building compassion and understanding.

Over the past 20 years, we have learned some important lessons about teaching Shakespeare in prison. What is most important is the value of the work for participants; this means meeting each person where they are and using Shakespeare as a tool to stimulate growth. Some actors are fulfilled by memorizing and performing large roles; for others, the experience of classroom exercises and being part of a team is the most impactful part of the program. The performance itself is secondary to the learning process. Of course, a wonderful performance brings personal fulfillment, and the respect of peers and staff and community members. But the performance is a means to an end—inspiring healing, and self-growth. We have also learned that promoting creative freedom is liberating to the mind and spirit; we encourage actors to make the work their own, add their own songs, poems, jokes, and ad libs. We recognize that Shakespeare is a dead white man; there is implicit racism, misogyny, and antisemitism in the texts. We use these as opportunities to discuss how these things continue to affect us today, and how they have changed over time. Some have questioned whether Shakespeare still has a place in a theater ecology dedicated to inclusion and diversity. We believe that there remains great power in engaging with Shakespeare's themes and language, while recognizing the many issues of importance to us today that are not in Shakespeare's texts. The scripts are so elastic—with opportunities to cut, adapt, add and delete characters, and add original material—that they remain powerful tools for working in prisons, with groups of typically 20 to 25 actors. Plus, they are in the public domain, so we can share videos of performances online. We have offered groups in prisons opportunities to take a break from Shakespeare and have found that while the artists love creating their own work, they still want to engage with Shakespeare's rich and rewarding texts.

The benefits to the Returned Artists of performing their own original work are similar and different from the benefits to performing artists inside prison. Both groups get to be part of a peer network, a "family" of support, people who have faced similar challenges and can provide wisdom and love. In addition, there is the benefit of continuing self-reflection, self-expression, teamwork, problem-solving, and appreciation. These build self-confidence, give actors a sense of worth, and reduce anxiety, loneliness, depression, and the concurrent threats of self-medication and self-harm.

Yet the work outside is different from the work inside as well. Participants are facing a myriad of different challenges—and the threats in a world that is far less controlled than the world of prison. Participants have different needs—for cash, for specific information, and for legitimacy. The RCTT allows members to earn money, learn from each other in different ways, and to establish themselves as part of MSC, which gives them artistic and personal respect. Importantly, it allows them to continue self-reflection and emotional intelligence building through theater, and to engage in dialogue with each other and audiences about the issues that are most important to them. Actor Joey Pagaduan, who participated in our Shakespeare at Solano program for five years, has been involved with MSC in a variety of artistic capacities since his release. He tells us that, "MSC has cultivated a strong peer support network that has been instrumental in my reintegration into society. Being part of this troupe has allowed me to uplift my artistic voice and share my experiences through powerful performances, contributing to my sense of purpose and identity."

Members of RCTT have been involved with other exciting creative projects. Two members toured the U.S. as part of the cast of "The Box," a play about solitary confinement. Several other members are part of the Formerly Incarcerated People's Project, which now is associated with Berkeley Repertory Theatre, one of the nation's most successful LORT Theaters. Several artists have been hired by a former MSC Board Member who is the Head of a prestigious Marin private high school; they engage with students in arts classes and share their own lived experiences. Some RCTT members also serve as Artistic Associates for MSC, work that, as Pagaduan describes it:

> gives me a platform to influence the artistic direction of the company. This role has enabled me to collaborate with a diverse group of artists and administrators, ensuring that a wide range of perspectives and stories are represented in MSC's productions. The inclusive and supportive environment at MSC encourages artistic innovation and fosters a vibrant cultural community.

Other RCTT members are pursuing theater, video, painting, music and other art forms in a variety of ways.

When members of the public engage with Returning Artists—as audience members, or through their association with MSC or other organizations—it breaks down stigmas and barriers. After one performance, an audience member shared that a RCTT member's description of depression as "feeling like being in a dark hole it is impossible to climb out of" mirrored her own experience of depression. Following another performance, an audience member remarked that they didn't expect to hear stories that resonated with their own life at a Shakespeare theater; they were surprised by the vulnerability and honesty of the RCTT actors, which made them feel more comfortable talking about their own similar life challenges. Community members meet and learn to love and respect people who have survived incarceration; they learn about the detrimental effect of California laws such as the Three Strikes law passed by voters a couple decades ago after the brutal abduction and murder of Polly Klass. Community members develop compassion and understanding for people who have experienced the trauma of poverty, racism, and discrimination—all of which lead to the scourge of mass incarceration.

MSC and its programs don't solve all of the myriad challenges faced by Returned Artists. Although we pay these Returned Artists a higher hourly wage than the professional Actors we employ (members of Actors Equity Association), we have only rarely been able to hire Returned Artists as full-time employees. Often, the expectations participants have while inside do not match the realities of what MSC can provide outside. For example, we can't provide many of the basic needs—a full-time job, a place to live, a car. But we can provide a peer support network of people who have faced, survived, and thrived despite the post-incarceration challenges, the feelings of self-worth that comes from being a paid artist, and a platform to speak up about personal challenges and social change.

Programs that serve Returned Artists help the individuals themselves, but they also help us on the outside learn firsthand about the social issues that influence all of us today—and hopefully help us become more informed voters and more engaged citizens.

Bibliography

Ahnert, Ruth. *The Rise of Prison Literature in the Sixteenth Century* (Cambridge, UK: Cambridge University Press, 2013).

Alexander, Michelle. *The New Jim Crow: Mass Incarceration in the Age of Colorblindness* (New York: New Books, 2010).

Alexander, Patrick Elliot. "Education as Liberation: African American Literature and Abolition Pedagogy in the Sunbelt Prison Classroom," *South: A Scholarly Journal* 50, no. 1 (2017): 9–21.

Artze-Vega, Isis, et al. *The Norton Guide to Equity-Minded Teaching* (New York: Norton, 2023).

Atwood, Margaret. *Hag-Seed: The Tempest Retold* (London: Hogarth, 2016).

Bakhtin, Mikhael M. *Problems of Dostoevsky's Poetics*, ed. and trans. Caryl Emerson (Minneapolis: University of Minnesota Press, 2013).

Baldwin, James. "Why I Stopped Hating Shakespeare," *The Cross of Redemption: Uncollected Writings*, ed. Randall Kenan (New York: Pantheon, 2010).

Bates, Laura. *Shakespeare Saved My Life: Ten Years in Solitary with the Bard* (Naperville: Sourcebooks, 2013).

Belknap, Joanne. *The Invisible Woman: Gender, Crime and Justice*, 4th ed. (Los Angeles: SAGE Publications, 2015).

Benedetti, Jean. *Stanislavski & the Actor* (London: Methuen, 1998).

Betts, Reginald Dwayne. "Freedom Reads Project," www.freedomreads.org.

Betts, Reginald Dwayne. "Incarcerated Language," *The Yale Review*, October 1, 2018, https://yalereview.org/article/incarcerated-language.

Blagden, Nicholas, Jake Jones, and Kirsten Wilson. "'It Doesn't Matter What You've Done You're Accepted Here': A Multi-Site Qualitative Exploration of the Experiences of Being Incarcerated in Prisons for Individuals with Sexual Convictions," *Sexual Crime and the Experience of Imprisonment*, eds. Nicholas Blagden, Belinda Winder, et al. (Cham: Palgrave Macmillan, 2019).

Blank, David L. "The Arousal of Emotion in Plato's Dialogues," *The Classical Quarterly* 43, no. 2 (2009): 428–439.

Borrello, Stevie, Daniel Fetherston, and Katherine Tutrone. "Prisoners Are Going Viral on TikTok," *Vice News*, November 12, 2020, https://www.vice.com/en/article/7k9bzd/prison-inmates-are-going-viral-on-tiktok.

Boutry, Katherine. "Creativity Studies and Shakespeare at the Urban Community College," *Shakespeare and the 99%: Literary Studies, the Profession, and the Production of Inequity*, eds. Sharon O'Dair and Timothy Francisco (Cham: Palgrave Macmillan, 2019), 121–142.

Brown, David Sterling. "(Early) Modern Literature: Crossing the Color-Line," *Radical Teacher* 105 (2016): 69–77.

Brown, David Sterling. "'Unicorns and Fairy Dust': Talking Shakespeare, Performance, and Social (In)Justice with Ayanna Thompson and Farah Karim-Cooper," *Shakespeare Bulletin* 39, no. 4 (2021): 537–558.

Brown, David Sterling, Patricia Akhimie, and Arthur L. Little, Jr. "Seeking the (In)Visible: Whiteness and Shakespeare Studies," *Shakespeare Studies* 50, no. 3 (2022): 17–23.

Caliguiri, Zeke. "Foreword," *American Precariat: Parables of Exclusion*, ed. Zeke Caliguiri, et al. (Minneapolis: Coffee House Press, 2023), ix–xvi.

Castro, Erin L. "Racism, the Language of Reduced Recidivism, and Higher Education in Prison: Toward an Anti-Racist Praxis," *Critical Education* 9, no. 17 (2018): 1–14.

Cavanagh Sheila T., and Steve Rowland. "'Those Twins of Learning': Cognitive and Affective Learning in an Inclusive Shakespearean Curriculum," *Critical Survey* 31, no. 4 (2019): 54–64.

Cavecchi, Mariacristinia. "Brave New Worlds. Shakespearean Tempests in Italian Prisons," Special Issue, *Other Modernities: Journal of Literary and Cultural Studies* (2017): 1–21.

Chekhov, Michael. *Lessons For the Professional Actor* (New York: Performing Arts Journal Publications, 1985).

Chekhov, Michael. *On the Technique of Acting* (New York: Harper Collins, 1991).

Chekhov, Michael. *To the Actor* (Abington: Routledge, 2002).

Cheung, Caroline. "Abolition Pedagogy is Necessary," *Journal of Higher Education in Prison* 1, no. 1 (2021): 51–68.

Connell, R. W. *Masculinities* (Cambridge, UK: Polity, 1995).

Crenshaw, Kimberlé Williams, Luke Charles Harris, Daniel Martinez HoSang, and George Lipsitz, eds. *Seeing Race Again: Countering Colorblindness Across the Disciplines* (Oakland: University of California Press, 2019).

Crewe, Ben, Anna Schliehe, and Daria Aleksandra Przybylska. "'It Causes a Lot of Problems': Relational Ambiguities and Dynamics between Prisoners and Staff in a Women's Prison," *European Journal of Criminology* 20, no. 3 (2022): 925–946.

Dalton, Michael. *The Country Justice, Containing the Practice of the Justices of the Peace …* (London: Printed by the Company of Stationers, 1661).

Davis, Angela Y. *Are Prisons Obsolete?* (New York: Seven Stories Press, 2003).

Davis, Angela Y., Gina Dent, Erica Meiners, and Beth Richie. *Abolition. Feminism. Now* (Haymarket Books, 2022).

Davis III, James. "Law, Prison, and Double-Double Consciousness: A Phenomenological View of the Black Prisoner's Experience," *Yale Law Journal Forum* 128 (2018–2019): 1126–1144.

Davis, Simone Weil, and Barbara Sherr Roswell. *Turning Teaching Inside Out: A Pedagogy of Transformation for Community-Based Education* (London: Palgrave Macmillan, 2013).

Devereaux, Simon, and Paul Griffiths, eds. *Penal Practice and Culture, 1500–1900* (New York: Palgrave Macmillan, 2004).

Dobson, Michael. "James I Theory," *The Oxford Companion to Shakespeare*, ed. Michael Dobson (Oxford: Oxford University Press, 2015).

Dreier, Jenna. "Decolonising Pedagogies in Prison Performance Programmes: Making Shakespeare Secondary," *Research in Drama Education* 26, no. 3 (2021): 477–493.

Dreier, Jenna. "From Apprentice to Master: Casting Men to Play Shakespeare's Women in Prison," *Humanities* 8, no. 3 (2019): 1–24.

Dyson, Tony, and Derek Gadd. "Excavations at 9–11 Bridewell Place and 1–3 Tudor Street, City of London, 1978," *Post-Medieval Archaeology* 15 (1981): 1–79.

Edelstein, Barry, host. "Becoming King," *Where There's A Will* (podcast), November 2022, https://www.pushkin.fm/podcasts/where-theres-a-will-finding-shakespeare/becoming-king.

Eklund, Hilary, and Wendy Beth Hyman. "Introduction: Making Meaning and Doing Justice with Early Modern Text," *Teaching Social Justice Through Shakespeare: Why Renaissance Literature Matters Now*, eds. Hilary Eklund and

Wendy Beth Hyman (Edinburgh: Edinburgh University Press, 2020), 1–23.

Eschenbaum, Natalie K. "Modernising Misogyny in Shakespeare's Shrew," *Critical Survey* 33, no. 2 (2021): 31–42.

Evans, David. "The Elevating Connection of Higher Education in Prison: An Incarcerated Student's Perspective," *Critical Education* 9, no. 11 (2018): 1–14.

Filippine, Haley. "The Return to Tough-on-Crime: The Media's Role in Rolling Back Reform," *Criminal Law Practitioner*, March 20, 2024, https://www.crimlawpractitioner.org/post/the-return-to-tough-on-crime-the-media-s-role-in-rolling-back-reform.

Fisher-Grant, Kyle, Frannie Shepherd-Bates, and Matthew Van Meter. *Self-Efficacy, Empathy, and Community: The Long Term Benefits of Shakespeare in Prison involvement* (Detroit: Detroit Public Theatre, 2021).

Fisher-Grant, Kyle, Frannie Shepherd-Bates, and Matthew Van Meter. *Shakespeare in Prison Case Study Report* (Detroit: Detroit Public Theatre, 2019).

Fossati, Marta. "Transforming *Romeo and Juliet* in a Juvenile Detention Centre in Italy: A Decolonising Approach to Prison Shakespeare," *Shakespeare in Southern Africa* 36 (2023): 33–45.

Foucault, Michel. *Discipline and Punish: The Birth of the Prison*, trans. Alan Sheridan (New York: Vintage Books, 1995).

Foucault, Michel. *The History of Sexuality, vol. 1*, trans. Robert Hurley (New York: Vintage Books, 1990).

Freire, Paulo. *Pedagogy of the Oppressed* (New York: Bloomsbury Academic, 2014).

Gaither, Carl C. "Education Behind Bars: An Overview," *Journal of Correctional Education* 33, no. 2 (1982): 19–23.

Garner, Jane. "'Almost Like Freedom': Prison Libraries and Reading as Facilitators of Escape," *Library Quarterly: Information, Community, Policy* 90, no. 1 (2020): 5–19.

Gehring, Thom. "Post-Secondary Education for Inmates: An Historical Inquiry," *Journal of Correctional Education* 48, no. 2 (1997): 46–55.

Gilligan, James. *Violence: Reflections on a National Epidemic* (New York: Vintage Books, 1996).

Givens, Jarvis R., and Ashley Ison. "Toward New Beginnings: A Review of Native, White, and Black American Education Through the 19th Century," *Review of Education Research* 93, no. 3 (2023): 319–352.

Glass, Ira, and Jack Hitt, hosts. "Act V," *This American Life* (podcast), August 9, 2002, https://www.thisamericanlife.org/218/act-v.

Gorski, Philip. *The Disciplinary Revolution: Calvinism and the Rise of the State in Early Modern Europe* (Chicago: University of Chicago Press, 2003).

Gramlich, John. "What the Data Says About Crime in the U.S." April 24, 2024, https://www.pewresearch.org/short-reads/2024/04/24/what-the-data-says-about-crime-in-the-us/.

Greenlaw, Justin. Interview by Frannie Shepherd-Bates and Ashley Poulin, August 7, 2023, video, 00:49:20.

Griffiths, Paul. *Lost Londons: Change, Crime and Control in the Capital City, 1550–1660* (Cambridge, UK: Cambridge University Press, 2008).

Guan, Fang, et al. "Awe and Prosocial Tendency," *Current Psychology* 38, no. 2 (2019): 1033–1041.

Hall, Kim F. *Things of Darkness: Economies of Race and Gender in Early Modern England* (Ithaca: Cornell University Press, 1995).

Heard, Emma Marie, et al. "Shakespeare in Prison: Affecting Health and Wellbeing," *International Journal of Prisoner Health* 9, no. 3 (2013): 111–123.

Hendricks, Margo. "'I Saw Them in My Visage': Whiteness, Early Modern Race Studies, and Me," *White People in Shakespeare: Essays on Race, Culture, and the Elite*, ed. Arthur L. Little, Jr. (London: Bloomsbury, 2023), 191–198.

Herold, Niels. "Movers and Losers: Shakespeare in Charge and Shakespeare Behind Bars," *Native Shakespeares: Indigenous Appropriations on a Global Stage*, eds. Craig Dionne and Parmita Kapadia (Aldershot: Ashgate, 2008).

Herold, Niels. *Prison Shakespeare and the Purpose of Performance: Repentance Rituals and the Early Modern* (New York: Palgrave Macmillan, 2014).

Higinbotham, Sarah. "Education as Repair," *To Repair the Ruins: Reading Milton*, eds. Mary C. Fenton and Louis Schwartz (Pittsburgh: Duquesne University Press, 2012), 339–358.

Hirsch, Foster. *A Method to Their Madness: A History of the Actor's Studio* (Cambridge, MA: Da Capo, 2002).

Hoath, Ashley. Jpay message to Frannie Shepherd-Bates, January 25, 2024.

Hoffman, Diane M. "Reflecting on Social Emotional Learning: A Critical Perspective on Trends in the United States," *Review of Educational Research* 79, no. 2 (2017): 533–556.

hooks, bell. *Teaching to Transgress: Education as the Practice of Freedom* (London: Routledge, 1994).

Horstman, Fritzi. "Afterword," The Good Prison Officer: Inside Perspectives, ed. Andi Brierley (London: Routledge, 2023).

Howard, Jean E. "The White Shakespearean and Daily Practice," White People in Shakespeare: Essays on Race, Culture, and the Elite, ed. Arthur L. Little, Jr. (London: Bloomsbury, 2023), 265–276.

Howes, John. John Howes' MS, 1582: Being a Brief Note of the Order and Manner of the Proceedings in the First Erection of the Three Royal Hospitals, ed. William Lempriere (London: Septimus Morgan, 1904).

Ievins, A. "Prison Officers, Professionalism and Moral Judgement," Sexual Crime and the Experience of Imprisonment, eds. Nicholas Blagden, Belinda Winder et al. (Cham: Palgrave Macmillan, 2019).

Ignatieff, Michael. A Just Measure of Pain: The Penitentiary in the Industrial Revolution, 1750–1850 (New York: Penguin, 1978).

Jennings, Sue. Dramatherapy: Theory and Practice Volume 2 (London: Routledge).

Jiand, Tonglin, and Constantine Sedikides. "Awe Motivates Authentic-Self Pursuit via Self-Transcendence: Implications for Prosociality," Journal of Personality and Social Psychology 123, no. 3 (2022): 576–596.

Jones, Trevin. "The Ideological and Spiritual Transformation of Malcolm X," Journal of African American Studies 24 (2020): 417–433.

Jordan, June. Civil Wars (Boston: Beacon Press, 1969), 52.

Karim-Cooper, Farah. The Great White Bard: How to Love Shakespeare While Talking About Race (London: Viking 2023).

Keltner, Dacher. Awe: The New Science of Everyday Wonder and How It Can Transform Your Life (New York: Penguin Press, 2023).

Keltner, Dacher, and Jonathan Haidt. "Approaching Awe, a Moral, Spiritual, and Aesthetic Emotion," Cognition and Emotion 17, no. 2 (2003): 297–314.

Kendi, Ibram X. How to Be an Antiracist (New York: Random House Publishing Group, 2019).

Kilgore, James. "Bringing Freire Behind the Walls: The Perils and Pluses of Critical Pedagogy in Prison Education," The Radical Teacher 90 (2011): 57–66.

Kilgore, James. Understanding E-Carceration: Electronic Monitoring, the Surveillance State, and the Future of Mass Incarceration (New York: The New Press, 2022).

Kingdon, John Abernathy. Richard Grafton, Citizen and Grocer of London (London: Rixon and Arnold, 1901).

Kolb, Laura. "Feminine Performance in The Taming of the Shrew: Finale Speech and Missing Soliloquy," Renaissance Drama 50, no. 2 (2022): 133–158.

Lagemann, Ellen Condliffe. *Liberating Minds: The Case for College in Prison* (New York: The New Press, 2016).

Lee, Rachel, and Lisa Callahan. *Trauma-Informed Approaches Across the Sequential Intercept Model* (New York: The Council of State Governments Justice Center, 2022).

Lennon, John J. "The Prisoner and the Pen," *Esquire*, September 29, 2023, https://www.esquire.com/news-politics/a45191144/prison-free-writing-laws/.

Li, Jin. "The Effect of Preceding Self-Control on Prosocial Behaviors: The Moderating Role of Awe," *Frontiers in Psychology* 10 (2019): 1–9.

Little, Jr., Arthur L. "Introduction: Assembling an Aristocracy of Skin," *White People in Shakespeare: Essays on Race, Culture, and the Elite*, ed. Arthur L. Little, Jr. (London: Bloomsbury, 2023), 1–26.

MacFarquhar, Larissa. "Out and Up," *The New Yorker*, December 12, 2016.

Mackenzie, Rowan. *Creating Space for Shakespeare: Working with Marginalized Communities* (London: Bloomsbury, 2023).

Mackenzie, Rowan. "Producing Space for Shakespeare," *Critical Survey* 31, no. 4 (2019): 65–76.

Mackenzie, Rowan. "'Study Is Like Heaven's Glorious Sun'—Learning Through Shakespeare for Men Convicted of Sexual Offenses," *Humanities* 10, no. 1 (2021): 1–16.

Mackenzie, Rowan, Pheelix Obun, and Ralph Lubkowski, "'If to Do Were as Easy as to Know What Were Good to Do': The Rehabilitative Potential of Collaborative Theatre Companies in English Prisons," *Advances in Preventing and Treating Violence and Aggression*, ed. Madhumita Pandey (London: Springer, 2023), 209–226.

Marin Shakespeare Company. "Racial Equity Action Plan," https://www.marinshakespeare.org/wp-content/uploads/2021/06/Racial-Equity-Action-Plan-Policies-%E2%80%93-Final-6-1-21.pdf.

Mayo Clinic Staff. "Stress Relief from Laughter? It's No Joke," MayoClinic.org, https://www.mayoclinic.org/healthy-lifestyle/stress-management/in-depth/stress-relief/art-20044456.

Meisner, Sanford, and Dennis Longwell. *Sanford Meisner on Acting* (New York: Random House, 1987).

Melossi, Dario, and Massimo Pavarini. *The Prison and the Factory: Origins of the Penitentiary System, 40th Anniversary Edition* (London: Palgrave Macmillan, 2018).

Michaels, Samantha. "Books Have the Power to Rehabilitate. But Prisons Are Blocking Access to Them," *Mother Jones*, 2020.

Miller, Reuben Jonathan. *Halfway Home: Race, Punishment, and the Afterlife of Mass Incarceration* (New York: Little, Brown & Company, 2021).

Monaco, Pamela J. "Removing the Bars of Collaborative Shakespeare," *Actes des congress de la Societe Francaise Shakespeare* 37 (2019): https://doi.org/10.4000/shakespeare.4630.

Moody, Myles. "From Under-Diagnoses to Over-Representation: Black Children, ADHD, and the School-to-Prison Pipeline," *Journal of African American Studies* 20, no. 2 (2016): 152–163.

Moore, Sarah, and Tanya Erzen. "The Relationship Between Liberal Arts Classroom Experiences and the Development of Agency-related Wellbeing for Incarcerated Students," *Journal of Higher Education in Prison* 1, no. 1 (2021): 30–49.

Mullaney, Stephen. *The Place of the Stage: License, Play and Power in Renaissance England* (Ann Arbor: University of Michigan Press, 1988).

Murray, Molly. "Measured Sentences: Forming Literature in the Early Modern Prison," *Huntington Library Quarterly* 72, no. 2 (2009): 147–167.

Newman, Karen. "*The Taming of the Shrew*: A Modern Perspective," *The Taming of the Shrew*, eds. Barbara A. Mowat and Paul Werstine (New York: Simon & Schuster, 2014).

Nicklin, Laura Louise. "'Make Not Your Prisons Your Prisons': Participant-Perceived Potential Outcomes of a Shakespeare Focused Alternative to Juvenile Incarceration in the USA," *Emotional & Behavioural Difficulties* 22, no. 1 (2017): 1–16.

O'Dair, Sharon, and Timothy Francisco, eds. *Shakespeare and the 99%: Literary Studies, the Profession, and the Production of Inequity* (Cham: Palgrave Macmillan, 2019).

Orders Appointed to Be Executed in the Citie of London, for Setting Roges and Idles Persons to Worke, and for the Releefe of the Poore (London: Printed by J.Charlewood for Hugh Singleton, 1587), B2^v.

Orr, Gregory. *Poetry as Survival* (Athens: University of Georgia Press, 2002).

Papenfuss, Mary. "Shakespeare's Sonnets Are Banned In Texas Prisons. But Hitler's 'Mein Kampf' Is Allowed," *HuffPost US*, 2017.

Parker, Patricia A. *Literary Fat Ladies: Rhetoric, Gender, Property* (London: Methuen, 1987).

Pensalfini, Rob. *Prison Shakespeare: For These Deep Shames and Great Indignities* (New York: Palgrave MacMillan, 2016).

Perlin, Joshua D., and Leon Li. "Why Does Awe Have Prosocial Effects? New Perspectives on Awe and the Small Self," *Perspectives on Psychological Science* 15, no. 2 (2020): 291–308.

Pica-Smith, Cinzia, and Christian Scannell. "Teaching and Learning for this Moment: How a Trauma Informed Lens Can Guide Our Praxis," *International Journal of Multidisciplinary Perspectives in Higher Education* 5, no. 1 (2021): 76–83.

Pierce, Andre. "The Violence of Carceral Logics," *Resentencing: Poetry, Stories, Essays, and Visual Arts Reflecting on Incarceration with a Different Type of Sentence* 1, (2022): 151–152.

Piff, Paul K., et al. "Awe, the Small Self, and Prosocial Behavior," *Journal of Personality and Social Psychology* 108, no. 6 (2015): 883–899.

Pokornowski, Ess and Kurtis Tanaka. "Between Two Systems: Navigating Censorship and Self-Censorship in Higher Education in Prisons," *Ithaka S+R*, April 3, 2024.

Prior, Karen Swallow. "Why Shakespeare Belongs in Prison," *The Atlantic*, April 23, 2014.

Prison Policy Initiative. "Mass Incarceration: The Whole Pie 2024," https://www.prisonpolicy.org/reports/pie2024.html.

Quarmby, Kevin A. "Shakespeare in Prison: A South African Social Justice Alternative," *The Arden Research Handbook of Shakespeare and Social Justice*, ed. David Ruiter (London: Bloomsbury, 2021), 190–206.

Rackin, Phyllis. *Shakespeare and Women* (Oxford: Oxford University Press, 2005).

Roberts, Peter. *Religion, Culture, and Society in Early Modern Britain*, ed. Anthony Fletcher and Peter Roberts (Cambridge, UK: Cambridge University Press, 1994).

Rodenburg, Patsy. *Presence: How to Use Positive Energy for Success in Every Situation* (New York: Penguin Books, 2009).

Rogerson, Hank, director. *Shakespeare Behind Bars*. Philomath Films, 2006.

Rolston, Simon. *Prison Life Writing: Conversion and the Literary Roots of the U.S. Prison System* (Waterloo: Wilfrid Laurier University Press, 2021).

Rowland, Steve, director. *Time Out of Joint: Prison Reflections on Shakespeare*. CultureWorks, 2021, https://www.tooj.org/.

Ruiter, David. "This Is Real Life: Shakespeare and Social Justice as a Field of Play," *The Arden Research Handbook of Shakespeare and Social Justice*, ed. David Ruiter (London: Bloomsbury, 2022), 1–23.

Sanders, Julie. "In the Friars: The Spatial and Cultural Geography of an Indoor Playhouse," *Cahiers Élisabéthains* 88, no. 1 (2015): 19–33.

Scott, Robert. "Distinguishing Radical Teaching from Merely Having Intense Experiences While Teaching in Prison," *The Radical Teacher* 95 (2013): 22–32.

Scott, Simon. "Go in Young, Come out Old: The Challenges Facing People Serving Life Sentences," *Clinks Blog*, June 2023, https://www.clinks.org/community/blog-posts/go-young-come-out-old-challenges-facing-people-serving-life-sentences.

Scott-Douglass, Amy. *Shakespeare Inside: The Bard Behind Bars* (London: Continuum, 2007).

Schalkwyk, David. *Hamlet's Dreams: The Robben Island Shakespeare* (London: Bloomsbury, 2013).

The Sentencing Project. "Growth in Mass Incarceration," https://www.sentencingproject.org/research/.

Sered, Danielle. *Until We Reckon: Violence, Mass Incarceration, and a Road to Repair* (New York: The New Press, 2019).

Shailor, Jonathan. "Humanizing Education Behind Bars: Shakespeare and the Theater of Empowerment," *Challenging the Prison-Industrial Complex: Activism, Arts, and Educational Alternatives*, ed. Stephen John Hartnett (Urbana: University of Illinois Press, 2011).

Shailor, Jonathan. *Performing New Lives: Prison Theatre* (London: Jessica Kingsley Publishers, 2011).

Sharpe, J. A. *Crime in Early Modern England, 1550–1750*, 2nd ed. (New York: Longman, 1999).

Shakespeare in Prison blog, Detroit Public Theatre, https://www.detroitpublictheatre.org/the-sip-blog-parnall/tag/prison.

Skotnicki, Andrew. *Conversion and the Rehabilitation of the Penal System* (Oxford: Oxford University Press, 2019).

Slack, Paul. "Hospitals, Workhouses, and the Relief of the Poor in Early Modern London," *Health Care and Poor Relief in Protestant Europe, 1500–1700*, eds. Andrew Cunningham and Ole Peter Grell (London: Routledge, 1997), 229–246.

Smith, Amy L. "Performing Marriage with a Difference: Wooing, Wedding, and Bedding in 'The Taming of the Shrew,'" *Comparative Drama* 36, no. 3/4 (2002–2003): 289–320.

Smith, Ashley A. "Report Shows Benefits of Prison Education," *Inside Higher Education*, January 16, 2019.

Smith, Ian. *Black Shakespeare: Reading and Misreading Race* (Cambridge, UK: Cambridge University Press, 2022).

Spierenberg, Pieter. "Four Centuries of Prison History: Punishment, Suffering, the Body, and Power," *Institutions of Confinement: Hospitals and Prisons in Western Europe and North America, 1500–1950*, eds. Norbert Finzsch and Robert Jütte (Cambridge, UK: Cambridge University Press, 1996), 17–36.

Spivak, Gayatri Chakravorty. "The Rani of Sirmur: An Essay in Reading the Archives," *History and Theory* 24, no. 3 (1985): 247–272.

Stanislavski, Konstantin. *An Actor Prepares* (New York: Routledge, 2003).

Stein, Sharon. "Beyond Higher Education as We Know it: Gesturing Towards Decolonial Horizons of Possibility," *Studies in Philosophy and Education* 38, no. 3 (2019): 143–161.

Stellar, Jennifer E., et al. "Self-Transcendent Emotions and Their Social Functions: Compassion, Gratitude, and Awe Bind Us to Others Through Prosociality," *Emotion Review* 9, no. 3 (2017): 200–207.

"Steven Czifra on Shakespeare, Solitary Confinement and Marveling at the Ordinary," *Berkeley City College Voice*, December 7, 2018, https://bccvoice.wordpress.com/2018/12/07/steven-czifra-on-shakespeare-solitary-confinement-and-marveling-at-the-ordinary/.

Sweeney, Megan. "Books as Bombs: Incendiary Reading Practices in Women's Prisons," *PMLA* 123, no. 3 (2008): 666–673.

Tarwater, Charles. "The Mind Oppressed: Recidivism as a Learned Behavior," *Wake Forest Journal of Law and Policy* 6 (2016): 357–369.

Tawney, R. H., ed. *Tudor Economic Documents: Being Select Documents Illustrating the Economic and Social History of Tudor England*, 3 (London: Longmans, 1924).

Taylor, Charlie. *HM Chief Inspector of Prisons for England and Wales Annual Report 2022–2023* (London: Crown Copyright, July 2023), https://assets.publishing.service.gov.uk/government/uploads/system/uploads/attachment_data/file/1167739/hmip-annual-report-2022-23.pdf.

Taylor, Jon Marc. "Alternative Funding Options for Post-Secondary Correctional Education," *Journal of Correctional Education* 56, no. 1 (2005): 6–17.

Taylor, Satra, et al. "Why Race Matters for Higher Education in Prison," *Peabody Journal of Education* 96, no. 5 (2021): 588–597.

Thibodeau, Paul H., and Lera Boroditsky. "Metaphors we Think with: The Role of Metaphor in Reasoning," PLoS One 6, no. 2 (2011): https://doi.org/10.1371/journal.pone.0016782.

Thieme, Nick. "Georgia Prison Libraries Short on Books and Titles, AJC Analysis Finds," Atlanta Journal-Constitution, May 10, 2019.

Thompson, Ayanna, and Laura Turchi. Teaching Shakespeare with Purpose: A Student-Centered Approach (London: Bloomsbury, 2016).

Thompson, James, ed. Prison Theatre: Perspectives and Practices (London: Jessica Kingsley, 1998).

Tobin, Thomas J., and Kirsten T. Behling. Reach Everyone, Teach Everyone: Universal Design for Learning in Higher Education (Morgantown: West Virginia University Press, 2018).

Trounstine, Jean. "Beyond Prison Education," PMLA 123, no. 3 (2008): 674–677.

Trounstine, Jean. "Changing Women's Lives Through Literature," The Women's Review of Books 32, no. 3 (2015): 27–29.

Trounstine, Jean. Shakespeare Behind Bars: The Power of Drama in a Women's Prison (New York: St. Martin's Press, 2001).

Tucker, Jed B. "Malcolm X, the Prison Years: The Relentless Pursuit of Formal Education," The Journal of African American History 101 (2017): 184–212.

Ugelvik, Thomas. Power and Resistance in Prison: Doing Time, Doing Freedom (Cham: Palgrave Macmillan, 2014).

Ujiyediin, Nomin. "Missouri Prisons Ban Friends and Family from Sending Books to Prisoners," KCUR, August 29, 2023.

Underground Scholars Language Guide: A Guide For Communicating About People Involved in the Carceral System, March 26, 2019, https://undergroundscholars.berkeley.edu/blog/2019/3/6/language-guide-for-communicating-about-those-involved-in-the-carceral-system.

van der Kolk, Bessel. The Body Keeps the Score (New York: Penguin, 2014).

Wachter, Rachel De. "Power and Gender in The Taming of the Shrew," British Library, 2016, https://www.bl.uk/shakespeare/articles/power-and-gender-in-the-taming-of-the-shrew.

Wacquant, Loïc. "Class, Race, and Hyperincarceration in Revanchist America," Socialism and Democracy 28, no. 3 (2014): 35–56.

Walker, Brenda L. Townsend. "Teacher Education and African American Males: Deconstructing Pathways from the Schoolhouse to the 'Big House'," Teacher Education and Special Education 35, no. 4 (2012): 320–332.

Wang, Jackie. *Carceral Capitalism* (Cambridge, MA: Massachusetts Institute of Technology Press, 2018).

Ward, Sophie, and Roy Connolly. "The Play Is a Prison: The Discourse of Prison Shakespeare," *Studies in Theatre and Performance* 40, no. 2 (2020): 128–144.

Warr, Jason. "The Prisoner: Inside and Out," *Handbook on Prisons: Second Edition*, eds. Yvonne Jewkes, Jamie Bennett, and Ben Crewe (Abingdon: Routledge, 2016).

Wilcox, Agnes. "Denmark Is a Prison, and You Are There," *The Journal of the Midwest Modern Language Association* 38, no. 1 (2005): 116–122.

Wilson, Meagan, et al. "Unbarring Access: A Landscape Review of Postsecondary Education in Prison and Its Pedagogical Support," *Ithaka S+R*, May 30, 2019.

Wolff, Nancy and Jing Shi. "Adult Behavioral Health Problems and Treatment," *International Journal of Environmental Research and Public Health* 9, no. 2 (2012): 1908–1926.

Woodson, Carter G. *The Miseducation of the Negro* (Buffalo: E World Inc., 2012).

Wray, Ramona. "The Morals of Macbeth and Peace as Process: Adapting Shakespeare in Northern Ireland's Maximum Security Prison," *Shakespeare Quarterly* 62, no. 3 (2011): 340–363.

X, Malcolm, and Alex Haley. *The Autobiography of Malcolm X* (New York: Ballantine Books, 1992).

Yang, Ying, et al. "Elicited Awe Decreases Aggression," *Journal of Pacific Rim Psychology* 10 (2016): https://doi.org/10.1017/prp.2016.8.

Yeo, Jayme M. "Teaching Shakespeare Inside-Out: Creating a Dialogue Between Traditional and Incarcerated Students," *Teaching Social Justice through Shakespeare: Why Renaissance Literature Matters Now*, eds. Hilary Eklund and Wendy Beth Hyman (Edinburgh: Edinburgh University Press, 2021), 197–205.

Zelon, Helen. "The Shakespeare Redemption: Inmates in a Kentucky Prison Grapple with the Truths of Human Existence," *American Theater* 18, no. 8 (2001): 132–135.

Zim, Rivkah. *The Consolations of Writing: Literary Strategies of Resistance from Boethius to Primo Levi* (Princeton: Princeton University Press, 2014).

Index

abolition: movements and critiques 1–2, 5, 9, 82, 200, 218; education as a pathway 6–7
"Act V" podcast 108–110, 112–114
acting exercises and techniques 131; atmospheres 138–139; breathing techniques 165–166; Imaginary Bodies 140; Meisner Technique 133–136; memory and 132–133; The Method 132–133; Michael Chekhov Technique 134–136; "Muse of Fire mad libs" 167; *Presence* 165–166; sensations 137–138; Six Directions 136–137; stick/veil/ball 139–140; the "System" 132–133, 135; "Zip! Zap! Zop!" 166; *see also* Michael Chekhov Technique
affective memory 132–133, 135
"as if" 133–134
Atwood, Margaret 101–102
Auburn Correctional Facility 91, 100–101
awe 54–57, 61–63; prosocial effects 58; psychological studies 58–60

Blackfriars 31, 35
Brand, Phoebe 132–133
Bridewell prison 12, 31–34, 38

carceral system: arts programs 6–7, 13, 17–18, 72–73, 82–84, 189–190; education programs 6–7, 13, 69–70, 189–190; mass incarceration and systemic inequities 1–3, 5–6, 71–73; rehabilitation and punishment 4–6, 11, 37, 82–84, 102–103, 105–115
Center for Performing Arts, Education, and Social Justice 239–240
check-in/check-out, Redeeming Time Project (RTP) 163–164, 166–167, 170–171
Chekhov, Michael 134; *see also* Michael Chekhov Technique
childhood trauma 219, 222–223; *see also* trauma
Circle of Truth 218–220
college-in-prison programs 6–7, 13, 15–17, 57, 119–120, 195; inclusivity 125; inside-out model 14, 105–107, 113–114, 177; *see also* Liberal Arts in Prison Program (LAPP); Cornell University: Cornell Prison Education Program (CPEP); Engaging, Educating, and Empowering Means Change Program (E3MC)
colonialism 70–71, 81, 84–85, 100

community 56, 59, 63, 102, 121; post-incarceration 243–244
Cornell University 91; Cornell Prison Education Program (CPEP) 91–92
COVID-19 pandemic 17, 210–211, 215–216, 242–243
critical race studies 76–77, 80, 84–85
culture/cultural 28; capital 4, 10–12, 28; invasion 69–71, 74–75
Czifra, Steven 197–199

decarceration 17, 20; role of education and arts in 81–89, 243–244
decolonial practices: addressing colonial narratives 70–71, 83–84; facilitators' roles in decolonisation 72–77, 85; prison arts/education programs 81–89, 100–101
Detroit Public Theatre 15, 130; Shakespeare in Prison (SiP) 7, 15, 69–71, 130
Drake, Trevor 203–204, 206, 210
drama/dramatic: distancing 154, 156; therapy 81, 87
Dreier, Jenna 82, 87

early modern period 12, 28–29, 233; Bridewell 31–34, 38; English language 92, 193, 205; London 30–31
e-carceration 29
Emergency Shakespeare 16, 145, 149, 158; Creative Workshop programs 150; impact on actors 152; inaugural production of *Macbeth* 150–152; mentoring 152–153; performances 157; teamwork 152–153, 156–157
emotions 57, 97, 134–136, 166, 170–171; sensations 137–138;

shame 164–165; *see also* awe; trauma
empathy: building through theater 100, 121, 153; role in restorative justice 169–170, 219; fostering connections in carceral education 224
Engaging, Educating, and Empowering Means Change Program (E3MC) 105–108
ethics: challenges 35; in prison arts and education programs 14, 107
expansion mindset xviii, 3–5, 11, 105–108

facilitator(s): role in prison arts/education programs 71–77, 85, 88; forgiveness 50–52, 54–55, 94–96, 110, 115, 218–219
Formerly Incarcerated People's Project 246
Formerly Incarcerated Teachers (FITs) 18, 230–231, 233–234; Prison Monologues 232–233; *see also* Time Out Of Joint (TOOJ)
Foucault, Michel 28–29, 33, 84
Freire, Paulo 14, 84; "cultural invasion" 69–71, 74–75

gang violence 93, 98
gender, stereotypes 44, 175–176; *see also* women
Gilligan, James 165; *Preventing Violence* 107, 173
Greenwich Village, House of Detention 30
Grinnell College 117; Liberal Arts in Prison Program (LAPP) 117, 119–120

hard labor 31–32, 35
healing 47, 49, 74, 82, 88, 99, 219
heroism: explored through Shakespearean characters

15; reimagined in carceral settings 125
Herold, Neils 84, 114
Hitt, Jack 108, 111–114
Hodge, Dan 206, 208–209
house of correction 34–35, 37; *see also* Bridewell prison; prison
House of Detention 30–31
human flourishing: through education and arts 13, 73; role in prison programs in 83
human nature 13, 50, 52
humanism: building empathy 8, 12–13, 122–124; liberation through education and arts 4–5, 8–9, 54–57; redefining identity through Shakespeare 3, 9–10, 146–147
Hutchinson, Derrick 109–110

"ideal center" 136–137
identity 87, 154–155; clothing 179–181; incarcerated people 126–128, 147; relationship with language 183–184; memory and 118–119; narrative 130
incarcerated people 19, 129; clothing 179–181; English writers 27–28; identity 126–128, 147; infantilization 149–150; stereotypes 101, 103, 106, 120–121, 124–125; traumatic experiences 131–132; vulnerability 52–53, 131–132
inclusive/inclusivity: college-in-prison programs 125; pedagogy 85–86; prison arts/education programs 75–76, 80–81
infantilization 147, 149–150, 153
injustice 38, 71, 83, 88–89
inside-out model 14, 105, 113, 177; student training 106–107; teaching 114–115
institutional racism 71–73

James I Theory 193–195
justice 5, 88, 101; restorative 169–170, 172; social 7–9, 18–19, 235–236; *see also* injustice

language 19–20, 93, 100, 167–169, 175–176, 194; controlling 179–182, 185–186; early modern English 92, 193, 205; identity and 183–184; metaphors 182–183
learning 57, 74, 91; through failure 164
Liberal Arts in Prison Program (LAPP) 117, 127
liberties, London 31
London: Bridewell prison 31–34, 38; early modern prison 30–31; liberties 31
Luther Luckett Correctional Facility 7, 43, 46, 220

Mackenzie, Rowan 8, 146, 149–150
Malcolm X 17, 191; *Autobiography of Malcolm X* 192, 194; James I Theory 193–194
Manhattan College 106; Engaging, Educating, and Empowering Means Change Program (E3MC) 105
Marin Shakespeare Company 87; paid opportunities for Returned Artists 242–243; peer support network 245–246; performances 239–240; Returned Citizens Theatre Troupe (RCTT) 241–247; Shakespeare for Social Justice (SSJ) 240–241
mass incarceration 1–2, 120, 128–129; racial disparity and systemic racism 2, 9, 71–73; reform challenges 5–6, 84,

192–196; systemic inequities 7–9, 83, 88, 100
meaning making 93, 102
memory/ies: affective 132–133, 135; and identity 118–119; traumatic 131, 133–136
men convicted of sexual offences (MCoSOs): rehabilitation 146, 148–149; stigma 145; vulnerability 146–147; *see also* Emergency Shakespeare; incarcerated people; MCoSO prison
mentoring: in carceral settings 118–119
metaphor/s 182–183; prison 36–37
Method acting 132–133
Michael Chekhov Technique 131, 134–135, 141; atmospheres 138–139; "ideal center" 136–137; Imaginary Bodies exercise 140; sensations 137–138; Six Directions 136–137; stick/veil/ball exercise 139–140
Milton, John: *On Education* 57; *Paradise Lost* 60
Missouri Eastern Correctional Center 14
Moose Lake Correctional Facility 162–163
motivation: extrinsic 120–121; intrinsic 121

narrative identity 130
Norfolk Prison Colony 192; "The Great Books" 194

O'Connor, Flannery 175, 185–186
Othello's Tribunal 17, 215, 220–223, 225–227

Pagaduan, Joey 245–246
pairing texts 231–232

parole hearing 53, 71, 82–83
participant motivations 13, 83, 84, 86, 122, 150
patriarchy 103, 184–185
pedagogy/ies 14, 85, 86, 101, 106, 111, 113, 230; building trust with students 121–122; "critical teachers" 111–112; decolonial practices 81–89; facilitator 72–77, 85, 88; inclusive 85–86; inclusivity 75–76, 80–81; social justice 7–9; teaching 56–59; trauma-informed 57
Pensalfini, Rob 4, 81, 162, 172; *Prison Shakespeare* 120–121
perspective 53, 100
Pierce, Andre 71–72
positive autonomy 149, 153–154, 158
Prichard, James 48–49
prison 36–37, 62; abolition 82, 200; debates 192–196; early modern 28, 30–31; education 69–70, 72, 189–190; forms of control 179–182; hard labor 31–32; institutional racism 71–73; leaving 239; MCoSO *see* MCoSO prison; metaphor 36–37; officers, compassion fatigue 149; security concerns 209–210; social hierarchy 109–110; staff attitudes 148–149; theater programs 6–7, 16–17; in the United States 28–29; Vulnerable Prisoner Units (VPUs) 145; writing 28–30, 91–92, 99
prison library 17, 189–190, 200; banned texts 188; independent reading 191–192, 194–199; Shakespeare's works 190
Prison Performing Arts Programs 2, 14–16, 114; *see also* Shakespeare Behind Bars (SBB); Emergency

Shakespeare; Returned Citizens
Theatre Troupe (RCTT);
Redeeming Time Project (RTP);
Shakespeare in Prison (SiP)
psychology/psychological: of awe
58–60; transformation 81–82,
99; *see also* healing
punishment 28, 30, 32–34, 36,
120–121, 180

race/racism 9, 13, 74, 75, 88,
100; institutional 71–73;
systemic whiteness 80; white
supremacy 72
Radford University 177
reading Shakespeare: library setting
191–192, 194–199; Malcolm
X's account 193, 195–197;
prison classroom setting 191
recidivism 5, 35, 61, 84
recruitment: prison arts/education
programs 147–148; Time Out
Of Joint (TOOJ) 229–230
Redeeming Time Project (RTP)
16, 162, 169, 174; check-in
163–164; check-out 166–167,
170; "Muse of Fire mad libs"
167; performances 171–172;
preliminary session 163;
Presence exercise 165; "Zip! Zap!
Zop! 166
redemption 5, 50, 52, 105;
remembrance and 118–119
reform 5, 37; penal 33–34;
prison 2
rehabilitation 3, 5–6, 11, 19,
37, 71–72, 82–84, 102,
115, 194; role of college
education 6–7; empathy and
perspective-building 153; men
convicted of sexual offences
(MCoSOs) 148–149
rehearsal: *Julius Caesar* 207–211;
Shakespeare Behind Bars (SBB)

46; challenges in carceral
settings 146–147, 209;
collaborative practices 149,
152–154, 157; ensemble trust-
building 170–171; reflections
on process 205; participants'
transformation 86, 211
remembrance 118–119
remorse 94–95; *see also* forgiveness
resistance 3, 13–14
responsibility 94; personal 50, 53
restorative justice (RJ): applications
in prisons arts programs 172,
193; theory and practice
169–170
Returned Citizens Theatre Troupe
(RCTT) 18, 241–247
returning citizens 19, 235–236
revenge 50–51
rich, dave 80–81, 83–86, 88
Rikers Island *see* Engaging,
Educating, and Empowering
Means Change Program (E3MC)
Robben Island Bible 6, 189

salvation stories 4–5
San Quentin 241–242; *Shakespeare for
Social Justice* (SSJ) 240–241
scholarship, prison arts/
education programs 80–82,
84–85, 189–190
SCI-Graterford 203–204
SCI-Phoenix 17, 204
Scott, Robert 108, 111
Scott-Douglass, Amy 74–76, 101
self-discovery 52–53
self-reflection 85, 154–156, 233
sensations, Michael Chekhov
Technique 137–138
sentencing: connections to
Shakespearean narratives,
94–95; mandatory minimums
and justice system complexities,
177; restorative justice

discussions, 170; representations of justice in early modern plays, 34–35, 39; transformation narratives and emotional impact, 86, 95

Shakespeare, William 10, 31–32, 103, 192–193; *Coriolanus* 122–124; *Hamlet* 14, 44–45, 54–55, 69, 93, 96–98, 105–106, 108–111, 113, 118–119; *Henry IV, Part 1* 35, 126; *Julius Caesar* 206–211; *King Lear* 52, 59; *Macbeth* 150, 204–206; *Measure for Measure* 55, 62–63; *Richard II* 198, 236–237; *The Taming of the Shrew* 156, 179–185; *The Tempest* 46–48, 50–52, 99–102; *The Tragedy of Othello* 92–96, 221–224; *Two Gentlemen of Verona* 74; *The Winter's Tale* 35–38, 47–48; *As You Like It* 45; see also reading Shakespeare

Shakespeare Behind Bars (documentary) 46–47, 118–119

Shakespeare Behind Bars (SBB) 7, 12–13, 17, 43, 215, 240; 25 Year Retrospective 48, 50–51; Circle of Truth 218–220; core values 218–220; cultural invasion 74–75; female roles 43–46; healing 49; mission 216; Othello's Tribunal 17, 215, 220–223, 225–227; redemption 50, 52; reenacting crime 47–48; rehearsals 46; vision 218; vulnerability 52–53

Shakespeare BEYOND Bars 216

Shakespeare for Social Justice (SSJ) 240–241

Shakespeare in Prison (SiP) 7, 15, 69–71, 130; acting exercises 131–132; facilitator 73–74; Method acting 133; Michael Chekhov Technique 134–140; *See also* Michael Chekhov Technique

slavery 1, 18–19, 70; *See also* race/racism

social justice: foundational principles 18–19; pedagogies and applications 7–9, 70–73, 170–171, 216–217; TOOJ core beliefs 234–236; Shakespeare as a tool for justice 46–48, 149, 232; community building and reentry 75, 169, 216–217; *see also* Shakespeare for Social Justice (SSJ)

solitary confinement 197–199, 246

Stanislavski, Konstantin, the "System" 132–134

stereotypes: gender 175–176; incarcerated people 101, 103, 106, 120–121, 124–125

Strasberg, Lee 132–133

surveillance 147; e-carceration 29

teachers/teaching 61–62, 91; building trust with students 121–122; "critical" 111–112; female 119–120; inside-out model 14, 105–106, 114–115; *see also* Formerly Incarcerated Teachers (FITs); pedagogy/ies

teamwork 173; Emergency Shakespeare 152–153, 156–157

therapy 131, 155, 173–174; *see also* rehabilitation

This American Life 14, 105–106; "Act V" 108–110, 112–114

Time Out of Joint: Prison Reflections on Shakespeare 228–229

Time Out Of Joint (TOOJ) 18, 228; community support 235; core beliefs 235–236; discussions 232–233; Formerly Incarcerated Teachers (FITs) 230–231, 233–234; grant funding 235; impact 233–235; pairing texts 231–232; Prison Monologues

232–233; recruitment 229–230; self-reflection 233; workshops 230
Tofteland, Curt L. 7, 17, 44, 162, 215; *see also* Shakespeare Behind Bars (SBB)
transformation: critical perspectives xvii–xviii; personal growth 52; systemic critique 70, 73–75; education and incarceration 82, 88; justice and rehabilitation 98; trust-building 169; reentry and community 216–217; theater practices 232
trauma 18, 96–99, 124, 139–141, 219, 222, 224, 247; -informed pedagogy 57; memory 131, 133–136; reactivation 135, 137–138; *see also* Michael Chekhov Technique
Trounstine, Jean 7, 75, 87

Underground Scholars Language Guide 19–20
uniforms 180–181
United States: 1994 Crime Bill 6–7; American education 70–71; prison system 28–29

University of California, Berkeley 197–198

van der Kolk, Bessel, *The Body Keeps the Score* 131–132, 134–136
violence 19, 96–97, 105, 107, 112, 173, 208, 223, 229; domestic 156; gang 93, 98; sexual 100; shame and 165
vulnerability: incarcerated people 52–53, 131–132; men convicted of sexual offences (MCoSOs) 146–147
Vulnerable Prisoner Units (VPUs) 145

white supremacy 72, 80, 85, 196
women 100; gendered expectations 175–178, 182, 184–186; men's portrayal of 43–46, 206; narrative identity 130; teachers 119–120
workshops: Emergency Shakespeare 150; Redeeming Time Project (RTP) 162–163, 167, 170–171, 173–174; Time Out Of Joint (TOOJ) 230
writing 98; creative 233; prison 28–30, 91–92, 99

For Product Safety Concerns and Information please contact our EU representative GPSR@taylorandfrancis.com
Taylor & Francis Verlag GmbH, Kaufingerstraße 24, 80331 München, Germany

www.ingramcontent.com/pod-product-compliance
Lightning Source LLC
Chambersburg PA
CBHW050529300426
44113CB00012B/2021